A-level Study Guide

Psychology

Revised and updated for 2008 by

Andrew Favager

John Griffin

Sandra Latham

Rhiannon Murray

Mark Cardwell

Alison Wadeley

Revision Express

Series Consultants: Geoff Black and Stuart Wall

Pearson Education Limited

Edinburgh Gate, Harlow

Essex CM20 2JE, England

and Associated Companies throughout the world

© Pearson Education Limited 2000, 2004, 2008

British Library Cataloguing in Publication Data

A catalogue entry for this title is available from the British Library.

ISBN 978-1-4082-0665-2

First published 2000

Reprinted 2001

Updated 2004

Second edition 2006

New Edition 2008

Set by Juice Creative Ltd.

Printed by Ashford Colour Press Ltd., Gosport

Contents

How to use this book

Specification match

Provides a quick and easy overview of the topics that you need to study for the specification you are studying (see pages 6–7)

Exam themes

At the beginning of each chapter, these give a quick overview of the key themes that will be covered in the exam

Exam themes

- Stress
- Healthy living

Measuring and managing stress

Psychologists need valid ways of measuring stress, so that the effects of stress and stress management techniques can be identified. The potentially harmful effects of stress mean that effective techniques for stress management are essential. Some techniques are physical (such as the use of drugs) whilst others are psychological (such as meditation).

Measuring stress

Physiological measures of stress can overcome the subjectivity of the self-report by relying on scientific measurements of hormones, chemicals, heart rate, blood pressure, etc. Geer and Maisels's study measured the stress in their participants using a polygraph to collect psychophysiological data.

Self-report methods can include questionnaires, interviews and diary-keeping. Holmes and Rahe used a self-report measure with their Self-Readjustment Rating Scale (SRRS). They felt that readjustment needed to cope with such an event causes stress. The more adjustment you have to make the more stressed you are. Each life event was given a score and a score of 300 would predict a strong risk of physical or psychological illness.

It is possible to **combine methods** of measuring stress, as in Johansson's study on work stressors. They used a combined method of physical tests of cortisol and self-reports of mood, plus statistics of absenteeism. Increases in cortisol levels indicate a higher stress level in the person and, as there is a link between stress and illness, more stress could cause a person to have more time off work. Using a combined method should increase the validity of their measures.

Managing stress

Physical approaches include using drugs such as Benzodiazepine (BZ) and anti-anxiety drugs such as Librium and Valium. These drugs work by reducing the activity of the neurotransmitter serotonin. This has an inhibitory effect on the brain, producing muscle relaxation and an overall calming effect. Beta-blockers such as Inderal work by reducing activity in the pathways of the sympathetic nervous system and are therefore effective against raised heart rate and blood pressure.

Biofeedback is a technique for controlling physiological responses by receiving information about the body's stress response as it occurs. Monitoring devices track responses such as heart rate and blood pressure. These provide the person with feedback in the form of a light or audible tone whenever they change the response in the desired direction. The aim of this technique is to find a strategy to reduce a particular stress-related response (such as increased heart rate) which can then be transferred to the outside world and used regularly to relieve stress.

Budzynski's (1970) study compared patients with tension headaches and found that biofeedback reduced the amount of headaches, their severity and the amount of medication people had to take. These effects were still noticeable three months after the treatment.

Links

Cross-reference links to other relevant sections in the book

Link

See Geer and Meisel's study showing a cause of stress on page 137.

Checkpoint

Quick question to check your understanding with full answers given at the end of the chapter

Checkpoint 1

What are the ways of measuring stress?

Grade booster

Examiner suggestions on how to get the top grade

Grade booster

What are the strengths and weaknesses of each method of measuring stress? At least 2 of each are needed to gain full marks in an evaluation essay.

Check the net

Suggestions for useful websites related to the topic

Check the net

For advice on understanding, recognising and managing stress:
www.mindtools.com/smpage.html

The jargon

A clear outline of what subject-related and examination-related jargon means

The jargon

Beta-blocker. A drug that prevents the stimulation of increased cardiac action.

138

Topic checklist

A topic overview of the content covered and how it matches to the specification you are studying

Topic checklist

	Edexcel		AQA		AQA/ B		OCR		WJEC	
	AS	A2	AS	A2	AS	A2	AS	A2	AS	A2
Mood disorders – depression		●		●		●		●		●
Anxiety disorders – phobias		●		●	○			●		

Revision checklists

Allow you to monitor your progress and revise the areas that you are not confident on

By the end of this chapter you should be able to:

1	Describe and evaluate theories and causes of stress.	Confident	Not confident **Revise** page 136
2	Describe and evaluate techniques of measuring and managing stress.	Confident	Not confident **Revise** page 139

Psychological approaches to stress management can be either general, such as using relaxation techniques or meditation to reduce the body's state of arousal, or specific, using cognitive and behavioural training. Progressive muscle relaxation is an active approach to reducing bodily arousal. In a typical relaxation session a client would be trained to progressively tense and relax muscles, working up the body from the legs to the facial muscles. Eventually the person can use the technique as a way of reducing bodily arousal. During the relaxation state, stress response mechanisms are inactive and the parasympathetic nervous system is dominant.

A **cognitive approach** to stress management is Meichenbaum's (1972) stress-inoculation training. This technique has three phases:

→ **Conceptualisation** – the cognitive element, in which the client is encouraged to relive stressful situations, analysing what was stressful about them and how they attempted to deal with them.
→ **Skills training and practice** – the client is taught a variety of techniques (e.g. relaxation, social skills and time management) in the therapeutic setting.
→ **Real-life application** – following training, the client can put what they have learned into practice in the real world. Reinforcement of techniques learned in therapy makes the practices self-sustaining.

Social support networks have also been seen to decrease illness associated with stress. Waxler Morrison's (1993) projective study of women with breast cancer found that women with larger social networks tended to have better survival rates and, as there is a link between stress and cancer, it is logical to believe that if the reduction of the disease is found in women with stronger social support, then this could indicate less stress in these women.

The concept of 'hardiness' is taken to mean resistance to illness, or ability to deal with stress. From studies of highly stressed executives, Kobasa and Maddi (1977) were able to identify the characteristics of those who handled stress well from those who did not. Those who reported the fewest illnesses showed three kinds of hardiness.

They showed an openness to change, a sense of purpose in their activities and a sense of control over their lives. Kobasa proposed three ways in which people's hardiness could be improved – by recognising stressful events then reliving stressful encounters and identifying whether their techniques were effective. This is followed by self-improvement and being encouraged to take on challenges that they can cope with.

Folkman (1984) identified problem-focused and emotion-focused coping strategies for managing stress. Problem-focused coping means behaving in such a way that the stressful situation is reduced or eliminated. With emotion-focused coping, the behaviours will simply reduce the negativity of the emotions by avoidance, distraction or rethinking the situation, i.e. the situation doesn't change but the person's feelings do.

Take note

Concentrating on one thing, or emptying the mind of thoughts to aid relaxation is meditating.

Action point

Summarise the assumptions of the cognitive approach to human behaviour.

Checkpoint 2

What advice would you give to someone who was suffering from stress, based on Waxler Morrison's research?

Watch out!

Kobasa's original studies were of highly-stressed executives. This may not generalise easily to other occupational groups.

Examiner's secret

Compare and contrast these techniques, looking for similarities and differences.

Take note

Extension notes on the core content

Action point

A suggested activity linked to the content

Watch out!

Flags up common mistakes and gives hints on how to avoid them

Examiner's secrets

Hints and tips for exam success

Exam practice

Exam-style questions to check your understanding of the topic content with full answers given at the end of the chapter

Exam practice answers: page 168

(a) Describe research into managing stress. (10 marks)
(b) Evaluate the effectiveness of measurements of stress. (15 marks)

139

Specification map

Perspectives, physiological psychology and issues	Perspectives
	Biological rhythms
	Sleep
	Sleep disorders and dreaming
	Gender and cultural bias
	Ethical issues and the use of animals
	Free will and determinism
	Reductionism
	Psychology as science
	Nature-nurture

Core studies	Baron-Cohen, Jolliffe, Mortimore and Robertson (1997)
	Gardner and Gardner (1969)
	Loftus and Palmer (1974)
	Savage-Rumbaugh et al (1986)
	Bandura, Ross and Ross (1961)
	Freud (1909)
	Gibson and Walk (1960)
	Langer and Rodin (1976)
	Samuel and Bryant (1984)
	Bennett-Levy and Marteau (1984)
	Dement and Kleitman (1957)
	Maguire, Gadian, Johnsrude, Good, Ashburner, Frackowiak and Frith (2000)
	Rahe, Mahan and Arthur (1970)
	Sperry (1968)
	Asch (1955)
	Milgram (1963)
	Piliavin, Rodin and Piliavin (1969)
	Reicher and Haslam (2006)
	Buss (1989)
	Griffiths (1994)
	Rosenhan (1973)
	Thigpen and Cleckley (1954)

Social psychology and research methods	Interpersonal relationships
	The formation, maintenance and dissolution of relationships
	Cultural and sub-cultural differences in relationships
	The causes of aggression
	Conformity
	Obedience to authority
	Explaining and resisting obedience
	Ethical issues
	Dealing with ethical issues
	Quantitative research methods
	Qualitative research methods
	Research planning
	Research design
	Analysing quantitative data
	Analysing qualitative data

Cognitive and developmental psychology	Remembering and forgetting
	Models of memory
	The role of emotion in memory
	Eyewitness testimony
	Cognition and the law
	Perceptual organisation
	Perceptual development
	Cognitive development
	The development of social cognition
	Attachment
	Daycare
	Sex and gender
	Theories of gender development
	Development of moral understanding
	Theories of the nature of intelligence
	Genetic and environmental effects on intelligence
	Erikson and lifespan theories
	Adolescence
	Middle and late adulthood

Health, clinical and sport psychology	Stress as a biological response, factors affecting stress
	Measuring and managing stress
	Healthy living
	Definitions of abnormality
	Models of abnormality – assumptions
	Models of abnormality – treatments
	Psychotic disorders – schizophrenia
	Mood disorders – depression
	Anxiety disorders – phobias
	Eating disorders
	Autism
	Substance abuse
	Sport and the individual
	Sport performance
	Social psychology of sport
	Exercise psychology

Educational and forensic psychology	Teaching and learning
	Social world of learning
	Student participation
	Enabling learning
	Causes of crime
	Making a case
	Reaching a verdict
	Sentencing and treatments

○		○		○		○		○	
○			●						●
○			●						●
○			●						●
			●			○			●
○	●		●		●	○			●
			●		●	○			●
			●		●	○			●
	●		●		●	○			●
○	●		●		●	○			
						○			
								○	
						○		○	
						○			
						○			
						○			
								○	
								○	
						○			
								○	
						○			
						○			
								○	
								○	
						○		○	
						○			
						○			
								○	
						○			
						○		○	
						○			
		○	●					○	●
		○	●					○	●
		○	●					○	●
		○	●			○	●		
○		○	●	○	●				
○		○	●						
○		○	●						
○	●	○	●			○	●	○	●
○	●	○	●			○	●	○	●
○	●	○	●	○	●	○	●	○	●
○	●	○	●	○	●	○	●	○	●
○	●	○	●	○	●	○	●	○	●
○	●	○	●	○	●	○	●	○	●
○	●	○	●	○	●	○	●	○	●
○		○		○		●			●
○				○					●
				○					●
○	●	○				○	●	○	●
○	●	○			●	○	●	○	●
			●	○					
			●						
	●		●		●		●		●
			●		●				
	●	○	●		●				
	●	○	●						
○			●	○	●		●		
			●	○	●				
			●		●		●		●
			●						●
			●						●
			●						●
			●						●
			●						●
		○			●		●	○	
		○			●		●		●
							●		●
	●	○					●		●
	●	○					●	○	
	●	○					●	○	
	●		●		●		●		●
	●		●	○			●		
	●			○					
	●		●		●				●
	●						●		●
	●						●		●
	●						●		●
		○					●		●
							●		
							●		
							●		
					●		●		●
					●		●		●
					●		●		●

Perspectives, physiological psychology and issues

Within psychology we have several different explanations to explain human behaviour and specific disorders. Each explanation is known as a perspective. Psychology is like a tower with different windows – when you look out of each window you get a different view, or perspective. Within psychology there are five different views. Each view will explain behaviour in a different way and consequently will offer a different therapy.

This chapter also looks at one of the more popular areas of physiological psychology – biological rhythms, sleep and dreaming – and deals with issues and debates within psychology.

Exam themes

- Biological, behavioural, psychodynamic, cognitive and humanistic perspectives: theory, therapy and evaluation
- Biological rhythms
- Theories of the function of sleep and dreaming
- Gender and cultural bias in psychological theory and research
- Ethical issues
- Issues and debates in psychology

Topic checklist

	Edexcel		AQA/A		AQA/B		OCR		WJEC	
	AS	A2	AS	A2	AS	A2	AS	A2	AS	A2
Perspectives: The biological approach	O		O		O		O		O	
Perspectives: The behavioural approach	O		O		O		O		O	
Perspectives: The cognitive approach	O		O		O		O		O	
Perspectives: The psychodynamic approach	O		O		O		O		O	
Perspectives: The humanistic approach and research methods	O		O		O		O		O	
Biological rhythms	O			●						●
Sleep	O			●						●
Sleep disorders and dreaming	O			●						●
Gender and cultural bias				●			O			●
Ethical issues and the use of animals		●		●		●	O			●
Free will and determinism				●		●	O			●
Reductionism				●		●	O			●
Psychology as science		●		●		●	O		●	●
Nature-nurture		●		●		●	O			●

Perspectives: The biological approach

The biological approach looks at psychology from a biological perspective. All behaviour is explained in terms of genetics, chemicals and neuroanatomy.

Probability

We may inherit predispositions to certain illnesses which are carried on genes from one generation to the next. Research by Holland et al (1988) has found evidence to support the genetic basis of behaviour. He studied twins who had developed eating disorders and found that the concordance rate for anorexia between MZ (identical) twins was 56% while for DZ (non-identical) it was 7%. Family and adoption studies have also been used to support the genetic argument. Egeland et al (1987) studied the Amish community and found that 11 out of 81 members of a family had manic depression. Wender et al (1986) found that adopted children who developed depression had biological parents who were eight times more likely than their adopted parents to have depression.

Checkpoint

Name two biological therapies.

Chemicals

There are two communication systems within the body. Neurons make up our **nervous system** and consist of an axon that transmits an electrical message to the next neuron via the interconnection called the synapse. The electrical message is transferred to the next neuron by chemicals called neurotransmitters. The other communication system is the **endocrine system**, which is a set of glands around the body that release hormones. Hormones are chemicals that travel in the bloodstream and affect certain organs. Research has linked some mental disorders with high or low levels of certain chemical substances in the brain, such as dopamine and the neurotransmitter serotonin.

Take note

A basic understanding of the nervous system is needed to understand how the biological approach works.

Neuroanatomy

The central nervous system consists of the spinal cord and the brain. Four parts of the brain have been linked to different functions within the body (known as localisation) – the frontal, parietal, occipital and temporal lobes.

Damage or abnormal development in any of these areas can affect a person's functioning and consequently their behaviour.

Take note

The frontal lobe is linked to speech and movement.
The parietal lobe is linked to senses.
The occipital lobe is linked to vision.
The temporal lobe is linked to understanding language and hearing.

Theory

Selye's research on stress is the theory that supports this perspective. In order to understand the effect stress has on the body we have to understand how it becomes aroused due to stress. The nervous system is divided into two areas: the central nervous system (the brain and spinal cord) and the peripheral nervous system, which is further divided into the following two systems:

→ The **somatic nervous system** is concerned with voluntary movements such as walking.

→ The **autonomic nervous system** is concerned with involuntary movements, e.g. heart rate and breathing.

There are two branches to the autonomic nervous system. The sympathetic branch activates internal organs when energy is needed e.g. increased heart rate and breathing (the flight or fight syndrome). The parasympathetic branch is concerned with storing energy, e.g. monitoring the relaxed state, promoting digestion and metabolism.

General adaptation syndrome or GAS was developed after Selye exposed rats to severe stressors and found that they went through three stages.

In evaluation:

Selye identified the body's response to stress, the dangers of prolonged stress and the importance of specific hormones when we are stressed. He also showed how stress can suppress the immune system.

However, Selye's work ignored individual differences and the fact that personality plays a role in how we deal with stress. He was criticised for using non-human animals to support research on human responses to stress.

Therapies

Psychosurgery

Because parts of the brain control different functions of the body, it was thought that those of us with abnormal disorders could have them treated by the use of surgery. Psychosurgery or lobotomy, developed by Moniz (1937), involves sections of the brain being removed or lesions made separating regions of the brain. It was first used on aggressive lab chimpanzees and was found to calm them. It has since been used on patients who are emotionally unstable and violent.

In evaluation:

→ Findings from chimpanzees cannot be applied to humans.
→ It is a quick option to control unmanageable patients and so can be seen as unethical. Lobotomies can lead to side effects such as personality changes, with the person becoming apathetic and lethargic. With some cases it has even lead to coma and death.

Chemotherapy

If the chemicals in our body can cause certain psychological illnesses, changing the levels of these chemicals could be effective in treating mental illness.

Certain drugs resemble neurotransmitters and work in two ways – by mimicking neurotransmitters and therefore causing stimulation, and by blocking receptors and therefore preventing an increase in that particular neurotransmitter. For example, the disorder schizophrenia is linked to a high level of the neurotransmitter dopamine. Certain drugs block dopamine receptor sites and reduce levels of dopamine and consequently symptoms of schizophrenia. In depressed patients the neurotransmitter serotonin is low and a drug called selective serotonin reuptake inhibitors increases the serotonin levels and again reduces the symptoms.

In evaluation:

→ Drugs can reduce symptoms, more ethical method than a lobotomy.
→ Drug treatment stops the symptoms but does not explain the cause. It does not work on all sufferers, so individual differences must play a role.
→ The use of drugs can have side effects.

Perspectives: The behavioural approach

According to the behavioural approach, developed by Watson and Skinner, all behaviour is learnt by either classical conditioning or operant conditioning.

Classical conditioning

Classical conditioning is automatic learning. It was identified by Ivan Pavlov (1927), who found that animals produce saliva in response to food. Pavlov then paired the food to a bell. After a while the dogs would salivate to the sound of the bell alone. Pavlov had conditioned the dog to respond to the bell. The bell was the conditioned stimulus and the salivation was the conditioning response.

Watson and Raynor (1920) also researched classical conditioning and showed how a human could learn a fear response. Their famous study was on little Albert. Albert was a baby who was shown a white rat which provoked no fear response. He was then repeatedly shown the white rat and an iron bar was struck near his head. After some time he began to fear the rat as he associated the frightening sound of the iron bar being struck with the sight of the rat. The rat had become the conditioned stimulus which produced a conditioned fear response. Albert had learned to fear the rat and other things that were white (generalisation). He had been conditioned and had developed a phobia.

Operant conditioning

Another way we learn is by operant conditioning, or reinforcement. This develops around reward and punishment, which takes place throughout our lives. If behaviour is reinforced (rewarded) then it will be repeated but if behaviour has unpleasant effects (punishment) then the behaviour will not be repeated. These ideas were developed by B.F. Skinner who carried out a lot of his research on animals. He devised the Skinner box in which pigeons or rats were placed and if they pressed a lever they could get a food pellet. The animals learned to press the lever so that they could get the food (a reward).

Theory

A third way we learn is by the social learning theory developed by Bandura (1961) who stressed the importance of observational learning or modelling, i.e. we learn by imitating the behaviour of others. In Bandura's study on aggression he got children to watch an adult kick and punch a Bobo doll. The children were then allowed to play with the doll and they also kicked and punched it. They had imitated the aggressive acts of the adult model. Bandura identified four stages in the learning process:

→ attention
→ retention
→ reproduction
→ motivation.

The likelihood that an observer will perform a behaviour that they have observed is increased if the model observed is of the same gender and age, of a high status and friendly.

Bandura also found that observational learning was likely to influence

Checkpoint 1

Outline two assumptions of the behaviourist approach.

Take note

Classical conditioning is an automatic response while **operant conditioning** is due to reward and punishment.

Take note

Social learning theory can involve thinking about copying someone's behaviour and therefore incorporates some of the cognitive model.

behaviour when we see the other person being rewarded for their behaviour (vicarious reinforcement).

Evaluation

A lot of evidence supports this theory, including Bandura's studies. However, his studies were artificial and not real life, and maybe the children felt they were being invited to hit the doll, which could make the study unethical. Other research by Eron et al (1972) did find a positive correlation between the aggressive levels of children and the amount of violent TV they watched (though correlation evidence only shows a relationship and not cause and effect).

It is not only television that can provide inappropriate models for social learning. It has been found that children who live in violent households have a higher level of violence (Ehrensaft et al 2003).

Checkpoint 2

Describe the social learning theory of aggression.

The jargon

A **correlation** is a relationship.

Therapy

Aversion therapy

If behaviour can be learnt then it can be unlearnt. One method of achieving this is by aversion therapy. A behaviour that needs to be eliminated, e.g. smoking, is paired with an unpleasant stimulus – for example, every time a person smokes a cigarette they are given an emetic (a tablet that makes you vomit). They then associate smoking with being sick and the behaviour is extinguished.

Grade booster

The biological approach is a good perspective to compare with the behavioural approach.

Evaluation

This therapy has been used effectively. Weinrott et al (1997) treated sex offenders by pairing the negative effects of sex offences with their own sexual arousal. Afterwards they demonstrated less physiological and self-reported arousal. A problem with this therapy is that it does not treat the causes of the problem only the symptoms. Aversion therapy is also unpleasant, raising ethical issues, and spontaneous recovery of a recently unlearned behaviour can occur.

Systematic desensitisation

Developed by Wolpe (1958) and used to treat phobias, this involves the use of an anxiety hierarchy developed between the phobic and the therapist. It is a series of situations involving the fear that gradually increase in intensity, e.g. with a fear of spiders stage 1 might be to look at drawings of spiders. The phobic does this until they feel relaxed, when they can move on to stage 2, which might be looking at photographs of spiders, and so on. The aim is to desensitise the patient about each item on the hierarchy.

Take note

A third therapy to treat phobias is Implosion, or Flooding, when a person is constantly exposed to the fear of stimulus.

Evaluation

Rothbaum et al (2000) successfully used this therapy to treat people who had a fear of flying, though again this removes the symptom not the cause. If the behaviour has been learned then it can be unlearned, but if caused by some unconscious problem, e.g. from childhood, the treatment may not last and the phobic behaviour may return.

Perspectives: The cognitive approach

This approach developed out of the behavioural approach. All behaviour is learned, but if we do not think about our behaviour, what then affects what we do? The cognitive approach argues that mental disorders are caused by distorted or irrational thinking.

This approach compares the way the mind works to that of a computer and emphasises the internal processes of the mind and how information is processed. It also stresses the importance of the ways that information is processed so we can make sense of our environment. We understand the world through our perception, attention and memory and these can be seen as a series of processing systems.

Theory

Attribution theory

When we meet people we process information about their behaviour in an attempt to decide why they behave the way they do. This is called attribution theory. A person can have internal attributions, e.g. their behaviour is because of their personality, or external attributions, e.g. their behaviour was because of the hot weather. We also make judgements about someone based on a single incident. This is called correspondence inference – e.g. when someone shouts we make an inference that they have a moody personality (a judgement is made that the behaviour corresponds to the person's character).

Evaluation

Other factors can also affect correspondent inference theory, e.g. if the person belongs to a certain group such as a gender group. Also, the theory does not take into account cultural factors.

Therapy

Cognitive therapy (CT)

Beck (1976) was concerned with depression and how negative thoughts can lead to this disorder. He put forward his theory of the **cognitive triad**, where a person has negative view of themselves, the world and their future. Cognitive therapy aims to change the sort of cognitions that lead to mental illness. The therapy challenges the negative thoughts people have by getting them to experience real life situations. For example, a patient may say that going out with friends is not enjoyable. Cognitive theory would test this assertion by having the person socialise with friends and then state whether they enjoyed it or not.

Evaluation

Cognitive therapy has been found to work on depressive patients, with Cahill et al (2003) reporting that 71% of patients receiving therapy reported fewer depressive symptoms.

Checkpoint

Describe the three parts of the cognitive triad.

Cognitive behavioural therapy (CBT) and rational emotive behaviour therapy (REBT)

CBT is based on the idea that altering patients' cognitions will alter their behaviour. This theory is based around REBT and Beck's cognitive therapy (CT). CBT attempts to alter the way people think as that then affects their emotional state and therefore their behaviour.

REBT was developed by Ellis (1977). He looked at how people reacted to negative events, specifically their emotions. Ellis focused on stoicism – being able to remain emotionally stable when confronted by trauma. He believed it is more efficient to deal with mental illness by confronting the irrational beliefs that people have and making them more stoical. If you are rational in your thinking then your behaviour and emotional state will be normal, hence the REBT theory.

Evaluation

REBT has been found to be successful in treating anxiety (Engels et al 1993) and as an aid to anger management (Adelman et al 2005).

However, REBT forces patients to change their outlook on life, which raises ethical issues as many may not want to do this.

Take note

The cognitive approach is concerned with the thought processes that we have and how these influence our behaviour.

Examiner's secrets

Make sure you can compare and contrast all the perspectives with each other.

Exam practice   answer: page 38

Evaluate **two** weaknesses of the cognitive approach. (4 marks)

Perspectives: The psychodynamic approach

This model was developed by Sigmund Freud (1915), who argued that mental illnesses arise out of unresolved unconscious conflicts that form in early childhood.

Freud's theory

Freud's theory has three parts, which all contribute to the development of the personality. The first is that during childhood a child goes through five psychosexual stages that can have an effect on their personality. Each stage is a source of pleasure but a child might get fixated in a stage which can then affect their personality development. Later in life, when they get stressed, they regress to that particular stage, e.g. the oral stage, and may suck their thumb.

The five psychosexual stages are:

1 **Oral** – from birth to 18 months – the focus is on the mouth, e.g. food and drink.
2 **Anal** –18 to 36 months – the focus is on bowel movements.
3 **Phallic** – 3 to 6 years – the focus is on gender and relationships. Boys go through the Oedipus complex, where they are attracted to their mother but fear that their father will castrate them. They deal with this by identifying with their father. Girls go thought the Electra complex, where they desire their father and suffer penis envy. They resolve this by identifying with their mother.
4 **Latency** – this lasts until puberty. Boys and girls spend very little time together.
5 **Genital** – this is from puberty onwards, where the main focus of pleasure is on the genitals.

The second part of Freud's theory is the personality structure. According to Freud we have three parts to our personality – the id, the ego and the superego. The id develops from birth and works in accord with the pleasure principle. It needs immediate satisfaction and is the selfish part of us. It contains innate sexual and aggressive instincts and is located in the unconscious mind. The ego develops at about age 2 and works on the reality principle. Finally the superego develops at about age 5 and is our moral compass, our sense of right and wrong.

The ego is the logical part of our personality and tries to keep the id and superego balanced. For example, if you drive your car down the motorway your id wants to go as fast as possible, e.g. 120mph. Your superego wants you to abide by the speed limit of 70mph. Your ego balances these both out and is in touch with reality, what is going on in the environment. You therefore drive at a speed that most people do on the motorway, of between 80 and 90mph. Personality is like a seesaw, with the ego being the pivot. An over-developed id will tip the person's personality towards selfishness.

The third part of Freud's theory is based around the conscious and unconscious mind. Our personality must be in our mind and it is within our unconscious mind that we have our defence mechanisms, which our ego uses when we suffer anxiety. These defence mechanisms contribute towards our adult personality.

Grade booster

Show your insider knowledge of Freud, e.g. there are three parts to the unconscious mind – the conscious, the pre-conscious and the unconscious.

The jargon

We always have access to the **conscious mind** (it is what we are currently thinking) while the **unconscious mind** is locked and we only gain access to it in our dreams.

Some of these defence mechanisms include:

→ repression – keeping threatening thoughts out of the consciousness
→ displacement – unconsciously moving impulses away from a threatening object and towards a less threatening object.

Take note

Other defence mechanisms include projection, denial, intellectualisation.

Evaluation

→ Freud came up with an explanation of personality which works and can explain behaviour. However, many modern psychologists would be more interested in looking at traits when attempting to explain personality.
→ Freud also identified traumatic childhood experiences as a factor in the development of adult disorders and this is supported by a lot of research, e.g. Kendler et al 1996 (though the evidence is only correlational and cannot show cause and effect).
→ A lot of Freud's evidence is gained from individual case studies, e.g. Little Hans. This study gives us a lot of detail but can a whole theory of child development be written using one study?

Weaknesses of this approach are:

→ Too little focus on the problems a patient may currently be facing.
→ Possible genetic factors are ignored.
→ Freud focused too much on sexual factors as a cause of mental illnesses, neo-Freudians such as Erikson (1959) have adapted Freud's ideas and focused more on social rather than sexual influences (Erikson's psychosocial theory).
→ Finally, and most importantly, there is no evidence for any of Freud's research, making it hard to prove or disprove.

Checkpoint

Outline one psychodynamic theory.

Therapies: psychoanalysis

Free association
If most of our problems are in the unconscious mind then the job of therapy would be to unlock that unconscious mind. One way is by free association. In this therapy the patient would lie on a couch with the therapist behind them and say anything that comes into their mind, with the idea that things linked to their problem would flood out of their unconscious mind.

Dream analysis
Another way to unlock the unconscious mind is through dream analysis. Freud called dreams 'the royal road to the unconscious'. He argued that any dream contains both the manifest content (the actual dream) and the latent content (the actual meaning behind the dream). The dream needs to be analysed to discover this latent content.

Take note

One issue with psychoanalysis is false memory syndrome. This is where patients who are undergoing psychoanalysis are led to believe that their problems are caused by physical or sexual abuse they suffered as a child. There are instances where these allegations have later been found to be false.

Evaluation
Again, no scientific proof exists to disagree or agree with the findings of these therapies – we all dream but do our dreams reflect our unconscious desires and thoughts? Although psychoanalysis has helped some people, it can lead to ethical issues.

Perspectives: The humanistic approach

The humanistic approach explains abnormality by saying it is due to a lack of contented existence.

Theory

The theory was devised by Rogers and Maslow (1959), who felt that we all try to achieve self-actualisation (self-fulfilment). According to this theory, normal psychological development takes place when a child receives unconditional positive regard from its parents, which leads to high self-esteem. If we only receive conditional love, e.g. 'we will only love you if you are good', then this leads to conflict between the self-concept and the ideal self – the person is trying to be someone they are not, in order to receive love. For example, you might work in your dad's firm not because that is what you want to do but to keep him happy. That way, you will never achieve your ideal self.

Maslow argues that at first we are driven by our basic needs, such as hunger. The higher motives such as love then take over. The highest motive of all is self-actualisation (fulfilment of one's potential). Rogers and Maslow felt that self-actualisation was what was needed for ideal mental health. This was the ultimate goal of human behaviour and abnormality would develop as a result of failing to achieve this.

Therapy

Humanistic therapists would attempt to get clients to view themselves and their situations with greater insight and acceptance so as to fulfil their potential as human beings. This is known as client-centred therapy. With this approach the client decides their own goals in order to allow them to grow as a person and achieve self-actualisation.

Evaluation

This therapy has been found to help people unhappy in their life but cannot help those with severe mental illness. The humanistic approach is also very vague, unscientific and untestable.

Research methods

Depending on the approach chosen the research method used will differ:

→ The biological and behavioural approaches both lend themselves to laboratory experiments.
→ The cognitive and humanistic approaches would use interviews to gain qualitative data.
→ The psychodynamic approach would use case studies.

> **Take note**
>
> The humanistic model does not carry out research. It is based around the individual achieving their potential (hard to study this premise).

and research methods

The biological approach:
This approach is suitable for experiments as it reduces behaviour to simple components. It could measure the stress response because it allows us to measure physiological reactions such as temperature, sweat and chemical levels within the blood.

The behavioural approach:
This approach also uses experiments because it believes that only observable behaviours count, and this model believes that behaviour can be reduced to simple cause and effect relationships. This could be investigating the effectiveness of reinforcement schedule by rewarding someone in lab conditions every time they answer a question correctly.

The cognitive approach:
This approach would use interviews to get people to describe their behaviour. They would probably use an unstructured interview technique in order to find out as much information as possible. Certain themes could be identified within the answers and then conclusions could be drawn.

The psychodynamic approach:
This approach would use the case study method to investigate behaviour. An individual would be studied over a period of time and their past life would be analysed. Early experiences in childhood would be focused on to uncover any repressed memories.

Psychodynamic	Biological	Behavioural	Cognitive
Idiographic	Twin studies	Controlled	Lab
Case studies	Brain scans	observations in	experiments
Clinical	Lab experiments	lab settings	Case studies
interviews		Animal research	

Take note

The research methods listed are not prescriptive but each perspective tends to lend itself to particular methods.

Take note

There are different kinds of research methods:
→ **structured** and **unstructured** interviews
→ **participant** and **non-participant** observations.

Grade booster

Be able to compare the different research methods used by each approach.

Take note

Most explanations of behaviour only use four perspectives. Most do not refer to the humanistic approach as there is little or no research to back it up.

Exam practice   answer: page 38

Compare and contrast the biological and psychodynamic approaches in terms of similarities and differences. (12 marks)

Biological rhythms

Many animal and human behaviours are governed by biological rhythms. The cycle for some of these behaviours is less than 24 hours, while for others it is seasonal. Whereas some rhythms appear to be endogenous, occurring independently of external changes, most are synchronised with changes in the external environment.

Types of biological rhythm

Ultradian rhythms

→ These have a frequency of more than one complete cycle every 24 hours (e.g. the cycle of sleep stages that occurs during a night's sleep).
→ They are also found in many complex human behaviours – EEG measures of alertness appear to vary with an ultradian rhythm.
→ Ultradian cycles are related to brain and body size – the smaller the animal the more rapid their ultradian cycles.
→ Ultradian rhythms appear to be controlled by different brain mechanisms than circadian rhythms. Destruction of brain mechanisms that control the latter does not seem to affect behaviours that have an ultradian rhythm.

Infradian rhythms

→ These are cycles which occur less than once every 24 hours (e.g. the human menstrual cycle).
→ Some infradian rhythms occur on a seasonal basis and are known as circannual rhythms (e.g. migration in birds).
→ Lesions in the SCN (see opposite) tend to disrupt circadian rhythms but do not disrupt circannual rhythms – thus they involve more than simply 'counting' 365 days.
→ Seasonal changes are also evident in human beings (e.g. seasonal affective disorder). People with SAD appear to have a high threshold for melatonin, a hormone which has an important regulatory role in sleep and is stimulated by exposure to darkness.

Circadian rhythms

→ These occur every 24 hours (e.g. the human sleep/wake cycle).
→ Other biological functions that display a circadian rhythm include body temperature, hormone secretion and blood pressure.
→ Circadian rhythms have great significance to animals. Nocturnal animals can avoid predators by remaining hidden during daylight hours, whereas diurnal animals are adapted to forage during the day.
→ These rhythms are controlled by endogenous pacemakers, so that animals can anticipate periodic events and engage in appropriate adaptive behaviours (e.g. sleeping when it gets dark).
→ The in-built biological nature of circadian rhythms is such that many will be maintained even when the light/dark cycle is manipulated artificially.

Checkpoint 1

How many complete cycles of sleep stages does someone go through in an average night's sleep?

Checkpoint 2

What other behaviours might occur in a circannual cycle?

Watch out!

A *circannual* rhythm is a type of *infradian* rhythm.

The jargon

Endogenous pacemaker. A physiological structure that regulates the timing of biological rhythms.

Checkpoint 3

What is the most powerful stimulus for resetting the circadian 'clock' in mammals?

Endogenous pacemakers

The pineal gland

In birds and reptiles, the most important endogenous pacemaker (biological clock) is the pineal gland. This contains light receptors, which respond to light penetrating the skull over the pineal. These then influence the activity of neurons in the pineal gland that convert the neurotransmitter serotonin into the hormone melatonin. Melatonin production and release is regulated by the amount of light falling on the pineal, *decreasing* as the level of light *increases*. When released into general circulation, melatonin acts on many organs and glands and is responsible for many of the body's rhythmic behaviours.

The supra-chiasmatic nucleus (SCN)

The SCN is part of the hypothalamus. The neurons of the SCN have an in-built circadian firing pattern. The SCN regulates the manufacture and secretion of melatonin in the pineal gland via an interconnecting pathway. The SCN also connects to the retina of the eye. Through these connections, the amount of light falling on the eye indirectly affects the release of melatonin from the pineal. Although the SCN and the pineal gland operate as endogenous pacemakers, their activity is synchronised with the light/dark rhythm of the external environment. Studies that have removed light as a zeitgeber have led to two conclusions:

→ Endogenous mechanisms are able to control the sleep/waking cycle even in the absence of light.

→ Light acts as a zeitgeber to reset the biological clock every day so that circadian rhythms are co-ordinated with the outside world.

Disruption of biological rhythms

The sensitivity of our bodily rhythms to zeitgebers is adaptive as long as external stimuli change only gradually. Sudden changes in zeitgebers (e.g. crossing time zones in air travel) mean we cannot adjust our bodily rhythms quickly enough, and our physiological activities are desynchronised for a while. This desynchronisation of the body's physiological rhythms from the external world gives rise to the feelings of tiredness and disorientation known as **jet lag**. After a few days the body and the external world re-synchronise, and we are again in tune with the external world and its zeitgebers. Studies of **shift work** (e.g. Czeisler et al 1982) show that switching shifts disrupts links between zeitgebers and biological rhythms, and that short-rotation shifts cause health problems, sleep difficulties and work-related stress.

> **Take note**
>
> Although the pineal gland has a role in sleep regulation in humans, it exerts control over the full daily cycle in other species (e.g. changes in blood pressure, body temperature etc.).

> **Take note**
>
> Human circadian rhythms may also shift when light is applied to the back of the knees.

> **The jargon**
>
> **Zeitgeber**. External cues (such as light) that help animals to maintain their circadian rhythms.

> **Grade booster**
>
> When outlining two or more theories, either do two in depth, or more than two in less depth but showing greater breadth.

> **Checkpoint 4**
>
> Why does jet lag tend to be greater when flying east to west than when flying west to east?

Exam practice   answers: page 38

(a) Describe **two** biological rhythms. (25 marks)

(b) Assess the consequences of disrupting biological rhythms. (25 marks)

Sleep

The sleep/waking cycle is an example of a circadian rhythm. Although we spend nearly one third of our lives asleep, psychologists are still unsure of its precise function. Sleep appears to be anything but a passive process, and the universality of sleep suggests that it is vital for all animals.

Restoration theories of sleep

This view of sleep proposes that the purpose of sleep is to restore the body after the exertions of the day. During sleep, growth hormone is released. Growth hormone has an important role in the metabolism of proteins. Proteins are relatively fragile and are constantly renewed during periods of slow-wave sleep (SWS).

Take note

Human sleep exhibits an alternating cycle of REM and SWS every 90–110 minutes. The cycle is shorter in smaller animals. Some species do not display REM sleep at all.

Oswald

→ Oswald (1980) claimed that the high levels of brain activity in REM are characteristics of brain recovery during REM sleep, while the increase in hormone activity during SWS reflects the restoration and recovery of the body.
→ REM is seen as essential for brain repair. REM sleep makes up for about half the total sleep time of newborn babies, when there is rapid growth and development of the brain.

The jargon

REM sleep. Rapid eye movement sleep, a stage of sleep that combines a state of body relaxation with an aroused EEG and rapid eye movements.

Horne

→ Horne (1988) proposes that in humans, only stage 4 sleep and REM sleep are *critical* for normal brain functioning.
→ This is supported by sleep deprivation studies which show that after deprivation, recovery is concentrated in stage 4 and REM sleep.
→ Horne claims that stage 4 and REM sleep make up **core sleep**, with the lighter stages of sleep (stages 1–3) making up **optional sleep**.
→ During core sleep, the brain restores itself after the activities of the day. Horne believes that body restoration is not the main purpose of sleep. This can be achieved during periods of quiet wakefulness.

Watch out!

Slow-wave sleep (SWS) is sometimes known as non-rapid eye movement (NREM) sleep.

Checkpoint 1

What are the characteristics of stage 4 sleep?

Evaluation of restoration theories

→ Evidence for the restoration theories only weakly supports these claims. Although intense exercise (increased metabolic expenditure) causes people to fall asleep more quickly, they do not sleep for longer.
→ Sleep deprivation does not appear to interfere with the ability to perform physical exercise and there is little evidence of a physiological stress response to the deprivation (Horne 1978).
→ Prolonged sleep deprivation in rats appears to interfere with the immune system, which may lead to death. In some species, sleep provides the only opportunity for tissue restoration, whereas in humans, a state of quiet wakefulness can serve the same purpose.
→ Restoration theories claim that a key function of sleep is protein synthesis. However, the main constituents of proteins (amino acids) are only freely available for five hours after eating (i.e. *before* sleep).

Take note

Rats may spend most of their waking life foraging or looking for mates, therefore sleep is the only inactive time they have for tissue restoration.

Ecological (evolutionary) theories of sleep

Despite the apparent universality of sleep, there are important differences in the amounts that animals sleep, and the relative proportion of SWS and REM sleep. Many of these differences can be attributed to differences in the ecological niche of these animals.

Meddis (1979) proposed that sleep evolved to keep animals safe from predators at times when their normal activities were impossible. Thus, diurnal and nocturnal animals which have evolved to be active at different parts of the 24-hour cycle are asleep at different parts of this cycle.

→ An animal's ecological niche affects the organisation of its sleep. Air-breathing aquatic mammals (such as dolphins and porpoises) must continue to come up to the surface to breathe; therefore prolonged sleep is dangerous. The Indus dolphin sleeps for seconds at a time repeatedly throughout the 24-hour day. The bottlenose dolphin 'switches off' one of its cerebral hemispheres at a time.

→ Because animals go to such lengths to sleep, this is a powerful argument for sleep being an essential function (Green 2000).

→ Smaller animals have higher metabolic rates, using up energy resources at a faster rate. Small animals, such as squirrels, sleep for much longer than larger animals, such as cows. Sleep may thus serve the double purpose of conserving resources at the same time as keeping the animal safe from predators.

→ REM sleep is common in birds and mammals (warm-blooded) but is absent in reptiles (cold-blooded). It has been proposed that REM sleep evolved to maintain the brain's temperature at night when otherwise it might fall to dangerously low levels.

Evaluation of ecological explanations of sleep

→ Research has not tended to support the exclusivity of sleep for preventing the attentions of predators. Although it is plausible that sleep would protect animals in this way, so would a state of behavioural inactivity. It is doubtful that such a complex response would evolve simply to protect animals from predators.

→ Sleep is also found in species which would clearly be better off without it. The Indus river dolphin is blind (the visibility in the river is extremely poor) but it has an excellent sonar system which it uses to navigate and catch prey. Vision has been 'selected out' because it was unnecessary. Despite the dangers of sleeping (e.g. the need to breathe, and the risk of injury from passing debris) the Indus dolphin still goes to great lengths to sleep. If sleep was simply adaptive, it would, as with vision, have been 'selected out'.

Checkpoint 2

When is a nocturnal animal asleep? When is a diurnal animal asleep?

The jargon

Ecological niche. An animal's habitat, to which it is adapted both physically and behaviourally.

Grade booster

Understand why each perspective would explain how we sleep.

Checkpoint 3

Why, according to this argument, would sleep have been 'selected out' in the Indus river dolphin?

Exam practice   answer: page 39

Outline and evaluate **two** theories relating to the functions of sleep. (25 marks)

Sleep disorders and dreaming

Dreams are a form of visual imagery experienced during REM sleep. Dreaming is also found in non-REM sleep, although not as regularly. The exact function of dreams is one of the oldest debates in psychology.

Watch out!

Although dreams commonly occur during REM sleep, dreaming and REM sleep are not one and the same thing.

Examiner's secrets

A lot of research has been done on sleep – do not just refer to those studies covered within your lessons.

Take note

When a person awakes from a nightmare, they may become aware of muscle paralysis (a characteristic of REM sleep). This can contribute to the frightening nature of the nightmare.

Explanations for disorders of sleep

Insomnia

This refers to a lack of sleep – not necessarily the length but the quality. One study by Carskadon et al (1974) found that people who considered themselves to have insomnia were actually only awake for up to 30 minutes during the night. Causes of insomnia can include lack of a regular sleep schedule, e.g. working shift work, too much alcohol and caffeine, and eating or exercising before bedtime. Another cause is apnea, which is when the individual stops breathing while asleep. They may have several hundred apneas per night, and with each one they wake up. This can lead to sufferers spending 12 hours or more in bed yet still feeling very sleepy throughout a normal day.

Sleepwalking

Dreams don't always occur during REM sleep, which is when the body is put in a state of paralysis for its own protection. People can also dream in non-REM and this can lead to sleepwalking. During non-REM sleep the person is not in a paralysed state and can therefore act out their dreams. Sleepwalking mainly affects children but a small number of adults also sleepwalk.

Narcolepsy

This is when a person may fall asleep at any time. This may happen several times a day and can last from a few seconds up to half an hour. Research by Hobson (1988) has found evidence that narcolepsy is caused genetically and runs in families.

The nature of dreams

→ Although sometimes people woken from non-REM sleep report having been dreaming, they are more likely to do this when woken from REM sleep. That dreams are not exclusive to REM sleep means it is inappropriate to describe it as merely 'dreaming sleep'.

→ Dreams may also occur in non-REM sleep, although these are usually less intense and less emotional in content than REM-based dreams. However, dreaming is clearly an important part of REM sleep, and is therefore considered to be one of the functions of REM.

→ Dreams are usually thought of as a series of visual images, but we also experience actions and emotions in dreams. Congenitally blind people have vivid dreams even though they see nothing in them.

→ Nightmares are dreams that contain a series of events that are associated with anxiety. They may become more frequent when the person has experienced considerable anxiety in their waking hours.

Psychological theories of dreams

Freud

Freud believed that dreams were the disguised fulfilment of a repressed desire (which was often sexual or aggressive and therefore would be unacceptable to the person when awake). Dreams thus have two roles:

→ They protect the dreamer from unacceptable impulses when awake.
→ They allow expression of these urges during sleep.

Dreams have a **manifest content**, which the person reports and which the analyst must interpret in order to get at the underlying **latent content**. The latent content reflects deep-seated desires and anxieties, which are transformed into the manifest content of dreams through 'dream-work'. The purpose of this dream-work is to prevent the dreamer becoming aware of the real (i.e. latent) desires and anxieties, and the role of the analyst is to reverse this process in order to get at what lies underneath.

Recent support for the Freudian explanation of dreaming comes from research with patients with brain damage in the cortical-limbic circuit in the forebrain. Damage to this area is characterised by a reported loss of dreaming. These circuits control our wishes and desires, whereas REM sleep is controlled by mechanisms in the brainstem.

Jung

Jung did not agree with Freud concerning the distinction between manifest and latent content. He saw dreams as reflecting the mind's current state rather than as having some underlying disguised content. The role of the analyst was to interpret the symbolic 'language' of the unconscious mind in dreams. Jung claimed that dreams contain certain universal archetypal symbols which are part of our collective unconscious. These include the *persona* (a drive to present oneself in the best light, which may give rise to dreams about anxiety in social situations) and the *anima/animus* (the male aspect of the female and the female aspect of the male – dreams help to balance these aspects for us).

Hypnosis

Freud called dreams 'the royal road to the unconscious'. Another way to unlock the unconscious is through hypnosis. Hypnosis is a relaxed state in which a person is out of touch with the outside world. Hilgard (1986) devised the neo-dissociation theory of hypnosis. This theory states that hypnosis is an altered state where consciousness is split into several independent streams; therefore hypnosis may give us access to memories that we could not normally remember.

Check the net

http://www.asdreams.org
The home page for the Association for the Study of Dreams.

"The interpretation of dreams is the royal road to a knowledge of the unconscious activities of the unconscious mind."

S. Freud (1909)

The jargon

Dream-work. The process by which underlying desires and anxieties are transformed into dream images.

Checkpoint

What is the significance of this finding for Freud's view of dreams and dreaming?

"The brain is so inexorably bent upon the quest for meaning that it attributes and even creates meaning when there is little or none in the data it is asked to process."

Hobson (1988)

Exam practice   answer: page 39

Describe Freud's theory of dreaming. (12 marks)

Gender and cultural bias

Gender bias is not a new thing. For centuries we have accepted assumptions about the differences between the sexes. Women are frequently 'pathologised' because of their physical differences from men, their pathology being seen as inescapably connected to their femaleness.

Gender bias

Some theories ignore the differences between men and women (**beta bias**), and some exaggerate them (**alpha bias**).

→ Alpha bias theories assume real and enduring differences between men and women. Within sociobiology, for example, differences in male and female behaviour may be attributed to genetic determinism. Thus male social dominance or sexual promiscuity might be seen as a product of their evolutionary history.

→ Beta bias theories have traditionally ignored or minimised sex differences. They have done this either by ignoring questions about women's lives or by assuming that findings from male studies apply equally well to females. Such theories may be described as **androcentric**.

Androcentric theories tend to offer an interpretation of women based on an understanding of the lives of men. Ideas of 'normal' behaviour may be drawn exclusively from studies of males. An example is Freud's theory, in which the young boy's identification with his father leads to the formation of a superego and of high moral standards. Girls, on the other hand, who do not experience the same Oedipal conflict as boys, cannot, it appears, develop their superego to the same degree as boys. Social psychologists have also typically developed theories from white, male undergraduates. This is then represented as 'human behaviour'.

Gender bias in psychological research

The main source of discontent with psychological research and its bias against women has centred around the use of traditional scientific method, most notably the use of the laboratory experiment.

Nicholson (1995) identifies two main problems with this adherence to an experimental science of psychology:

→ The experiment takes the *behaviour* of an individual research participant as the unit of study rather than the participant herself. This ignores the social, personal and cultural context in which the behaviour is enacted.

→ As a result of such research, women have been labelled as irrational, inappropriately volatile and easily depressed for no reason. They have been pathologised by the labels *pre-menstrual syndrome*, *post-natal depression* and *menopausal symptoms*.

Cultural bias

Cultural bias in psychological theory

Hofstede (1980) proposed that cultures could be classified on the dimension of individualism–collectivism. In making this distinction,

Watch out!

Many of our gender stereotypes have a long history!

Checkpoint 1

Can you find another example of an 'alpha bias' in your textbook?

Link

An example of a beta bias theory is Kohlberg's theory of moral development (see page 118).

Checkpoint 2

Can you find another example of a 'beta bias' in your textbook?

Action point

Read through your textbook – particularly the chapters on adult development. Can you find evidence of an 'androcentric bias'?

Watch out!

The laboratory experiment is seen as the essence of scientific 'proof' about human behaviour. For some reason there is more credibility and prestige associated with the results of laboratory experiments than there is with other methods in psychology.

Hofstede was careful to avoid what is known as the **ecological fallacy**. This would be the (mistaken) belief that if two cultures differ in terms of their individualist or collectivist bias, then any two individuals taken at random from those cultures would also differ in that way.

The **emic-etic** distinction (Berry 1969) focuses on the differences in our analysis of human behaviour.

→ Etic analyses focus on the universals of human behaviour. For example, Kohlberg's theory (page 118) sees moral development as a universal process. That is, all individuals, regardless of culture, would experience the same developmental processes.
→ An emic analysis of behaviour, on the other hand, would focus on the varied ways in which activities and development could be observed in any specific cultural setting.

Attempts to explain human behaviour in different parts of the world often involve using theories and research studies that have been developed within (predominantly) the USA. This **imposed etic** makes the assumption that whatever measures have been used in one cultural context, will have the same meaning when applied in another.

Cultural bias in psychological research

Replicating research studies across cultures presents psychologists with problems. Failure to ensure that participants and procedures are equivalent in different studies means that alternative explanations of the research findings (known as **plausible rival hypotheses**) must be addressed. Some of the problems are as follows:

→ **Translation** – instructions and responses must be faithfully translated for the purposes of comparison.
→ **Participants** – although these may be taken from similar social groups, they may have quite different social backgrounds and experiences in different cultural groups.
→ **Research tradition** – in many cultures people are used to scientific research and respond positively to participation. Inherent in this positive attitude is the belief that their responses will remain confidential. Trust in the research process cannot be taken for granted in other cultures where psychological research may be rare.

An example of cultural bias is Milgram's research into obedience. It has been replicated in a number of other cultures, but not always with direct equivalence of methods and participants.

Ethnocentrism

This is another area we have to be aware of when studying different cultures. It refers to the use of our own ethnic group as a basis for judgements about other ethnic groups. The other ethnic groups may be biased against, as their views, beliefs and customs may be considered as being abnormal when compared to our own. We may consider our own ethnic group as being somehow superior.

"Culture refers to the collective programming...which distinguishes members of one group from another."

Hofstede (1980)

> **Action point**
>
> Read through your textbooks to find cross-cultural replications of research (e.g. of obedience research). Make a list of any aspects of the research that were different in these studies. Are these factors likely to have affected the outcome of the study?

> **Exam practice** answer: page 39
>
> With reference to psychological theories and/or research, discuss the view that psychology offers a culturally biased view of behaviour. (25 marks)

Ethical issues and the use of animals

The ethical issues of psychological research are based on a number of fundamental moral principles. These are rules or standards that can be justified from a variety of theoretical perspectives. These principles underlie the issues that arise in research with human and animal participants.

Ethical issues in research with human participants

Deception

Baumrind (1985) suggests the following as consequences of deception:

→ It may decrease the number of naïve participants available for future research (i.e. those who do not suspect deception is taking place).
→ It may reduce support for psychological research in general (e.g. in the media and within the general population).
→ It may undermine the commitment of researchers to always telling the truth.
→ It removes the ability of research participants to give their fully informed consent to take part in an investigation.

Informed consent

The essence of the principle of informed consent is that the human subjects of research should be allowed to agree or refuse to participate in the light of comprehensive information concerning the nature and purpose of the research (Homan 1991).

→ To be informed means that all pertinent aspects of what is to happen and what *might* happen are disclosed to the participant. The participants should also be able to understand this information.
→ To give consent, the participant must be competent to make a rational and mature judgement. The agreement to participate should be voluntary, free from coercion and undue influence.

The greater the risk, the more meticulous should be the operation of informing potential participants.

Socially sensitive research

Socially sensitive research refers to '...studies in which there are potential social consequences or implications, either directly for the participants in research or the class of individuals represented by the research' (Sieber and Stanley 1988).

Specific issues of socially sensitive research include the following:

→ **Confidentiality** – in some areas of research, questions may reveal information of a sensitive nature. In such situations confidentiality is paramount. Otherwise, participants would be less willing to divulge this information in future research.
→ **Scientific freedom** – it is the role of the researcher to carry out scientific research. This freedom to pursue scientific research is balanced against the obligation to protect those who take part or the sectors of society that they represent.
→ **Ownership of data** – a major concern in the interpretation and

Watch out!

An ethical **issue** is not the same as an ethical **guideline**. Ethical guidelines are ways of resolving ethical issues.

Action point

Read through your textbook for examples of deception in psychological research. Do you feel these were justified given the aims of the research?

Grade booster

There are two sides to all of the ethical issues – arguments for and against.

Checkpoint 1

In what ways might we exert pressure on participants to take part (or continue) in a study?

Checkpoint 2

What types of research might be classified as 'socially sensitive' under this definition?

application of research findings in psychology is that they may be
used for reasons other than those for which they were originally
intended. It is the responsibility of researchers to consider in
advance the ways in which their research might be used.

→ **Ethical guidelines** may protect the immediate needs of research
participants, but may not deal with all the possible ways in which
research may inflict harm on a group of people or section of society.

The use of non-human animals in research

Arguments for animal research

→ Animals may be studied because they are fascinating in their own
right (ethology).

→ Animals offer the opportunity for greater control and objectivity in
research procedures.

→ Human beings and non-human animals have sufficient of their
physiology and evolutionary past in common to justify conclusions
drawn from the one being applied to the other.

→ Animal research has produced benefits to humans and to animals.

→ Researchers are sensitive to the suffering experienced by animals
and use procedures that ensure animals are humanely treated.

→ Researchers have developed alternative procedures which have led
to a reduction in the use of animals. Therefore animals are only used
when no other suitable procedure is available (*reduction, refinement*
and *replacement*).

Arguments against animal research

→ Animals have rights by virtue of their 'inherent value'. These rights
include the right to be treated with respect and not harmed.

→ The traditional scientific position on animal research treats animals
as 'renewable resources' rather than as organisms of value whose
rights we must respect.

→ The benefits of animal research have often been accomplished at
considerable expense in terms of animal suffering. By calculating the
benefits to humankind, but not the costs to animals, we might be
committing speciesism.

→ Critics of animal research often assert that the assumed similarities
between human beings and other animals do not exist. Green (1994)
argues otherwise: the basic physiology of the brain and nervous
systems of all mammals is essentially the same.

Take note

The Canadian Psychological Association
advises its members to 'analyse likely
short-term, ongoing, and long-term risks
and benefits of each course of action on
the individual(s) or group(s) involved or
likely to be affected'.

*"Animal liberators
need to accept that
animal research is
beneficial to humans.
Animal researchers
need to admit that
if animals are close
enough to humans...
then ethical dilemmas
surely arise in using
them".*

B. Orlans (1997)

Checkpoint 3

What is meant by the terms 'reduction,
refinement and replacement' in this
context?

Watch out!

There are strict laws (e.g. the 1986 Use
of Animals Act) and codes of conduct
(e.g. BPS and ASAB guidelines) to protect
animals that are used in research.

Exam practice   answer: pages 39–40

Describe and assess arguments for and against animal research in
psychology. (25 marks)

Free will and determinism

The idea that we are able to have some choice in how we act is fundamental in most common-sense theories of psychology. The free will versus determinism debate examines the degree to which human behaviour is freed from the causal influences of past events.

Checkpoint 1

In what ways might human behaviour be influenced by past events?

Free will

The notion of 'free will' allows us to separate out what is clearly the intention of an individual, from what has been caused by some internal or external event. The idea of free will is inconsistent with the opposite idea of determinism, because under the latter view of human behaviour, individuals act as a result of some prior cause. The term 'free' is taken to mean that a person or their behaviour is independent from the causal determinism of past events. The term 'will' refers to the idea that people make decisions about the goals they are seeking to achieve.

Action point

Mostly we act in ways that are consistent with our past (e.g. habits, previously reinforced behaviours etc.). Think of examples of your behaviour that could not be explained in this way.

→ Free will enables people to choose a path that is inconsistent with their past. If we do not accept that we are bound to the past, but accept that we have the capacity to formulate plans and goals and act accordingly, we are proposing the existence and influence of free will.

→ The concept of free will is therefore not only compatible with a wider view of determinism, but is also very important if we are to view individuals as being morally responsible for their own actions. If our actions are merely the product of some past event or of our biological 'programming', then we cannot be held responsible for our behaviours.

Determinism

Checkpoint 2

The notion of free will is particularly important for the issue of moral responsibility. If criminality was genetically determined, what issues would this raise?

When most people talk about determinism, they are, in fact, talking about **efficient causality**, a definition of causality originally put forward by Hume (1951). To say that one event has been determined by another, Hume wrote, meant that:

→ two events must be highly correlated (i.e. when one occurs, so does the other)

→ they must appear in chronological order (i.e. one after the other)

→ they must be located near to one another.

Take note

Every time John goes into a room, everybody leaves. They always leave just after he enters the room, and only the people in the room he enters leave. Could he be causing this behaviour?

Although the presence of these three criteria does not necessarily imply a cause-effect relationship, this belief in the importance of efficient causality has been enough to convince many scientists that the only appropriate way of determining the cause of events is to examine events in the past.

Some approaches tend to see the source of this determinism as being outside the individual, a position known as 'environmental determinism'. Others propose the source of this determinism as coming from inside the organism, e.g. in the form of unconscious motivation or genetic determinism – a position known as 'biological determinism'.

Link

See 'nature-nurture' on pages 36–37 for a more detailed discussion on the degree to which our behaviour is a product of 'biology' or 'experience'.

Major approaches and the free will debate

The psychodynamic approach

Freud believed that we are controlled by unconscious forces over which we have no control, and of which we are largely unaware. In psychoanalytic theory, events are not seen as occurring by chance; they are purposeful, being related to unconscious processes ('psychic determinism'). This view of human behaviour is in contrast to the belief that we are rational, thinking beings, fully in control of our own actions.

The behavioural approach

Behaviourists believe that our behaviour is a product of the reinforcement provided by the environment. Within our own reinforcement history, we have been conditioned into behaving in specific ways. Most human beings somehow believe that they are both free to choose yet, at the same time, controlled. For behaviourists, however, our actions are solely determined by factors in our environment, which directly or indirectly, mould our behaviour.

The humanistic approach

This approach believes that human beings are free to plan their own actions. People are seen as struggling to grow and to make difficult decisions that will profoundly affect their lives. As a result of these decisions, each of us becomes unique and responsible for our own behaviour. Humanistic therapies such as person-centred therapy are based on the assumption of free will.

The cognitive approach

Cognitive theorists reject biological and environmental determinism. They stress that human beings have a wide range of cognitive schemata that they use in their everyday life. When individuals face new events in their environment, they experience *freedom of decision* as to how they will behave, but are limited (i.e. their behaviour is determined to some extent) by the schemata they possess to organise their behaviour.

Conclusion

Scientists who accept a view of humans being guided by their own conscious planning have embraced a less radical view of determinism. This 'soft' determinism view proposes that people act consistently with their character. It is less difficult to reconcile this view of determinism with the idea of free will than it is with the 'hard' determinism view that behaviour is caused by environmental or biological factors.

Take note

This approach is an example of environmental determinism.

Grade booster

Each perspective has its own viewpoint on the free will/determinism debate – know what they are.

Examiner's secrets

Make sure you can expand each of these descriptions – exam questions frequently state a certain number of approaches from which to draw your material.

The jargon

Schemata. Cognitive 'structures' that act in much the same way as a computer programme. They act as a framework for interpreting incoming information and guide our actions.

Watch out!

Cognitive theorists do not see behaviour as a product of free will or determinism alone, but as a combination of the two.

Exam practice answer: page 40

With reference to **two or more** approaches, discuss the free will versus determinism debate in psychology. (25 marks)

Reductionsim

Psychologists frequently reduce their level of explanation to its simplest level (i.e. biological or mechanical processes). Following a reductionist line of thinking, we might always look for something more basic underneath whatever it is we are trying to explain – that is, the real cause of the event we are experiencing.

Psychologists frequently reduce their level of explanation to its simplest level (i.e. biological or mechanical processes). Following a reductionist line of thinking, we might always look for something more basic underneath whatever it is we are trying to explain – that is, the real cause of the event we are experiencing.

Physiological reductionism

As humans are biological organisms, it should be possible to reduce even complex behaviours to their constituent neurophysiological components. There is a clear advantage to this, as it leads to the application of concise and concrete terms, which are then susceptible to scientific methods of research (Wadeley et al 1997).

Scientists interested in the causes of schizophrenia have found evidence that excess activity of the biochemical neurotransmitter dopamine is a characteristic of schizophrenia. Such a 'biochemical' theory of schizophrenia would effectively de-emphasise the importance of environmental factors in the development of the disorder.

Evaluation of physiological reductionism

→ The view that disorders such as schizophrenia can be neatly explained in terms of biochemical deficiencies is changing. Most theorists now agree that schizophrenia is probably 'caused' by a combination of factors. Genetic and biological factors may establish a predisposition to develop the disorder, but psychological factors help to bring the disorder to fruition. Other factors, such as societal labelling, help maintain and, in some cases, worsen the symptoms.

→ Examples such as schizophrenia show us that complex phenomena cannot easily be explained simply by reference to a physiological imbalance. The influence of brain chemicals in disorders such as schizophrenia is indisputable, but to argue that they cause schizophrenia is to neglect all other potential influences in the course of this disorder.

Biological reductionism

In Darwinian theory, behaviours that can be shown to arise from genetic factors must have some 'survival value'. It is possible that many human behaviours have also evolved because of their survival value or their ability to increase an individual's opportunities for passing on their genes. The principles of kin selection suggest that in helping biological relatives, with whom we share genes, we are also ensuring the survival of our own genetic code. This, according to Wilson (1975), is the primary motivation behind much of human social behaviour from altruism to xenophobia (fear of strangers). According to sociobiologists, nature 'selects' certain psychological traits and social customs (such as kinship bonds and taboos against female adultery) because they help to ensure the transmission of an individual's genes.

Genetic explanations have also been advanced for behaviours that

---

The jargon

Reductionism. A belief that complex phenomena are best understood by breaking them down into their fundamental components.

Checkpoint 1

What factors in the environment of the schizophrenic might influence the 'course of this disorder'?

Watch out!

Darwin was not aware of the mechanics of genetic transmission at the time of his writing.

The jargon

Sociobiology. A branch of biology that focuses on the biological basis of social behaviour.

contribute to some of society's most pressing problems, such as drug abuse, mental illness, and mental retardation. For example, twin and adoption studies suggest that familial resemblance for schizophrenia is due to heredity rather than to shared family environment. Although these data suggest that inheritance plays a major role in schizophrenia, it is also evident that non-genetic factors are of critical importance. A risk of 30% or 50% for an identical co-twin of a schizophrenic far exceeds the population risk of 1%, but is not the 100% concordance expected if schizophrenia was entirely a genetic disorder (Plomin 1990).

Evaluation of biological reductionism

→ Unlike physical characteristics, most behaviours and behavioural problems are not distributed in 'either/or' dichotomies.
→ The role of inheritance in behaviour has become widely accepted, even for sensitive topics such as IQ. Acceptance of genetic influence has even begun to outstrip the data in some cases.
→ For most behaviours, too few studies have been conducted to answer the question of whether genetic influence is significant.
→ Genetic variance rarely accounts for as much as half of the variance of behavioural traits. Evidence for significant genetic influence is often implicitly interpreted as if heritability were 100%, whereas heritabilities for behaviour seldom exceed 50% (Plomin 1990).

Environmental reductionism

Behaviourists believe that we are controlled by forces outside our control. The complex behaviour of humans is seen as learned 'performances' in response to signals which are present in the environment. The principles for learning behavioural sequences are seen as being the same for all species. The application of these principles in behaviour modification programmes has had considerable success, e.g. the effective control of aggressive behaviour requires a change in the pattern of rewards that aggression brings (Medcof and Roth 1979).

Evaluation of environmental reductionism

→ Restricting ourselves to the study of only one influence at a time may make sense within the context of a laboratory, but we may miss the complexity of influences on a behaviour at any one time.
→ In a world dominated by either reinforcement or punishment, it might appear that the only way to motivate people is with the 'carrot and the stick'. This distracts us from asking whether the behaviour being reinforced is worthwhile in the first place.

Check the net

Use the Internet to find out more about some of the genetic explanations for psychopathology. A good starting point is: www.mentalhealth.com

The jargon

Concordance. The degree to which genetically-related people share similar traits or characteristics.

Watch out!

High levels of concordance are often interpreted as if the trait was completely inherited. This is rarely the case.

Checkpoint 2

Behaviourists believe that learning principles are the same for all species. Why is this particularly significant for their view of behaviour and the methods they use to explore it?

Exam practice   answer: page 40

Discuss the nature and value of reductionist explanations of human behaviour. (25 marks)

Psychology as science

Watch out!

Not all psychologists accept scientific methods as the best way of exploring human behaviour.

Science is concerned with what we *know* to be true, rather than what we *believe* to be true, and so we attach considerable importance to science as a way of distinguishing what is true and real from what is not. Science is seen as both a body of knowledge that we accept as being trustworthy, as well as the method for attaining that knowledge.

The nature of science

What is science?

Science is often seen as both a body of knowledge that we accept as being trustworthy, and also the method for attaining that knowledge (i.e. the scientific method).

"Science is built up of facts, as a house is built of stones; but an accumulation of facts is no more a science than a heap of stones is a house."

Henri Poincaré (1905)

The characteristics of science

The most fundamental characteristic of science is its reliance on **empirical methods** of observation and investigation, i.e. observation through sensory experience rather than a reliance on thoughts and ideas. All scientific ideas must, at some point, be subjected to empirical investigation through careful observation of perceivable events. For science to 'make sense', it is necessary to explain the results of empirical observation. That means constructing theories, which can then be tested and refined through further empirical observation.

Slife and Williams (1995) identify further attributes of science.

→ Scientific observation is made under **objective** conditions.
→ Scientific observation takes place under **controlled** conditions.
→ Science involves making **predictions** about what is expected to happen under specified conditions. We can then **validate** or **falsify** whatever theory or hypothesis led to the observations being made.
→ Scientific investigations are open to public scrutiny. Confidence in results is increased when investigations can be **replicated**.

Psychology as science

Science as knowledge

Science is a body of knowledge that explains the nature of the world.

→ Scientific explanations reject, and are preferred to, other explanations of naturally-occurring phenomena (such as magic).
→ Scientific explanations are often stated as laws or general principles about the relationship between different events. Because of the regularity of the way in which these events occur together, it then becomes possible to control and predict them.

"Man is the interpreter of nature, science the right interpretation."

William Whewell (1840)

Despite significant advances in scientific psychology, it has yet to lead to the development of universal laws of human behaviour. Although most psychologists accept the idea that behaviour tends to be determined, the inability to control all the variables that underlie human behaviour means that accurate control and prediction is impossible.

Science as method

Scientific investigation involves empirical observation and the development of theories that are constantly tested and refined. In psychology, scientific methods are the preferred method of investigation for most psychologists, particularly the laboratory experiment, which offers the psychologist opportunities for control and prediction that are absent in less 'scientific' methods. However, the use of scientific methods is insufficient cause for labelling psychology a 'science'. Parapsychology has been subjected to rigorous scientific study, yet few psychologists would accept it as 'scientific'.

Problems with scientific psychology

Maintaining objectivity

Kuhn (1970) believed that total objectivity was never possible in science. The view that any particular scientific psychologist holds about the world (in Kuhn's terms, their 'paradigm') makes them think about the world in a specific way. This influences what they investigate, the methods they use to investigate it, and the sorts of explanations that are seen as acceptable for the results obtained. As all scientific knowledge emerges from within this specific set of influences, it is questionable whether it is possible to establish universal laws of behaviour.

Operationalisation

To carry out a scientific test, we must be able to observe whatever it is we are investigating. This is not always straightforward. For example, there are many events (such as emotion) that we cannot observe directly. Instead, we observe something else that we think represents the thing we are really interested in. Thus psychologists often explore the relationship between two things (e.g. love and happiness) without ever being able to measure either of these directly. As is the case with many investigations in psychology, our observations are always one step removed from the phenomenon that we are really interested in.

Establishing causality

It is generally accepted in scientific psychology that the only way to establish causality is to carry out an experiment. To be confident that any change in a dependent variable has been caused by manipulation of an independent variable, the researcher would need to control everything else that could possibly have a causal effect on the dependent variable. This is impossible when we are dealing with human beings. We cannot know all the possible ways in which any one individual might be influenced to behave at any given time.

Link

See Research planning and Research design on pages 78–81.

The jargon

Parapsychology. The study of paranormal phenomena (such as ESP and clairvoyance).

Checkpoint 1

In what ways might scientific psychology be influenced by the 'paradigm' of the researcher?

"As soon as questions of will or decision or reason or choice of action arise, human science is at a loss."

Noam Chomsky (1978)

Checkpoint 2

Correlational designs are criticised because they tell us nothing about causal relationships between variables. What important factor exists in experiments that enables us to make causal statements?

Exam practice   answer: page 41

Discuss the nature of psychology as science. (25 marks)

Nature-nurture

Action point

Use your textbook to find examples of theories that subscribe to each of these perspectives.

Throughout the development of psychology, there has been a tension between those who favour a view of behaviour as a product of heredity (nature) and those who favour the greater influence of environment (nurture). Those who adopted the former viewpoint were called nativists and those who adopted the latter were called empiricists.

Ethology versus behaviourism

Midway through the last century, there were two dominant schools of thought concerning human behaviour.

Watch out!

Behaviourists believed that differences between species were quantitative rather than qualitative – this was the justification for concentrating their experimental studies on animals.

→ **Behavourists**, as a result of extensive laboratory work with animals, concluded that all behaviour was the product of learning. This process was considered to be so universal that differences between species were regarded as irrelevant.

→ In contrast, the **ethological** school focused on natural behaviour. According to this position, organisms are born with 'fixed-action patterns' that are little changed by the environment. These fixed-action patterns are the result of evolutionary adaptations.

Although behaviourists accepted that evolution had some relevance in human behaviour, this was merely to acknowledge the continuity between humans and other animals. However, although evolution implies continuity between species, it also implies diversity, each organism being adapted to a specific way of life in a specific environment (De Waal 1999). Behaviourists were forced to adopt some of the ideas of evolutionary biology, especially with the discovery that learning is not the same for all species.

Ethologists also ran into problems explaining some aspects of animal and human behaviour. Behavioural traits such as the inhibition of aggression, or altruistic behaviour, were seen as being 'for the benefit of the species'. These ideas have now been replaced by theories of how an action benefits the individuals concerned and its genetic relatives.

The jargon

Altruistic behavior. Acting in some way to benefit another while incurring some cost to ourselves.

Checkpoint 1

In what ways might the inhibition of aggression or altruistic behaviour benefit the individual?

Nature-nurture and intelligence

Until the middle of the 20th century, intelligence was widely regarded as mainly biologically determined (the **nature** view). If intelligence, and therefore potential, was inherited, there seemed little one could do for individuals of low intelligence. A different perspective, which stretches back to the 17th century, proposed that intelligence was largely a product of experience and was, within limits, completely malleable (the **nurture** view). In the 1950s, the predominant view concerning the origins of intelligence shifted from the 'nature' to the 'nurture' side of the argument. Supporters of this view put forward arguments that intelligence was not genetically determined, but was due to the nature of an individual's experience. It was argued that intelligence was particularly malleable in early childhood. This led to the development of a number of compensatory education programmes such as the *Headstart* programme in the USA.

The jargon

Headstart. Originally the name of a programme in the 1960s designed to enrich the academic performance of children from underprivileged backgrounds, the term is now used to cover a range of social and educational programmes with the same broad aim.

Evaluation of the nature-nurture debate

Piaget and intelligence

Piaget's theory is significant for this debate for two reasons:

→ It bridges the gap between 'nature' and 'nurture' – biologically given structures unfold when placed in a nurturing environment.
→ Piaget proposed four mechanisms of cognitive development (e.g. maturation and equilibrium) through which the environment interacts with the internal structures of the individual.

The individual is the main focus, whereas the role of the environment is to facilitate the automatic unfolding of biological, cognitive structures.

Methodological difficulties in the nature-nurture debate

There is no agreement about how we might define or measure the environment in which a person grows up. Research using animals has been much more successful in defining and manipulating environmental variables. It is this kind of research that emphasises that much of behavioural development is subject to environmental influence in its development. Trying to understand how such environmental variables would affect *human* behavioural development is a more complex issue. It is at the cultural level that this difficulty becomes most pronounced, yet it is probably at the level of cultural influences that the most powerful and subtle environmental variables operate (Horowitz 1993).

Gene-environment interactions

When we say that a behavioural trait such as intelligence or depression is inherited, all we mean is that *part* of its variability is explained by genetic factors. The environment accounts for the rest of the variability. The interaction between genes and environment is complex, e.g. the balance between genetic and environmental influences on a particular behaviour appears to change as a person ages (Plomin 1994).

Research has suggested three types of gene-environment relationships:

→ A **passive** relationship between genes and environment may occur because parents transmit genes that promote a certain trait and also construct the rearing environment.
→ An **evocative** relationship between genes and environment may occur because genetically distinct individuals may evoke different reactions in those around them.
→ An **active** relationship between genes and environment may occur because individuals actively select experiences that fit in with their genetically influenced preferences.

Link

See Cognitive development on pages 106–107.

Grade booster

Use research on specific disorders to support either nature-nurture approach, e.g. studies done on eating disorders using MZ and DZ twins.

Checkpoint 2

Why do you think it is so difficult to assess the influence of cultural variables on behaviour?

"Life is like playing a violin solo in public and learning the instrument as one goes on."

Samuel Butler (1895)

Examiner's secrets

This question has a **synoptic** element, so make sure you can resource your answer with a range of different perspectives and topics in psychology.

Exam practice   answer: page 41

With reference to **two or more** areas of psychology, discuss the nature-nurture debate as it applies to an understanding of human behaviour. (25 marks)

Answers

Perspectives, physiological psychology and issues

Perspectives: The biological approach

Checkpoint

Psychosurgery and chemotherapy

Perspectives: The behavioural approach

Checkpoints

1 Credit could be given for the following:
- the role of external/environmental factors on learning
- classical conditioning
- operant conditioning
- social learning theory.

2 This is when we acquire new behaviours by observation. An individual acquires an ability by watching the behaviour of another (the model). This theory was developed by Bandura through his Bobo doll experiment (1977). Aggression can be learnt from the media such as TV, computer games and films.

Perspectives: The cognitive approach

Checkpoint

The cognitive triad includes a person's negative views about themselves, the world and their future.

Exam practice

Credit could be give for the following:
- the computer analogy
- determinism vs free will
- cognitive reductionism
- the relevance of social/cultural factors in influencing behaviour.

Perspectives: The psychodynamic approach

Checkpoint

The therapy that could be outlined includes
- free association – getting someone to unlock their unconscious by allowing them to say whatever comes into their head.
- dream analysis – understanding the unconscious by analysing someone's dreams.

Perspectives: The humanistic approach and research methods

Exam practice

Credit would be given for writing about the following:
- determinism vs free will
- practical applications (therapy)

- the methods used to study behaviour
- the scientific/objective nature
- reductionism
- the role of innate factors.

Biological rhythms

Checkpoints

1 The average person goes through between four and five complete cycles of sleep stages per night. Each complete cycle lasts about one and a half hours.
2 Another common behaviour that occurs on a circannual cycle is hibernation (e.g. in squirrels and bears).
3 Light, which enters through the eyes, then, via the supra-chiasmatic nucleus, affects the release of melatonin by the pineal gland.
4 The most likely explanation for this is that it is easier for the body to adjust its body clock when it is ahead of local time (known as 'phase delay') than when it is behind (known as 'phase advance').

Exam practice

(a) This only asks for a *description* of biological rhythms, so you should restrict your answer to that – don't be tempted to offer any evaluative content. We have covered three different types of rhythms, but you are only asked for two here. It is best not to do both infradian and circadian rhythms (as they are both infradian rhythms). You would only have 15 minutes to answer this part of the question (that's about 150 words for each rhythm), so you might construct your answer as follows:
- definition of infradian rhythms and relation with circannual rhythms. SAD in humans and difference in the physiological basis of infradian and circadian rhythms
- definition of circadian rhythms, examples of circadian rhythm, significance (e.g. for diurnal and nocturnal animals), role of endogenous pacemakers, and the role of the SCN.

(b) This part of the question gives you the chance to assess what would happen if biological rhythms were disrupted. The most common forms of disruption are jet lag and shift work. As the question asks you to 'assess' the consequences, don't just describe what they might be, but assess these (e.g. is there research evidence for this form of disruption, why would it happen, and so on).

Sleep

Checkpoints

1 Stage 4 sleep is characterised by an EEG of only delta waves, metabolic rate at its lowest and the highest arousal threshold (how difficult it is to wake the sleeper) of any of the stages.
2 A nocturnal animal sleeps during the day.
A diurnal animal sleeps during the night.

3 Because it served no advantage, but rather because of its disadvantages it would put dolphins in danger.

Exam practice

It is appropriate to choose either two named theories (such as Oswald and Horne) or two theoretical perspectives (such as 'restoration' and 'ecological' explanations). Whichever approach you take, it is vital that equal amounts of coverage are given to each theory, and to the descriptive and evaluative aspects of the question.

Examiner's secrets

Remember that questions such as this require a number of things (two theories, outline and evaluate), so effective time management is vital. Practise!

Sleep disorders and dreaming

Checkpoint

Previously, dreams were seen by many as an artefact of REM sleep, or as a simple way of clearing out unwanted information (and therefore of no significance). Although this finding does not directly support Freud's theory, it lends some support to Freud's proposal that dreams are located in that part which deals with our wishes and desires, a fundamental aspect of the Freudian view of dreaming.

Exam practice

This is a straight forward 'describe' question so you should describe Freud's theory about dreams, referring to the idea that they are repressed desires or memories. You also need to explain the manifest and latent content of the dream and the methods used by this approach to explain the meaning of the dream (no evaluation is needed).

Gender and cultural bias

Checkpoints

1 Gilligan's theory of moral development (see page 107) is an example of an 'alpha bias' theory. Gilligan claimed that women seem to centre their judgements more on care than do men.
2 Few theories in psychology draw a specific distinction between males and females, therefore most of psychology might be said to show a beta bias.

Exam practice

This is a fairly open-ended question as it invites you to draw on psychological theories and/or research. Try to remember, when selecting material for this answer, that this question has a synoptic element. This means that your answer will also be assessed for the range of theories, issues, methods etc. that you include in your answer. A suitable response to this question would be:

• the nature of cultural bias in psychological theory (e.g. the emic-etic distinction) or historical bias (e.g. 'Asch effect' in conformity and the era of McCarthyism in

the USA)
• examples of theories that demonstrate a cultural bias (e.g. social exchange theories of relationships and Kohlberg's theory of moral development)
• the nature of cultural bias in psychological research (e.g. problems of translation, research participants and cultural differences in the research tradition)
• discussion of research that has been replicated in other cultures (e.g. Milgram's work on obedience) – relate this to the cultural biases in the previous point.

Examiner's secrets

Questions in the AQA (A) 'Perspectives' section have a synoptic element. This means that, in addition to the material chosen to answer the question, you will be assessed on the breadth of approaches, issues and debates demonstrated in your answer.

Ethical issues and the use of animals

Checkpoints

1 There are a number of ways that participants can be pressurised to take part (or continue) in a study. These include selection of participants (e.g. in a school), or through payment of participants (when they may feel pressurised because of their part in a 'contract' with the researcher).
2 Research that might be classified as 'socially sensitive' would include research into racial and gender differences, and research into the nature and origins of sexual diversity.
3 Reduction involves using methods that obtain the same amount of information from fewer animals, or more information from the same number of animals. Replacement involves, for example, the increased use of brain imaging and scanning procedures (such as MRI and PET scans) in humans and the use of computer simulations.
Refinement involves using procedures that minimise stress and enhance animal well-being.

Exam practice

This question appears to ask for simply a list of arguments for and against animal research in psychology. However, it benefits from a closer second look. You are asked to describe and assess (i.e. give a considered appraisal of...) these arguments. This will require not only a description of arguments for and against animal research, but also a critical appraisal of these arguments. For example, an argument *for* animal research is that it has produced considerable benefits to humans. You might appraise this argument by giving examples of where animal research has proved useful to humans (e.g. in developing a better understanding of stress), but also point out that by judging the value of animal research solely in terms of its benefits to humans, we may be committing speciesism.

Although there is no prescribed order in which material need be presented, the following is a suggested route through the requirements of the question:

- description of the arguments *for* animal research in psychology
- critical appraisal of the arguments *for* animal research in psychology
- description of the arguments against *animal* research in psychology
- critical appraisal of the arguments *against* animal research in psychology.

Free will and determinism

Checkpoints

1 Biologically, it might be influenced by 'instinct' or inherited characteristics. Alternatively, we may be seen as a product of our reinforcement histories.
2 This may be seen to lessen the criminal's personal responsibility for their actions as well as causing anxiety in the genetic relatives of the criminal (who may also carry the same gene or genes). However, behaviour is rarely 'caused' by genes alone, so personal responsibility for behaviour would not be lost.

Exam practice

There is a reminder in this question to draw material from at least two approaches in psychology. If you feel you have sufficient relevant material from just two approaches (the question gives you the opportunity to include more than two) then don't feel that you have to write about more than this. Trying to cover too many different approaches may produce a superficial answer that would be worth fewer marks than a more detailed one that has a slightly narrower focus.

The material on pages 30–31 would cover all that is required in this answer, but you might like to include your responses to the checkpoints, as these extend the discussion of the topic. A suggested route through this answer would be:

- the nature of free will in psychological theory
- the nature of determinism in psychological theory
- review of the psychodynamic approach – an example of biological determinism
- review of the behavioural approach – an example of environmental determinism
- the humanistic and cognitive approaches – alternatives to purely deterministic theories
- conclusion – hard and soft determinism.

Reductionism

Checkpoints

1 Behaviourist explanations of schizophrenia claim that by failing to attend to relevant social cues, schizophrenics develop bizarre responses to the environment. Family explanations stress the role of the family environment in the development of schizophrenia. Sociocultural theorists suggest that many aspects of schizophrenia are caused by the diagnosis itself (e.g. labelling theory).
2 This justifies the use of animals in experimental studies of learning. Findings from animal studies can then be generalised to human beings.

Exam practice

As with the previous question (on free will), this is a fairly open-ended question, but unlike that question, it does not give the 'reminder' that you should draw from more than one approach in psychology. However, you should draw from at least two types of reductionism in order to satisfy the synoptic element of the question.

We have covered three types of reductionism and within these different types there are a number of different 'explanations' of human behaviour. Remember that half of the marks available for this question are for the critical part of your answer (the *value* of reductionist explanations), so balance your response accordingly.

A suitable response to this question might be:

- introduction – the nature of reductionism in psychology
- physiological reductionism – e.g. biochemical explanations of schizophrenia
- evaluation of physiological reductionism – e.g. neglect of other possible causes of schizophrenia
- biological reductionism – e.g. genetic explanations of behaviour
- evaluation of biological reductionism – e.g. overestimation of the degree of heritability in behavioural traits
- environmental reductionism – e.g. the universality of learning principles
- evaluation of environmental reductionism – e.g. it ignores the complexity of influences on a specific behaviour at any one time.

Psychology as science

Checkpoints

1 The paradigm of the researcher will influence the predictions made, the methods deemed appropriate to research these predictions, and the interpretation of the results gained. Results will either validate a particular point of view or falsify it. Even when research supports a particular theory, it is possible that other explanations (from outside the paradigm) might better explain the results obtained.

2 Because the independent variable can be systematically varied (i.e. the experimenter can manipulate it), it is possible to study its causal effect on the dependent variable.

Exam practice

Your answer to this question can be neatly split into three parts, each part being equivalent to about 13 minutes of writing time (about 200–300 words).

As the question asks you to discuss the nature of psychology as science, you should begin by considering what science actually is (including the characteristics of science), and then move on to consider the degree to which psychology satisfies these criteria. As this question also has a critical component, you should follow this with a detailed account of the problems of scientific psychology.

A suitable response to this question might be:

- what is science? – the characteristics of science (e.g. scientific observation takes place under objective and controlled conditions)
- arguments for psychology as science – science as knowledge and science as the preferred method in psychology
- problems with scientific psychology (e.g. maintaining objectivity and establishing causality).

Examiner's secrets

You may have come across references to 'post-modernists' and 'social-constructionism' as you have read around psychology. Although it is not required to include reference to these in your answer to this question, you may get some good critical commentary by reading a little about their views of science.

Nature-nurture

Checkpoints

1 By inhibiting aggression, the individual may be able to profit from the co-operation of others. In status conflicts, the loser who inhibits their aggression minimises the risk of expulsion from the group or further injury. Altruistic behaviour has a potential pay-off if it is reciprocated some time in the future (reciprocal altruism) or benefits those with whom the altruist shares genes (kin selection).

2 It is difficult to exactly replicate studies in different cultures, due to problems of translation, the nature of participants, etc. Researchers may be unaware of the subtle influences on behaviour within a particular culture.

Exam practice

As with the free will versus determinism question earlier, there is a specific requirement to draw your material from more than one area of psychology. Remember that in casting the net wide, you are satisfying the synoptic element of the question.

The question asks you to discuss the nature-nurture debate 'as it applies to psychology', so don't just write about it in the abstract. The material on pages xxx-x splits the relevant content quite neatly into descriptive material (e.g. nature-nurture and intelligence) and evaluative material (e.g. gene-environment interactions). It is important to point out that few theories in psychology rely on either/or explanations, but most accept the (often subtle) interactions of genes and environment.

A suitable response to this question might be:

- what is meant by 'nature' and 'nurture', and what characterises these different explanations of behaviour?
- ethology and behaviourism – conflicting views of behaviour
- nature-nurture and intelligence
- Piaget and intelligence – the interactionist perspective on intelligence
- methodological difficulties in exploring the nature-nurture debate
- gene-environment interactions.

Examiner's secrets

Remember, when discussing different explanations, that you are discussing the 'nature-nurture debate' rather than simply presenting alternative views of human behaviour. It is all too easy to get side-tracked, e.g. when discussing Piaget's views on intelligence, to become bogged down in a detailed description of his theory, rather than simply making a point about its position and significance in the nature-nurture debate and then moving on. That is another good reason for setting time limits for each part of your response. Stick to these and you won't go far wrong.

Revision checklist
Perspectives, physiological psychology and issues

By the end of this chapter you should be able to:

1	Understand all five perspectives and their relevant theories and therapies.	Confident	Not confident **Revise** pages 10–19
2	Understand what biological rhythms are and what different types exist.	Confident	Not confident **Revise** pages 20–21
3	Explain several reasons why we sleep.	Confident	Not confident **Revise** pages 22–23
4	Understand the role that dreaming plays in our sleep.	Confident	Not confident **Revise** pages 24–25
5	Discuss the effect of gender and culture on research.	Confident	Not confident **Revise** pages 26–27
6	Argue for and against the use of animals in psychological research.	Confident	Not confident **Revise** pages 28–29
7	Know about the free will versus determinism debate.	Confident	Not confident **Revise** pages 30–31
8	Be able to define and explain the term reductionism and how it applies to the five perspectives within psychology.	Confident	Not confident **Revise** pages 32–33
9	Discuss the arguments for and against psychology being a science.	Confident	Not confident **Revise** pages 34–35
10	Know about the nature-nurture debate.	Confident	Not confident **Revise** pages 36–37

Core studies

Core studies are an essential element of both OCR and WJEC specifications and by using the *Topic checklist* you can find out which of the core studies you need to know about for your examination. These summaries provide you with a brief snapshot of the context, aims, sample, method, findings and conclusions of each of the core studies.

Exam themes

The OCR specification expects you to be able to answer questions relating to:

- specific aspects of the core studies

- theories and research surrounding the core studies

- the approaches/perspectives, issues and methods arising from the core studies.

The WJEC specification expects you to be able to answer questions relating to:

- the aims and context, procedures and findings, and conclusions of the core studies

- the methodology used in the core study or findings in relation to alternative research findings.

Topic checklist

	Edexcel		AQA/A		AQA/B		OCR		WJEC	
	AS	A2	AS	A2	AS	A2	AS	A2	AS	A2
Baron-Cohen, Jolliffe, Mortimore and Robertson (1997)							○			
Gardner and Gardner (1969)									○	
Loftus and Palmer (1974)							○		○	
Savage-Rumbaugh et al (1986)							○			
Bandura, Ross and Ross (1961)							○			
Freud (1909)							○			
Gibson and Walk (1960)									○	
Langer and Rodin (1976)									○	
Samuel and Bryant (1984)							○			
Bennett-Levy and Marteau (1984)									○	
Dement and Kleitman (1957)							○			
Maguire, Gadian, Johnsrude, Good, Ashburner, Frackowiak and Frith (2000)							○			
Rahe, Mahan and Arthur (1970)									○	
Sperry (1968)							○			
Asch (1955)									○	
Milgram (1963)							○		○	
Piliavin, Rodin and Piliavin (1969)							○			
Reicher and Haslam (2006)							○			
Buss (1989)									○	
Griffiths (1994)							○			
Rosenhan (1973)							○		○	
Thigpen and Cleckley (1954)							○			

Cognitive psychology

Check the net

Check out the websites of the exam boards www.ocr.org.uk and www.wjec.co.uk for examples of the exam papers and the types of questions you can be asked.

Baron-Cohen, Jolliffe, Mortimore and Robertson (1997): *Another advanced test of theory of mind: evidence from very high functioning adults with autism or Asperger's syndrome*

'Theory of mind' (TOM) is the ability to understand that others' intentions, beliefs and desires may be different from our own. Children with autistic spectrum disorders (ASD) are unable to demonstrate TOM using traditional 1st order assessments (e.g. the Sally-Anne test). Baron-Cohen et al aimed to investigate if adults with ASD are able to interpret states of mind from 'reading eyes'.

Three groups of participants: 50 'normal' (25 male, 25 female); 16 'autistic' (13 male, 3 female); 10 'Tourette's' (8 male, 2 female). Participants were matched for intelligence and age.

Each participant was individually shown 25 photos of pairs of eyes, for 3 seconds each photo. The participant was asked 'Which word best describes what this person is thinking or feeling?' and then had to select the correct answer (target) from choice of two (incorrect answer called foil).

Baron-Cohen et al found the adults with autism were less likely to select the target word (mean 16.3) than the normal adults (mean 20.3) and adults with Tourette's (20.4). They also found that in the 'normal' group, females (mean 21.8) were better at 'reading minds' than males (mean 18.8). They concluded these results were evidence of slight 'mindreading' deficits in intelligent adults with ASD.

Gardner and Gardner (1969): *Teaching sign language to a chimpanzee*

After previously unsuccessful attempts to teach primates a vocal language, Gardner and Gardner aimed to investigate if they could teach a chimpanzee to communicate using American Sign Language (ASL).

Washoe was a wild-caught female infant chimpanzee who was approximately 8-14 months old when she arrived at the Gardners' laboratory.

Action point

Compare Gardner and Gardner's research with Savage-Rumbaugh et al. Both are using primates in language research, but what other similarities and differences are there in these two studies?

After establishing a routine, Washoe was always with at least one of her human companions, who would introduce games and activities and used ASL extensively in Washoe's presence. The methods used to encourage Washoe's companions to use ASL included: imitation of signs using the 'Do this' game; encouraging 'babbling'; and instrumental conditioning – tickling was the most effective reward to use with Washoe. Three observers had to note Washoe using the sign in context and spontaneously over a period of 15 consecutive days before it was considered as being learnt.

Within 22 months from the beginning of Washoe's training, 30 words met the criteria set by Gardner and Gardner. Washoe learnt 'Me' and 'You', which allowed her to form simple sentences. Gardner and Gardner are wary of answering the question of whether Washoe acquired language. However the fact that Washoe's signs do not remain specific to their original contexts suggests that she has indeed 'learnt' language.

Loftus and Palmer (1974): *Reconstruction of automobile destruction*

A leading question is one which suggests to the witness what answer is desired. Loftus and Palmer's investigation had two aims – whether leading questions can affect a witness's initial answer to that question and how questions are answered a week later. In Experiment 1, 45 students were selected and in Experiment 2, 150 students were selected.

In Experiment 1, five groups of participants were shown clips of a traffic accident and were asked 'About how fast were the cars going when they hit/smashed/collided/bumped/contacted each other?' In Experiment 2, all three groups were shown a car crash. One group was then asked 'How fast were the cars going when they smashed each other?'; the second group heard 'hit' not 'smashed': the third group were not asked a question. A week later they were all asked 'Did you see any broken glass?' (n.b. there had been no broken glass in the film).

In Experiment 1, mean mph estimates for the conditions were: smashed – 40.8; collided – 39.3; bumped – 38.1; hit – 34.0; contacted – 31.8. In Experiment 2, the number of participants reporting broken glass in the conditions were: smashed – 16; hit – 7; control – 6. People's accuracy for reporting the details of a complex event is potentially distorted through the use of leading questions.

Action point

Loftus and Palmer's research is sometimes criticised for lacking validity because the participants were shown film clips of car accidents in a laboratory. Do you think this is a fair criticism?

Savage-Rumbaugh et al (1986): *Spontaneous symbol acquisition and communicative use by pygmy chimpanzees*

There is much debate as to whether language is a learned phenomenon (nurture) or whether there is an innate feature in the brain that is responsible (nature). Much primate research has, with various degrees of success, tried to 'teach' a human language. This is an opportune case study of a pygmy chimpanzee that spontaneously began to use symbols to communicate.

Kanzi is a pygmy chimpanzee, born in captivity to a mother who was a 'language chimp' at the Yerkes National Primate Centre. At 6 months old, he was assigned to be reared in a language-using environment. At 2½ years of age (and separated from his mother) he was observed to be spontaneously using symbols.

Kanzi used a keyboard with geometric symbols that lit up when touched, and a speech synthesiser. For 17 months, from 2½ years of age, Kanzi's language usage was recorded by both observers and a computerised log of his keyboard usage. Symbol use was recorded as correct, incorrect, spontaneous, structured, imitation and whether the symbol used matched his behaviour.

Savage-Rumbaugh et al found that he was able to use symbols to: identify where food had been located in his 55-acre forest enclosure; guide a person to a specific location; and indicate where he wanted to go. Kanzi produced 2530 correct combinations of symbols. On 265 occasions, Kanzi imitated symbols. Savage-Rumbaugh et al concluded that Kanzi had learned to use symbols spontaneously and that pygmy chimpanzees, unlike other varieties of chimpanzees, learned and used language more like human children.

Check the net

www.bbc.co.uk/radio4/science/ lifewithkanzi.shtml – a radio programme which includes an interview with Sue Savage-Rumbaugh about her work with primates.

Developmental psychology

Bandura, Ross and Ross (1961): *Transmission of aggression through imitation of aggressive models*

Social learning theory, a behaviourist premise, explains human social behaviour through the observation and imitation of behaviour that we perceive as being rewarded, rather than through instinct. Bandura et al aimed to investigate whether children, when witness to aggressive role models, would imitate this aggressive behaviour.

Participants included 36 boys and 36 girls, aged between 37 and 69 months (mean age of 52 months). One adult male and one adult female acted as role models.

Participants were divided into one of three conditions in order to: observe an aggressive model; observe a non-aggressive model; or be a control group that did not observe a model. Participants in each of the aggressive and non-aggressive conditions were divided further into four subgroups: boys with same-sex model; boys with opposite-sex model; girls with same-sex model; girls with opposite-sex model. Each subgroup contained six participants. The children were observed in a playroom for: physical aggression; verbal aggression; aggression to inanimate objects; aggressive inhibition.

Bandura et al found that participants who observed aggressive models demonstrated more aggression; boys in the aggressive conditions demonstrated more aggression if the model was male; girls demonstrated more physical aggression if the model was male, but more verbal aggression if the model was female. Bandura et al concluded that the research showed how behaviours could be learned through the process of observation and imitation without any reinforcement.

Link

See the section on the Causes of aggression on pages 62–63 for more information on social learning theory explanations.

Freud (1909): *Analysis of a phobia of a five-year-old boy*

Freud believed that our adult personality was reliant on how well the emotional conflicts of childhood were resolved. Unresolved conflicts in our unconscious would appear in our fantasies and dreams in disguised forms and symbols. Freud used this research to illustrate his ideas on the theory of sexuality and the nature of phobias.

This research is a case history of a boy, Hans. Much of Freud's therapeutic assessment was derived from corresponding with Hans' father.

At the age of 3, Hans developed an active interest in his 'widdler' (penis). When he was 3½, his mother told him that if he continued to play with his widdler, she would call the doctor to cut it off. Hans had dreams about the death of his mother. When Hans was almost 5, his father reported that he also had a phobia of horses after being frightened by one's large penis. Soon Hans refused to go out for fear of the horses, he was particularly scared of them falling over. He then dreamed of a big giraffe and a crumpled one; the big giraffe called out because Hans had taken the crumpled one away. When Hans was taken to Freud, Hans described the black bits around horses' mouths as being frightening. His fear of horses then declined and he described a fantasy of marrying his mother and having children. He also fantasised that a plumber removed his widdler and bottom and replaced them with larger versions.

Check the net

www.bbc.co.uk/radio4/science/case_study.shtml – a radio programme that reviews and analyses the significance of the Little Hans case study.

Freud concluded that this supports his concept of Oedipus complex. In Hans' mind, the horse was his father (black bits around the mouth were his father's moustache); the big giraffe (his father) was upset over Hans taking the crumpled giraffe (his mother) away from him. Freud concluded that psychoanalysis was helpful if someone was to become a civilised and useful member of society.

Gibson and Walk (1960): *The visual cliff*

Gibson and Walk aimed to investigate whether infants could discriminate depth by the time they were able to move independently. Thirty-six human infants were selected, aged 6-14 months and able to crawl. Gibson and Walk also conducted the research using a variety of non-human animals including kittens, lambs, goats and chicks.

Infants were placed on the centre board of the visual cliff, apparatus which consisted of a large glass sheet above the floor with chequered patterned material directly beneath the glass on one side, and several feet below it on the other. This gave visual cues that one side was 'shallow' and the other side was 'deep'. Each child was observed to see if it would crawl onto the deep side to its beckoning mother or if it would crawl onto the shallow side.

Gibson and Walk found that all of the 27 infants who moved off the centre board crawled out onto the shallow side at least once. Only three attempted to crawl onto the deep side. They concluded that most human infants can discriminate depth by the time that they can crawl.

Take note

Chicks less than 24 hours old would always hop off the centre board on to the 'shallow' side, rather than the 'deep' side, whereas 24% of the aquatic turtles crawled off onto the 'deep' side. Does an aquatic turtle have poorer depth discrimination because its natural habitat does not really pose it with the opportunity to fall?

Langer and Rodin (1976): *The effects of choice and enhanced personal responsibility for the aged: A field experiment in an institutional setting*

Langer and Rodin aimed to investigate whether increased control has beneficial effects on the physical and mental alertness, activity, sociability and general satisfaction of nursing home patients. Residents on one floor in a nursing home were randomly assigned to be the experimental condition (responsibility-induced) and included 8 males and 39 females. 9 male and 35 female residents on another floor acted as a control condition.

Questionnaires assessing perceived control and happiness were administered by research assistants who were unaware of the experimental hypothesis. The Nursing Home administrator asked the responsibility-induced group for their opinions – selecting a plant to care for and choosing which night was to be 'movie night'. The comparison group were told that their complaints would be handled by staff; they were given a plant to be taken care of by someone else and were told which night would be 'movie night'.

48% of the residents in the responsibility-induced group and 25% of the residents of the comparison group reported feeling happier. Residents in the responsibility-induced group reported being significantly more active and alert after the experimental treatment than residents in the comparison group. Langer and Rodin concluded that a greater sense of personal responsibility produces improvement.

Action point

What implications does this research have for the living arrangements of elderly people?

Samuel and Bryant (1984): *Asking only one question in the conservation experiment*

Take note

Even though Samuel and Bryant seem to contradict Piaget's conclusions, they do support two major conclusions. Firstly, older children do better on conservation tasks than younger ones and secondly, children could conserve number before they could conserve mass and volume tasks.

In response to Piaget's conservation tasks, which require the researcher to ask a child the same question twice, Samuel and Bryant aimed to investigate whether the errors made by the children were due to the nature of the test rather than to a limitation of their thought processes.

252 children between the ages of 5 and 8½ years. were divided into four groups of 63 children, with mean ages of 5 years 3 months; 6 years 3 months; 7 years 3 months and 8 years 3 months.

Samuel and Bryant carried out mass, volume and number conservation tasks. Children from each age group were assigned to one of three conditions: standard (as Piaget, asked about objects before and after shape change); one judgement (asked about objects after witnessing transformation); fixed-array (asked about objects after transformation, not witnessed by child).

They found that each age group made fewer errors than the group(s) that were younger and that in all age groups, the children in the one judgement condition made fewer errors than the other two tasks e.g. in the 6 years 3 months age group, the mean number of errors made by the one judgement group was 4.3 errors, compared to 5.7 (standard) and 6.4 (fixed-array). Samuel and Bryant concluded that the important question is not whether the child possesses a particular intellectual skill, but how and when they decide to use it.

Physiological psychology

Bennett-Levy and Marteau (1984): *Fear of animals: what is prepared?*

Action point

Can you think of evolutionary explanations for other common phobias such as haemophobia (fear of blood) and claustrophobia (fear of enclosed spaces)?

Evolutionary psychology suggests phobias are once-adaptive behaviours which helped our ancestors to survive. Bennett-Levy and Marteau aimed to investigate whether human beings are biologically prepared to fear certain types of animals, and are meaningfully related to ratings of avoidance of these animals.

113 participants, attending a health centre, completed one of two questionnaires distributed in a random order. Questionnaire 1 was completed by 34 females and 30 males. Questionnaire 2 was completed by 25 females and 24 males.

Questionnaire 1 measured self-reported fear (three-point scale) and avoidance (five-point scale) of 29 small harmless animals and insects. Questionnaire 2 measured self-reported ratings for ugliness, sliminess, speed and suddenness of movement (three-point scale) for the same 29 animals and insects as used in Questionnaire 1.

Rats were feared the most; rabbits and ladybirds were feared the least. Ugliness and sliminess were significantly correlated with nearness and fear measures. Bennett-Levy and Marteau concluded feared animals had certain fear-evoking perceptual properties, most notably a discrepancy from the human form.

Dement and Kleitman (1957): *The relation of eye movements during sleep to dream activity*

Although much had previously been written about dreams, it was not until Dement and Kleitman aimed to investigate a possible connection between periods of rapid eye movement (REM) and our experience of dreaming, that any really empirical research was attempted. Nine participants (7 males, 2 females) were involved; however most of the data was taken from just 5 of the participants.

Participants were asked to eat normally, but to refrain from caffeine and alcohol before reporting to the laboratory just before their usual bedtime. Electrodes were attached near the eyes to detect eye movement and to the scalp to detect brain activity. These electrodes fed information to an electroencephalograph (EEG). Participants were woken by a bell near their bed, on average 5.7 times, and were asked to describe the content of any dream they had been having.

Dement and Kleitman found REM periods, lasting from 3 to 50 minutes, occurred regularly in each participant, every night. Although each participant had their own pattern, the average period between REM events was 90 minutes. Participants reported 152 accounts of dreams and 39 accounts of not dreaming during REM sleep, compared with 11 accounts of dreaming and 149 accounts of not dreaming during non-REM sleep. Dement and Kleitman also found that direction of eye movement was associated to the content of the dream. They concluded there was a clear connection between REM and dreaming.

Jargon

Electroencephalograph (EEG). A procedure used to measure the electrical activity produced by the brain, via electrodes placed on the scalp. Although the skull and cerebrospinal fluid can obscure the EEG signal, it is still considered to be one of the best 'direct' methods of looking at brain activity. Modern techniques have to rely on 'indirect' measurements such as changes in blood flow (fMRI) or metabolic rates (e.g. PET).

Maguire, Gadian, Johnsrude, Good, Ashburner, Frackowiak and Frith (2000): *Navigation-related structural changes in the hippocampi of taxi drivers*

Neuroplasticity or brain plasticity refers to the brain's amazing ability to reorganise itself by forming new connections between brain cells (neurons). Maguire et al aimed to investigate whether these changes in the brain could be detected, by investigating those with extensive navigational knowledge.

There were two groups of participants. Group 1 consisted of 16 right-handed males (mean age 44), who had all been licensed taxi drivers for more than 18 months (mean taxi experience 14.3). Group 2 were 16 right-handed males who were not taxi drivers, but had been matched for age.

MRI brain scans of 50 healthy, non-taxi drivers aged between 33 and 61 years were examined and a database of the structure and volume of their hippocampi was established. MRI brain scans were then conducted on the taxi drivers and their age-matched controls.

Maguire et al found that in the taxi drivers' brains there was an increased volume of grey matter in both the left and right hippocampi. They also reported a correlation between time spent as a taxi driver and the size of the right posterior hippocampus. Non-taxi drivers had more grey matter in the anterior hippocampus, whereas taxi drivers had more grey matter in the posterior hippocampus. Maguire et al concluded this was evidence that the brain changed in response to environmental demands.

Jargon

Magnetic resonance imaging (MRI). A technique which allows us to visualise the different soft tissues of the body. Although MRI scanners are very expensive, and are mainly used for clinical rather than research purposes, they are safer than many other scans as they do not expose participants to ionising radiation.

Rahe, Mahan and Arthur (1970): *Prediction of near-future health change from subjects' preceding life changes*

Much retrospective research suggests a relationship between stress and illness. Rahe et al, using prospective methods, aimed to investigate whether a relationship between pre-deployment life events and reported illnesses during deployment existed.

2664 naval personnel, mean age 22.3 years, aboard three US Navy aircraft carriers were involved. Two carriers were deployed in operations off the coast of Vietnam and the third in the Mediterranean.

Participants completed a military version of the Schedule of Recent Experience (SRE) every 6 months for two years prior to a 6–8 month deployment. This self-administered questionnaire assessed the severity and adjustment needed in Life Change Units (LCU). A research physician reviewed all of the sailors' health records, which noted even the most minor health changes reported by crew members.

A significant positive correlation coefficient of 0.118 ($p < 0.01$) was found between the LCU totals for the six months prior to deployment and illness. Rahe et al concluded the results support a linear relationship between participants' total LCU and illness rate; however the illnesses experienced by the men were generally minor and their pre-deployment life changes were often few and of low significance.

Sperry (1968): *Hemisphere deconnection and unity in consciousness*

Following the examination of many case studies of individuals affected by accidental brain damage, different cognitive functions of the two hemispheres was suspected. Following the development of a therapeutic technique for severe epilepsy, the commissurotomy, Sperry aimed to investigate the functions of the different hemispheres through a variety of tasks in a more controlled environment.

There were 11 participants of various ages, gender and stages of recovery from a 'commissurotomy' procedure. Using the divided visual field technique, Sperry was able to present information to either the left or the right of the visual field for 1/10th of a second, to test the participant's language skills, visuo-tactile associations and motor control.

Participants verbally reported information sent to the left hemisphere; however information relayed to the right hemisphere was not reported. Participants were able to correctly select objects when using their left hands (controlled by the right hemisphere). Sperry concluded the left hemisphere is equipped for language; although the right hemisphere can't express itself verbally, it can respond non-verbally.

Action point

What are the strengths and limitations in the sample selected by Rahe, Mahan and Arthur (1970)?

Watch out

Sperry did not cut his participants' brains in half just to conduct his research! He took advantage of a group of people who had undergone a commissurotomy to help with their severe epilepsy.

Social psychology

Asch (1955): *Opinions and social pressure*

Asch believed that Sherif's research using the autokinetic effect did not reflect real conformity. Asch aimed to investigate whether group pressure on an individual in an unambiguous situation would lead the individual to give a conforming or an independent response.

123 male students volunteered to take part in what they thought was a 'psychological experiment in visual judgement'. In a laboratory environment, a group of 7-9 participants was shown one card with a single vertical line, the *standard* line, and a second card with three vertical lines of varying lengths. Participants verbally reported which line on the second card was the same length as the standard line. The last but one participant in each group was a naïve participant, as the other participants in the group were confederates of the investigator who had been told to give the same obviously wrong answer on 12 of the 18 trials.

Asch found the naïve participants conformed on 36.8% of the critical trials. Although ¼ of the naïve participants never gave a conforming response, some individuals conformed nearly all the time. Asch concluded there was a strong tendency for conformity.

Milgram (1963): *Behavioural study of obedience*

Before Milgram's research, it was thought that the sort of obedience required to perpetuate the Holocaust was due to the fact that 'Germans are different'; it was thought the German population consisted of authoritarian personality types. Milgram aimed to quantifiably assess how obedient individuals would be in a controlled situation.

Forty males between the ages of 20 and 50 with a variety of educational and occupational backgrounds volunteered, via a newspaper advert, to take part in what they thought was research about memory and learning.

Each participant saw another participant (actually a confederate of Milgram) attached to an electrode which they were told linked to a shock generator in an adjoining room. The participant sat in front of this machine which had 30 switches on it, going from 15 to 450 volts. When the learner (Milgram's confederate) got an answer wrong, the participant was told to give a shock and to 'move one level higher on the shock generator each time'. Eventually the learner screamed and begged to be let out. An experimenter verbally prodded the participant if they hesitated or protested. The whole situation was contrived by Milgram, the learner actually receiving no electric shocks.

Milgram found that none of the participants stopped administering shocks before 300 volts (where five stopped) and that 26 of the 40 participants administered 450 volts. Milgram concluded that various elements of the situation contrived to produce such high levels of obedience.

Piliavin, Rodin and Piliavin (1969): *Good Samaritanism; an underground phenomenon?*

In a laboratory environment, social psychologists observed a lack of assistance being offered to 'victims', which they attributed to explanations such as diffusion of responsibility. Piliavin et al aimed to investigate, in a real world setting, the conditions under which people would offer help.

Take note

When Asch gave the naïve participant a *truthful* partner, their number of incorrect answers dropped to a quarter of the level of the incorrect answers offered by naïve participants with no partner. Perhaps having someone who thinks like us depletes the influence of the majority?

Links

See the section on Conformity on pages 64–65 for criticisms of Asch's research.

Action point

Milgram's research is frequently criticised for having many ethical issues. However, might it not have been more unethical for him not to have conducted the research and for us to continue to underestimate the power of the situation to produce obedience?

Link

See the section on Obedience to authority on pages 66–67 for criticisms of Milgram's research.

Approximately 4450 New York subway commuters, travelling between 11am and 3pm during two months in 1968, took part. On average, each train carriage contained 43 people, with 8.5 people in the critical area. 45% of the train passengers were black, 55% were white.

Teams of four researchers (two male, two female) would board a train. The females would observe from outside the critical area. 70 seconds after the train left the station, the first of the male researchers would play the 'victim', stagger forward, collapse and stay on the floor until offered assistance. If not helped by a member of the public, the second male researcher would help the victim to his feet and help him off the train at the next station. The victims were always male, however the ethnicity (black or white) and condition (drunk or carrying a cane) was varied. The observers noted the sex, age and ethnicity of every passenger and any helping behaviour that was demonstrated.

Passengers were more helpful than predicted. In the cane condition, the victim received help during 62 of the 65 trials, compared with only 19 of the 38 occasions when the victim was supposedly drunk. Help was offered by more than one helper on 60% of the occasions when spontaneous help was offered. Males were more likely to firstly offer help than females and there was a slight tendency for people to help those of their own ethnicity in the drunk condition. They concluded that this research refutes the diffusion of responsibility hypothesis.

Action point

What advantages and disadvantages do you think conducting research in the real world has?

Reicher and Haslam (2006): *Rethinking the psychology of tyranny: The BBC prison study*

Following the Stanford Prison Experiment, social psychologists proposed many explanations such as deindividuation to explain tyranny. Reicher and Haslam investigated whether participants accepted roles they were assigned uncritically; whether those given power were able to exercise it with moderation and those without power would accept without protest.

332 male applicants applied through national press adverts. Clinical, medical and background screening reduced the number to 27. From this group, 15 men were chosen to reflect age, class and ethnic diversity. Five from the 15 were selected as guards, the others were assigned to be prisoners.

Guards were informed of their duties and responsibilities the night before the study. They had superior accommodation and facilities and, although allowed to draw up their own rules and punishments, were not allowed to use physical violence. Prisoners had their head shaved on arrival and were issued a T-shirt with a 3-digit number. They were told that no violence was allowed and had a poster with rules and rights in each three-man cell. Participants were told prisoners could be promoted to a guard role on day 3 but on day 3 prisoners were told that there were no real differences between prisoners and guards and that it was impractical to reassign roles. On day 4 a new prisoner (with a trade union background) was introduced to organise 'collective action'.

Reicher and Haslam found that the guards did not form a coherent group identity and did not internalise the power role. Until day 3, prisoners promoted their individual self-interests by aspiring to promotion. However, after day 3 when the roles were fixed, the prisoners did develop a group identity and they challenged the guards. On day 6, the prisoners broke out of their cells, the guards' rule was over and, although the leaders from the prisoners' group were not cooperative, a self-governing commune was established. By the end, on day 8, some group members were suggesting a more authoritarian system. Reicher and Haslam concluded that the norms of the group were responsible for the pro- or anti-social behaviours of its members, and that the breakdown of groups and powerlessness created conditions ripe for tyranny.

Check the net

www.bbcprisonstudy.org – an excellent site with lots of extra information and activities related to the research.

Psychology of individual differences

Buss (1989): *Sex differences in human mate preferences*

Do men and women look for similar or different characteristics in a potential mate? Buss aimed to investigate if similar sex differences in human mate preferences were found in cultures with varying ecologies, locations, ethnic makeup, religious orientations and political inclinations.

There were 10,047 participants from 37 samples from 33 countries, located on six continents and five islands. Sampling techniques varied across the different countries: in Estonia, it was couples applying for a marriage licence and high school students; in West Germany, the sample was selected through newspaper advertisements; in New Zealand the sample consisted of high school students.

Participants completed a questionnaire consisting of: biographical data; marriage preferences; a four-point rating scale for 18 characteristics, including good financial prospects; chastity; good looks and ambition and industriousness; a rank order of 13 characteristics desired in a potential mate. Sometimes questionnaires were amended to reflect cultural differences, e.g. polygamy in Nigeria. Data was collected by native residents (unaware of hypothesis) and mailed to the US for analysis.

In 36 samples, females valued good financial prospects in a mate more highly than males did. Samples varied tremendously in the value placed on chastity. In 37 samples, males rated good looks higher than females did. In 34 samples, females expressed a higher valuation for 'ambition and industriousness' in a mate than did males. Buss concluded that evolutionary explanations of mating behaviour, specifically differences in the reproductive capacities of males and females, are evident.

Action point

When we initially look at Buss' sample it seems to be quite impressive, due to its many participants taken from a range of different cultures, but what limitations are evident with the different techniques used by Buss to select his participants?

Griffiths (1994): *The role of cognitive bias and skill in fruit machine gambling*

Rational Choice Theory (RCT) suggests that people make decisions about how they should act by comparing the perceived costs and benefits of different courses of action. RCT suggests that regular gamblers have a cognitive bias which distorts their reasoning, as the most rational course of action is not to gamble. Griffiths aimed to investigate whether regular gamblers perceive and act differently to non-regular gamblers.

Two groups of volunteer participants were selected via a poster; regular gamblers consisted of 29 males and one female all of whom gambled at least once a week; non-regular gamblers consisted of 15 male and 15 females who gambled once a month or less.

Participants were given £3 each and asked to play on a fruit machine 'FRUITSKILL', which gave 30 free gambles. Each participant was asked to stay on the machine for 60 gambles, to break even and win back the £3. If they achieved 60 gambles they were told they could either keep the winnings or continue to gamble. They were randomly assigned to think aloud or not to think aloud.

Griffiths found that 14 regular and 7 non-regular gamblers managed to break even. 10 regular and 2 non-regular gamblers decided to continue on the machine until they lost all the money. 18 regular gamblers reported skill was involved, compared with 7 non-regulars. Regular gamblers were also more likely to personify and talk to the machine than non-regular gamblers. Even though the regular gamblers were more skilful, and

Take note

One of the most interesting aspects of Griffiths' research is the way in which he analyses the comments made by those participants who were asked to 'think aloud'. Using a content analysis we are able to see distinct differences in the 'thoughts' of the regular gamblers and the non-regular gamblers.

achieved higher numbers of gamble than non-regulars, they perceived their own skill level to be higher than it was. Griffiths concluded that regular gamblers do demonstrate a cognitive bias, as demonstrated by their irrational verbalisations, and as such were able to be helped through cognitive behavioural therapy.

Rosenhan (1973): *On being sane in insane places*

Rosenhan aimed to investigate whether psychiatrists could distinguish between people who are genuinely mentally ill and those who aren't.

In the initial research, three women and five men (three psychologists, a paediatrician, a psychiatrist, a painter and a housewife – the eighth being Rosenhan) attempted to be admitted to 12 different hospitals in five different states in the United States.

The participants (pseudopatients) stated they were hearing voices saying 'empty', 'hollow' and 'thud' but following admission to hospital no further symptoms were 'acted' out. They made notes of observations of patients and staff on the ward.

All the pseudopatients were admitted, except in one case, with a diagnosis of schizophrenia. Hospitalisation ranged from 7 to 52 days, averaging 19 days. Average daily contact with the psychiatrists was 6.8 minutes per day and they were given a total of 2,100 tablets. Each was eventually discharged with a diagnosis of 'schizophrenia in remission'. Rosenhan concluded that, having once been labelled schizophrenic, there was nothing the pseudopatients could do to overcome the label.

Thigpen & Cleckley (1954): *A case of multiple personality*

The concept that one individual can have more than one personality is an area of abnormality which many people are quite unconvinced by. Thigpen and Cleckley aimed to demonstrate the existence of an individual with multiple personalities.

One individual, known as Eve White in the case study, was referred because of blackouts and severe headaches. She was a modest woman suffering from some marital conflicts and a bout of amnesia from a recent trip. During the course of therapy, Eve was interviewed whilst conscious and whilst under hypnosis, tested using an electroencephalogram (EEG), and had IQ, memory function and Rorschach tests.

Thigpen and Cleckley became concerned about Eve following the receipt of a letter where the handwriting was initially confident, but became more childish towards the end. When interviewed, Eve recalled starting the letter, but did not recall finishing or sending it. She became distressed and reported hearing a voice, she put her hands to her head but was then silent and then dropped her hands, smiled and said 'Hi there, Doc!'. This confident, relaxed personality (known as Eve Black) had a very different voice, language structure and overall presence from Eve White. When Eve Black was 'out', Eve White was unaware of what was happening. Eve White had an IQ of 110, had a superior memory function test result and a repressive personality (Rorschach); Eve Black had an IQ of 104 and a regressive personality. During hypnosis, another personality called 'Jane' emerged. She claimed to be aware of Eve White and Eve Black, but they weren't aware of her. The EEG showed a clear difference between the readings of Eve Black and the other two personalities. Thigpen and Cleckley concluded that the Jane personality was most likely to produce an appropriate resolution, but reported they were uncertain of how to proceed, and acknowledged the moral issue of 'killing' some of Eve's personalities.

Social psychology and research methods

This section starts by looking at relationships – how they are formed and why some last but others don't. It also looks at aggression and what makes some people aggressive. It then moves on to the areas of conformity and obedience, looking at the role the majority plays in affecting our behaviour, as well as the role of the minority. It asks questions about why we obey even when the order may make us go against our own moral codes. The last section covers the research methods used in psychology to study human behaviour and how the results from such studies are then analysed.

Exam themes

- The formation, maintenance and dissolution of interpersonal relationships
- Cultural and sub-cultural differences in relationships
- Causes of aggression
- Conformity
- Obedience
- Ethics
- Quantitative research methods and analysis
- Qualitative research methods and analysis

Topic checklist

	Edexcel		AQA/A		AQA/B		OCR		WJEC	
	AS	A2	AS	A2	AS	A2	AS	A2	AS	A2
Interpersonal relationships			O	●					O	●
The formation, maintenance and dissolution of relationships			O	●					O	●
Cultural and sub-cultural differences in relationships			O	●					O	●
The causes of aggression			O	●			O	●		
Conformity	O		O	●	O	●				
Obedience to authority	O		O	●						
Explaining and resisting obedience	O		O	●						
Ethical issues	O	●	O	●			O	●	O	●
Dealing with ethical issues	O	●	O	●			O	●	O	●
Quantitative research methods	O	●	O	●	O	●	O	●	O	●
Qualitative research methods	O	●	O	●	O	●	O	●	O	●
Research planning	O	●	O	●	O	●	O	●	O	●
Research design	O	●	O	●	O	●	O	●	O	●
Analysing quantitative data	O	●	O	●	O	●	O	●	O	●
Analysing qualitative data	O	●	O	●	O	●	O	●	O	●

Interpersonal relationships

People are initially attracted to each other for a number of reasons. Theories of attraction stress the initial factors that are important in drawing people together. Theories of relationships explain why attraction may sometimes lead to more enduring partnerships.

Attraction

There are several factors involved in the formation of interpersonal relationships. This section focuses on six factors involved in initial attraction that can lead to a relationship.

The first of these factors is **proximity** – we are attracted to those we see every day. Festinger et al (1950) studied student relationships and found that those who had become close friends were living on the same floor in the student accommodation. Bossard (1932) in his research on marriage found that those who got married had often lived close to each other.

A second factor is **physical attraction**. It is often said that first impressions count and, when we meet someone for the first time, we generally notice how attractive or unattractive they are. Research by Dion (1972) found that we think of attractive people as being special and that they are often rated as being interesting, exciting and warm. This is known as the Halo-Effect – 'What is beautiful is good'.

Research by Walster et al (1969) also proposed that we are attracted to people of a similar attractiveness level. From his computer dance study he found that students were attractive to other students of a similar level of physical attractiveness; he called this the matching hypothesis.

Three other factors involved in attraction all involve the couples being similar in several ways. The first two are similarity in **personality** and **attitude**. Most research supports the fact that we tend to get intimately involved with those who are similar to us in personality. Burgess and Wallin (1953) measured 42 personality characteristics of 1000 engaged couples and found that there was significant within-couple similarity for at least 14 personality characteristics indicating a similarity in personality.

According to Byrne et al (1968) we are attracted to people that also have a similar attitude and belief system to our own and we dislike those who disagree with us. Research by Hill and Stull (1981) seemed to support this. They questioned female college students and found that those who had chosen to share a room had very similar values and attitudes.

Take note

Proximity/nearness often determines who you are likely to meet, and is also important in determining our choice of friends (Festinger et al 1950).

Take note

Some research may state that there are *five* factors involved in initial attraction, while other research states there are *seven* factors. Human behaviour is not an exact science!

Take note

Individual *differences* can also affect attraction.

A third factor based on similarity is similar **demographics**. We are attracted to someone who is of the same age, social class, ethnic background, etc. because we have more in common with them as a result.

The last factor involves **reciprocal liking** – the idea that we are attracted to people who like us. Backman and Secord (1959) found that members of a discussion group who are told that other members in the group like them are more likely to want to be in a group with those people at a later date.

Evaluation of factors of attraction

A lot of research seems to indicate that attraction depends upon how similar people find each other, although we do not always dislike people who are dissimilar. According to Novak and Lerner (1968) we even prefer people to have different attitudes from ours. Although Rubin (1973) put forward several reasons why being similar was so important, he stated that it is easier to communicate with people who are similar and who will often enjoy the same activities. Also, if most people like themselves, then it should follow that they like people who are similar to them.

Most of the research done lacks validity, is artificial and has mostly ignored individual differences, for example one person may think looks are more important another may prefer a similarity in personality.

Examiner's secrets

A range of factors can be accepted as being involved in interpersonal attraction, as long as each is backed up by research.

Exam practice   answer: page 86

'Women have more phobias than men.'

Design an experiment around this hypothesis. Include your experimental method and the advantages and disadvantages of using this design. (6 marks)

The formation, maintenance and dissolution of

Most people will enter some kind of relationship in their life but unfortunately almost 40% do not last. Several theories have been put forward to explain why some relationships stay the distance while others falter.

Formation

Sociobiological and evolutionary theories

Evolutionary theorists suggest that human beings select mates according to criteria that are important from an evolutionary point of view. The sex investing more in offspring will be selected to exert stronger preferences about mating partners. Buss (1989) found evidence that females seek to mate with males who have the ability and willingness to provide resources related to **parental investment**. Females should value attributes in potential mates that signal the likely possession of resources. Furthermore, females should compete to display the reproductively-linked cues that males desire in mates. Males and females also both seek healthy fit partners who are more likely to produce healthy fit offspring. Buss (1989) stated that men prefer women younger than themselves as they are more likely to be fertile. In evaluation:

→ Evolutionary explanations of human relationships presume heterosexuality. Attempting to explain homosexual relationships in such a way is more problematic.

→ Evolutionary theories presume that relationships are solely about 'reproduction'. For many people (particularly in the case of later life relationships), relationships are not about having children.

→ These explanations may be seen as endorsing 'natural' behaviours such as sexual promiscuity in males and 'coyness' in females.

Social exchange and equity theories

Social exchange theory suggests that we all try to maximise the rewards that we can get from a relationship, such as love, attention and sex, and we try to minimise the costs, such as time and effort. It is also expected that any rewards are reciprocated, for example 'I love you therefore you must say I love you back'. Thibaut and Kelley (1959) argued that relationships go though four phases as part of the social exchange theory.

1 The sampling stage, where costs and rewards are explored.
2 Bargaining, where rewards and costs are agreed.
3 Commitment, where rewards and costs are accepted.
4 Institutionalisation, where norms and expectations are firmly established.

Equity theory (Walster 1978) is a development of social exchange theory and is also an 'economic' theory. It focuses on the importance of balance in relationships. There are four principles:

→ Individuals attempt to maximise rewards and minimise losses in their relationships.

→ Rewards are 'distributed' within a relationship to ensure fairness.

→ Inequitable (i.e. unfair) relationships lead to dissatisfaction.

→ The 'loser' is motivated to re-establish the equity in the relationship. The greater the inequity, the greater the effort needed.

Checkpoint 1

In what different ways might partners attempt to achieve 'balance' in a relationship?

Grade booster

Make sure you are able to compare and contrast different explanations on why some relationships are maintained while others are not.

The jargon

False consensus effect. The tendency to over-estimate the degree to which our opinions and beliefs are shared by others.

relationships

In evaluation:
- → Many of the studies supporting exchange and equity theories have taken place in artificial 'laboratory' situations that have little relevance to relationships in the real world.
- → Clark and Mills (1979) have identified two types of couple, the communal couple and the exchange couple. Only in the exchange couple is 'score-keeping' evident. Communal couples are more relaxed about what is rewarding or equitable in their relationship.
- → Moghaddam et al (1993) argue that the preoccupation with exchange and equity is a feature of North America rather than more collectivist cultures.

Reinforcement and need satisfaction

This theory suggests that we are attracted to, and form relationships with, people who **reinforce** us in some way. The model proposes:
- → Our social environment contains experiences that can be evaluated as either 'good' or 'bad'.
- → We like things that make us feel good.
- → We associate people with these experiences, and are thus attracted to, or repelled by, them.

In evaluation:
- → Partners in relationships are frequently more concerned with equity and fairness than maximising their own rewards.
- → Many relationships in non-Western societies show little concern for personal reinforcement in relationships.
- → It is easy to find examples of things that might be considered reinforcing in existing relationships, but we cannot be sure that these are the factors that led to their original formation.

Maintenance and dissolution

For a relationship to be maintained a level of commitment is needed. This growth of commitment is affected by several factors. According to research by Rusbalt (1980) there are three important factors:
- → Satisfaction: the rewards a relationship provides.
- → Perceived quality of alternatives: a relationship is more attractive if there are no alternative options.
- → Investment size: the greater the investment in a relationship the more the commitment.

However, most of this research focused only on short-term relationships.

The stages of relationship breakdown were divided into phases by Duck (1988). If there is no resolution at each phase, it will probably lead on to the next phase. Lee (1984) argued that a relationship breaks down over a period of time and involves five stages. Both these models discuss stages of breakdown but neither explains why a relationship ends. Predisposing factors for a relationship breakdown include an untidy partner; or either being too young or from different social or cultural backgrounds.

The benefits of being in a relationship include an increase in self-esteem, the relationship can be a deterrent against stress, and the fact that a partner can help achieve goals.

> "The cost of indiscriminate mating will be less for the sex investing less and the benefits greater."
>
> Buss (1989)

Checkpoint 2

Why would homosexual relationships pose a problem for theories that explain the formation of relationships in this way?

Take note

Duck's phase model:
- → **The intra-psychic phase** One partner becomes increasingly dissatisfied with the relationship as it is.
- → **The dyadic phase** The other member of the relationship is now involved. Dissatisfaction can only be resolved by one or both partners changing.
- → **The social phase** The break-up becomes 'public'. Partners are forced to consider the possibility and potential impact of the break-up.
- → **The grave-dressing phase** Each partner organises their post-breakdown lives and creates their own version of who was responsible for the breakdown and why, probably minimising their own blame.

Take note

1 **Dissatisfaction**: problems within the relationship.
2 **Exposure**: the problem is brought out into the open.
3 **Negotiation**: discussion about problems.
4 **Resolution** attempts: the couple attempts to solve the issues.
5 **Termination**: problems cannot be solved and the relationship ends.

Grade booster

Be prepared to illustrate these theories with research studies that support or challenge the main assumptions.

Exam practice
answer: page 86

Outline and evaluate **two** explanations of personal attraction. (25 marks)

Cultural and sub-cultural differences in relationships

Take note

Although there may be differences between cultures, there are also many differences within cultures.

Whereas interpersonal relationships in Western cultures tend to be individualistic, voluntary and temporary, those in non-Western cultures tend to be collective, obligatory and permanent. Sub-cultural differences include those represented by men and women, homosexuals and heterosexuals, Asians and Afro-Caribbeans.

Differences between Western and non-Western cultures

Individualist and collectivist cultures

In individualist cultures, the emphasis is on the individual and their personal rights and achievements. There is an emphasis on autonomy and the 'I' is more important than the 'we'. Where there is a conflict between the interests of the individual and the collective, individuals prioritise their own needs. In contrast, in collectivist societies, the needs of the collective are prioritised over the needs of the individual. A marriage may be seen as a union between families as much as a union between individuals (Humphreys 2000).

Checkpoint 1

Give two examples of cultures that you consider to be 'individualistic' and two that you consider to be 'collectivistic'.

Take note

People in collectivist societies tend to have fewer, but closer, friendships than people in individualist societies (Goodwin, 1995).

Voluntary and involuntary relationships

Although marriage arrangements vary from those where partners have no choice at all to those where the choice is totally determined by the partners themselves, the majority of cultures have characteristics of each. The most common form of marriage is by arrangement, with parents having the most significant influence on the eventual choice (Ingoldsby 1995).

Take note

In some societies polygamy (where a man has more than one wife) is the norm.

→ A study of Sikhs, Hindus and Muslims living in Britain found that arranged marriages were common. The most important factors in partner choice were caste, social class and religion (Ghuman 1994).

→ A study of Hindu Gujarati couples found that only a small percentage had completely arranged marriages. Most had been introduced by a third party but had been given the option of refusal.

Permanent and impermanent relationships

Most cultures allow divorce although there is a greater stigma attached to divorce in cultures where marriages are arranged. There is considerable variation between different cultures for the main reasons for marital breakdown (Goodwin 1999).

Take note

Intra-cultural variations refers to differences within a single cultural type, whereas inter-cultural variations refers to differences between different cultural types.

→ In China (a collectivist culture) divorce rate is very low and is considered shameful for both the individuals concerned and their families.

→ In some African societies, increased urbanisation and greater educational opportunities for women have led to increases in divorce rates. This is seen as a reflection of the preoccupation within individualist societies to search for the 'ideal partner'.

Action point

You may know someone (or be such a person yourself) for whom such practices are the norm. Talk to them about arranged marriages and attitudes to divorce.

Evaluation of cross-cultural differences research

→ Smith and Bond (1999) argue that there are considerable problems faced by researchers when having to translate research designs into 'local' languages, and having to translate 'local' responses into a form where they make sense to the researchers. This may lead to a loss of the more subtle aspects of people's responses.

→ Some researchers (e.g. Buss 1989) have claimed that there are actually far more similarities among different cultures concerning those factors that are considered important for male-female relationships. In particular, Buss argues that there are strong male-female differences that are universal to most if not all cultures.

Understudied relationships

Gay and lesbian relationships

Homosexuality is still illegal in many cultures and was, until 1973, considered sufficiently 'abnormal' to be classified as a mental disorder on DSM (Diagnostic and Statistical Manual of Mental Disorders). There are some cultures where homosexuals are treated more sympathetically, and even some cultures where homosexuality is positively encouraged. Because gays and lesbians are exposed to so many negative stereotypes and prejudices, they may develop pride and dignity by maintaining privacy and secrecy about their sexual preference (Humphreys 2000). Humphreys identifies a number of problems faced by gay and lesbian couples:

→ The operation of pervasive stereotypes about gays and lesbians. These include the belief that they are incapable of sustaining long-term relationships and that these are inferior versions of heterosexual relationships.
→ Partners must continuously seek the support and sympathy of their partner rather than sharing the load with others (because of the fear of being 'outed').
→ Family and friends may hold unrealistic expectations about 'closeted' homosexuals and may continuously attempt to pair them off at social occasions.
→ They face a complex world of schools and other child-oriented networks. Those in shared custody arrangements with a former heterosexual spouse face losing custody of their children.

Mediated friendships

These are relationships where the friends or partners are brought together by means of an intervening agency, e.g. dating agencies, or electronic relationships through email and chat rooms. Chat rooms especially have been used as a means to start up relationships. Branwyn (1993) found that much of the focus of these chat rooms is on romantic and sexual encounters.

Relationships with parents and peers

Often relationships between parents and their offspring are seen as very volatile. Some studies have found conflict but many have found good strong relationships. Youniss (1989) found that many children and teenagers reported being very close to their parents. Peers also become increasingly important, especially during adolescence. Research by Buhrmester (1992) found a low level of anxiety and depression in adolescents who had good peer group relationships.

Take note

Buss tested this claim across 37 different cultures, and found strong support for these 'evolutionary significant' male-female differences.

Checkpoint 2

What do you think are the differences in male-female and female-male preferences that Buss found?

The jargon

Understudied relationships. Relationships such as gay and lesbian, relationships among the disabled, and internet relationships, that have traditionally been ignored by the majority of social psychologists.
Outed. Being 'exposed' as a homosexual by other people.

Examiner's secrets

Although this question mentions gay and lesbian relationships and internet relationships, they are merely included as examples of appropriate content.

Exam practice   answer: page 86

Discuss the effect that western and non-western cultures have on relationships. (25 marks)

The causes of aggression

Social psychological explanations of aggression see the causes of our aggressive behaviour as located within our social world, which is in stark contrast to psychodynamic and biological explanations.

Social learning theory (SLT) explanations

SLT explanations claim that aggressive behaviour is learned through:

→ direct experience – aggressive behaviour may be reinforced and is therefore more likely to reoccur in similar situations in the future
→ vicarious experience – the person observes a role model behaving aggressively and subsequently imitates the behaviour.

For behaviour to be imitated it must be seen to be rewarding. The likelihood of a person behaving aggressively in a situation depends on:

→ previous experience of aggressive behaviour (direct and vicarious)
→ how successful their aggressive behaviour has been in the past
→ the chance of aggressive behaviour being successful in this situation
→ other cognitive, social and environmental factors that are operating at the same time.

Evaluation of social learning theory explanations

→ Experimental studies that support SLT explanations (e.g. Bandura et al 1963) have been criticised as being artificial and lacking in **ecological validity** (i.e. not related to 'real-life' aggression).
→ SLT explanations can account for inconsistency in aggressive behaviour. It may be reinforced differently in different situations.
→ Biological factors, such as the male hormone **testosterone**, may also have a causal role in aggression. Pre-menstrual syndrome has been cited in criminal trials as a reason for aggressive behaviour. These cast doubt on aggression being purely a learned response.

Deindividuation

Zimbardo (1969) distinguished between **individual** behaviour, which is rational and conforms to acceptable social standards, and **deindividuated** behaviour, which is based on primitive urges and does not conform to **social norms**. People usually refrain from acting in anti-social ways because such behaviours are easily identifiable in a society that has strong norms against such 'uncivilised' behaviour. In some situations (e.g. crowds) these restraints may become relaxed and aggression might follow as a consequence.

Evaluation of deindividuation

→ Deindividuation may not only produce anti-social behaviour. Evidence also exists (e.g. Diener 1980) that deindividuation may produce increases in pro-social behaviour.
→ The deindividuation perspective argues that when we are deindividuated we are less likely to conform to social norms. However, an alternative view is that individuals are conforming

---

The jargon

Anti-social aggression. Behaviour that is intended to inflict physical or psychological harm on another individual who does not want to be so treated.

Checkpoint 1

When would children be likely to imitate the aggressive behaviour of models?

Checkpoint 2

Read about Bandura et al's research with 'Bobo' dolls. Why do you think this research 'lacks ecological validity'?

The jargon

Deindividuation. A process whereby people lose their sense of socialised individual identity and engage in unsocialised, often anti-social behaviours.

to 'local group norms', which may sometimes be anti-social and aggressive, and at other times pro-social and altruistic.

➔ Marsh et al (1978) found that, in most cases, 'deindividualised' football violence is highly organised rather than undisciplined, and ritualised rather than physically violent.

Institutional aggression

This refers to how society itself can foster aggression. In every part of daily life, at home, at school and at work, people are dealing with aggressive behaviour. Aggression is therefore becoming institutionalised into our everyday life. Institutional aggression can also refer to the violence that takes place within certain institutes such as mental facilities and prisons.

Biological explanations of aggression

➔ **Genetic approach** – Jacobs et al (1965) found that men in prison had XYY sex chromosome instead of normal XY. It is argued that it is this extra Y chromosome that increases aggression.

➔ **Evolutionary explanation** – This is based around Darwin's theory survival of the fittest, that all animals are biologically programmed to fight over resources and that therefore being aggressive is a highly adaptive response. It is the strongest that will feed and mate and therefore survive to reproduce.

➔ **Physiological approach** – Aggression has been linked to hormones with males having more of the male hormone testosterone. Research by Kalat (1998) found that the highest levels of violence was reported with men aged 15-25, who also have the highest levels of testosterone. Aggression has also been linked to the neurotransmitter serotonin. Research by Virkkunen et al (1987) has found that people with a history of violence have been found to have a low level of serotonin.

However, if aggression is caused by a chemical imbalance then it can be controlled by drugs. Also, the biological approach is highly deterministic and therefore takes the blame away from the person.

Other factors leading to aggressive behaviour

A range of other factors, for example jealousy and collective influence (e.g. group membership or lynch mobs), may also act as triggers for aggressive behaviour.

> *"Deindividuation may produce an orgy of aggressive, selfish and antisocial behaviour."*
>
> Hogg and Vaughan (1998)

Take note

Jealousy in relationships can lead to physical violence. According to Clanton and Smith (1977) it comes from the real or imagined attraction between a partner and a third party. Buss et al (1992) found that men are more upset by sexual infidelity while women are more upset by emotional infidelity.

Take note

Group membership, such as in crowds at sporting events, may contribute to aggressive behaviour. Wann (2006) found that sports fans admitted a willingness to injure a player, fan or coach of a rival team. The violence can fall into two categories – hostile spectator aggression and instrumental spectator aggression (Wann et al 1999).

Take note

Lynch mobs can also lead to aggression. They usually involve some sort of motive that provokes a group attack. The psychodynamics involve the raw power and excitement of the hunt and lynch mobs may take on a life of their own, leading to behaviour that individuals would not display if alone. More and more people may then be drawn in (Huntoon, 2007).

Grade booster

If a question asks you to evaluate a psychological explanation of aggression, you can bring in biological explanations as part of your evaluation.

Exam practice   answer: page 86

Describe and evaluate the social learning explanation of aggression. (25 marks)

Conformity

The jargon

Conformity. Also referred to as 'majority influence'.

Conformity is a form of social influence which results from exposure to the opinions of a majority. Zimbardo et al (1995) define it as a 'tendency for people to adopt the behaviour, attitudes and values of other members of a reference group'.

Research studies of conformity

Asch (1956)

In Asch's study, he showed a series of lines to participants seated around a table. All but one were confederates of the researcher. In each trial, participants were shown a 'test' line, and asked which of three other lines was the same length. On six neutral trials, the confederates gave correct answers; on the other twelve they unanimously agreed on the same incorrect answer.

The main results were:

→ In 32% of the trials where confederates had unanimously given a wrong answer, naïve participants conformed to the majority view.
→ 74% of the naïve participants conformed at least once (compared to a figure of only 5% when making decisions in private).
→ Some conforming participants went along with the majority because they believed that their perception must be inaccurate and the majority's accurate. Some yielded because they did not want to be in the minority and risk being ridiculed by the rest of the group.

Subsequent variations of Asch's procedures found that conformity could be raised or lowered according to certain conditions such as:

→ The size of the majority – conformity levels were close to zero when only one confederate was used, 12.8% when two were used, and 32% with three confederates. Further increases in the size of the majority did not produce significant increases in conformity.
→ A non-unanimous majority – the presence of another participant who also gave a response different to that of the majority caused a dramatic decrease in the levels of conformity in real participants.
→ Mode of response – when participants were required to write their answers down instead of calling them out, the levels of conformity dropped significantly.

Criticisms of Asch's research

→ Harris (1985) argues that, as the majority of trials in the Asch studies produced non-conforming responses, this was more a demonstration of independence than conformity.
→ Perrin and Spencer (1981) claim that the Asch studies reflect a particular historical and cultural perspective (the American era of McCarthyism) and suggest that such conformity effects are no longer evident in similar experimental studies.

Watch out!

Students frequently claim that 32% of *participants* conformed, whereas it should be 32% of *trials* produced conforming responses.

Checkpoint 1

How are these two explanations of conformity usually described?

Checkpoint 2

The level of conformity dropped when answers were written down. What does this tell you about conformity?

Take note

Perrin and Spencer referred to the Asch effect as a 'child of its time'.

→ Smith and Bond (1998), in a review of 31 studies of conformity, suggest that conformity to a majority is more likely in collectivist cultures than in individualist cultures (like the UK and USA).

Why do we conform?

Insko et al (1985) claim that there are two main reasons why we conform to social norms (i.e. the views of the majority). These are:

→ **Normative social influence** – we conform so that others will approve of us and accept us. This is also known as compliance: we go along to fit in with the majority, though in private we do not accept their values and opinions.
→ **Informational social influence** – we look to others to provide information about ambiguous situations. This is also known as internalisation, a type of social influence born out of our desire to be right in our opinions and values. The information is integrated and over time can become dissociated from the original source.

These two processes do not necessarily operate independently, but frequently operate together. Turner (1991) claims that belonging to a social group makes us conform to its social norms. We observe how other members of the group behave and we behave in the same way. He describes this as **referential informational influence**. Using others as a reference group sets the scene for normative and informational influence to be most effective.

Checkpoint 3

What is the main difference between a collectivist and an individualist culture?

Take note

Even studies that appear to be extremely unethical can have positive consequences.

Watch out!

This question is asking why people conform rather than asking you to describe research into conformity.

Exam practice   answer: page 87

Outline **two** reasons why people conform. (12 marks)

Obedience to authority

Watch out!

Make sure you don't confuse obedience with conformity.

Obedience refers to a type of social influence whereby somebody acts in response to a direct order from another person. There is also an implication that the person receiving the order is made to respond in a way that they would not otherwise have done without the order.

Milgram's research into obedience (1963)

Link

See Ethical issues on pages 70–71.

Milgram deceived 40 male volunteer participants into thinking they were giving gradually increasing electric shocks to another participant (an actor) during a word association task. The 'real' participant acted as the 'teacher' and the 'learner' was in fact an actor. In the baseline condition, the learner was in another room, with no voice contact with the teacher. After each wrong answer an electric shock was delivered (although none was really given) with an increase of 15 volts each time, up to 450 volts.

Take note

No shocks were really being delivered in this study. However, participants believed they were giving real electric shocks.

→ All 40 participants continued to at least the 300-volt level.
→ 65% continued to the full 450 volts.

Milgram extended his research to explore the different situational factors that led participants to obey or disobey. He found that the closer the 'teacher' was to the 'learner', the more likely they were to refuse the experimenter's command to deliver the shocks. Milgram also discovered that obedience levels were lower when the experimenter was not physically present and gave orders over the telephone.

Checkpoint 1

As the 'learner' was brought closer to the 'teacher', the level of obedience dropped. How would this be explained?

Criticisms of Milgram's research

Milgram's research was criticised on two main counts:

1 It was not a valid research study, in that the deception had not worked (experimental validity) and the study had little relevance outside of the experimental setting (ecological validity).
2 The study was unethical; it should not have been carried out because it compromised the trust between researchers and their participants. We can now look at each of these criticisms in turn.

Experimental and ecological validity of Milgram's research

The jargon

Experimental validity. Whether the observed effect really was caused by the experimental manipulation.
Ecological validity. Whether these results could be generalised out to other situations and settings.

→ Orne and Holland (1968) claimed that Milgram's research lacked experimental validity – the participants had not been deceived at all. Therefore conclusions drawn from the study were inappropriate.
→ Milgram defended his original claim through evidence from debriefing sessions (participants admitted they had believed they were giving shocks), and through film evidence where participants appeared in considerable distress when delivering the shocks.
→ Orne and Holland's second claim was that the study lacked ecological validity, having been carried out in the psychology lab of a prestigious American university (Yale).
→ Milgram carried out a replication in some run-down office buildings, and found that obedience levels, although lower, were still far higher than predicted at the beginning of the research.

Examiner's secrets

If you are asked to discuss the Milgram study, there are several variations of the study that can be accepted.

Ethical criticisms of Milgram's research

Baumrind (1964) criticised Milgram's research on the grounds that it was not ethically justified. She claimed that:

→ participants suffered considerable distress that was not justified given the aims of the research
→ participants would suffer permanent psychological harm from their participation in the study, including a loss of self-esteem and distrust of authority
→ Milgram failed to obtain informed consent from his participants – they may not have volunteered had they known what they had to do.

Milgram responded to each of these criticisms in turn.

→ In a follow-up survey, 84% of his participants indicated they were 'glad to have taken part', and felt they had learned something extremely valuable about themselves.
→ Psychiatric examinations one year later showed no sign of psychological damage attributable to participation in the research.
→ At no point were participants forced to do anything, and the fact that some had withdrawn meant that all were free to do so.

Checkpoint 2

If you were Milgram, how might you answer this second criticism?

Take note

By the use of experimental 'prods' – such as saying 'You must continue' – Milgram applied pressure on participants to continue.

Other research on obedience (Hofling et al 1966)

Hofling et al arranged for nurses in a hospital ward to receive a telephone call from an unknown doctor. Each unsuspecting nurse was asked to administer a drug to a patient before the doctor arrived. To have done so meant breaking a number of hospital rules, including:

→ giving twice the maximum dose for the drug
→ accepting a telephone instruction from an unknown doctor
→ acting without written instructions from a doctor.

Despite this, 21 out of 22 nurses agreed to administer the drug (a harmless placebo), thus lending some support to Milgram's claim that obedience would also be evident in natural settings.

Take note

This research is important as it involved obedience in a more natural setting than was the case in Milgram's study.

Criticisms of Hofling et al's research

Rank and Jacobson (1977) criticised the Hofling et al study because:

→ the nurses had no knowledge of the drug involved (Astroten)
→ they had no opportunity to seek advice before giving the drug.

In a replication of the study where the common drug Valium was used, and nurses were able to speak to other nurses before proceeding, only 2 out of 18 nurses gave the drug as requested by the absent doctor.

Examiner's secrets

When revising a research study, it is a good idea to revise the main aims, procedures, results and conclusions of the study.

Exam practice   answer: page 87

Describe the findings and conclusions of **two** studies that have investigated obedience. (12 marks)

Explaining and resisting obedience

In the light of Milgram's findings, psychologists have explored the reasons *why* people obey. A number of psychological processes operate that appear to both remove personal agency (freedom to direct our own behaviour) and bind people to an obedient relationship with the authority figure.

Watch out!

Make sure that you are clear about the distinction between conformity and obedience.

"Under conditions of tyranny it is far easier to act than to think."

H. Arendt (1970)

Checkpoint 1

What does 'foot in the door' mean in this context?

Action point

In all conflicts, war criminals make use of this defence. Look out for it when reading or watching stories about war atrocities.

Checkpoint 2

Think of some different ways in which military personnel are 'buffered' from the consequences of their actions during wartime.

Explaining obedience

A **socio-cultural perspective** suggests that we learn to obey authority and expect to encounter legitimate authority in many different contexts. The role of legitimate authority figures tends to be defined by society. This gives them the right to exert power over others, who in turn tend to accept the legitimacy of their power and act accordingly. Those who took part in Milgram's research had a long history of rewarded obedience.

Once subjects are actually in the experimental condition, **binding factors** begin to operate. Various cues (the experimenter's status and manner, the volunteer status of the subject and the learner's apparent willingness to receive punishment) increase the pressure on the participant to continue their role in the study. The gradual increase in shocks may be made more likely through a combination of factors ('foot in the door', embarrassment at non-continuation). It is perhaps this slow progression towards violence that explains destructive obedience in the real world.

The participant shifts the responsibility for their actions onto another person (in this case the experimenter) through the process of **agentic shift**. They now see themselves as the agents of another person (the authority figure) and no longer responsible for their own actions. This claim that the actual responsibility for actions lay elsewhere has been a common defence in war crimes trials.

Situational factors

Milgram (1974) stipulated three factors of a situation that affect obedience:

1 The role of buffers

A 'buffer' is defined as any aspect of a situation that protects people from having to confront the consequences of their actions (Meldrum 2000). In Milgram's original study, the teacher and learner were in different rooms, with the teacher protected (i.e. buffered) from having to see his 'victim', and the consequences of his electric shocks. When the learner was in the same room, this buffering effect was reduced, as was the tendency to obey the commands of the experimenter.

2 A socially obedient environment

We tend to obey legal authority as our experience has taught us that they are on the whole honest and trustworthy.

3 Graduated commitment

In Milgram's experiment the shocks began low and increased gradually so that the participants did not realise when they were beginning to behave in an unreasonable fashion.

Resisting obedience

→ Individuals can be reminded that it is they who are responsible for their actions, not the authority figures. Hamilton (1978) found that, under these conditions, agentic shift was reversed and sharp decreases in obedience could be obtained.

→ The presence of disobedient models (which might suggest that obedience was inappropriate) can also serve to reduce obedience. In Milgram's research the presence of two disobedient peers was sufficient to override all the binding and agentic shift dynamics that usually produce an obedient response.

→ There is growing evidence (e.g. Sherman 1980) that knowledge of results such as Milgram's may change people's behaviour. Knowing about the process of obedience may enhance people's ability to resist destructive obedience.

→ Kohlberg (1969) found that people who used more advanced stages of moral reasoning were more likely to disobey the commands of the experimenter than those who reasoned at lower levels.

→ Obedience can also lead to discrimination as we have seen with the authoritarian personality. Adorn et al (1950) believed those with authoritarian personality can also be prejudiced. He devised several questionnaires to research his theory. One of these was called the ethnocentrism scale (E scale) where a person believes that their ethnic group is superior to all others. Another was the F scale (Fascism scale) designed to measure the attitudes of those with so-called authoritarian personality. Adorno found that those who scored high on the scale tended to be more prejudiced.

Action point

Ask yourself why the presence of disobedient peers would override binding and agentic shift dynamics.

Link

See Cognitive development on pages 106–107.

Obedience research – the legacy

Research such as Milgram's has changed the way in which we view the nature of destructive obedience. It appears from these studies that many of us are capable of committing destructive acts, and that we fail to recognise our susceptibility to such influence. Prior to this research, it was traditional for social scientists to explain behaviour such as the Nazi war crimes in World War II in terms of the actions of deviant personalities.

The current view is that destructive obedience may be produced in the majority of people purely by situational factors (i.e. the orders of an authority figure). The capacity for moral decision-making may be suspended when an individual is embedded within a powerful social hierarchy. This has led some to comment upon the 'ordinariness' of such evil acts rather than seeing them as the product of pathological (i.e. 'disturbed') personalities (Arendt 1963).

"It was though... he [Eichmann] was summing up the lessons that this long course in human wickedness had taught us – the lesson of the fearsome, word-and-thought-defying banality of evil."

H. Arendt (1963)

Exam practice   answer: page 87

'Obedience research has only provoked controversy because of the results rather than the procedures used to gain them.'

To what extent might obedience research, such as that carried out by Milgram, be considered worthwhile? (25 marks)

Ethical issues

Watch out!

Ethical guidelines are just one way in which psychologists try to resolve ethical issues.

Historically, the role of ethics has been in the promotion and maintenance of competence in a particular discipline or activity. One consequence of research such as Milgram's work on obedience has been the development of ethical guidelines for the treatment of human participants. The 'role' of these ethical guidelines is summarised in the BPS Code of Conduct: 'To preserve an overriding high regard for the well-being and dignity of research participants'.

Ethical issues in social influence research

Deception

One of Baumrind's main objections to Milgram's study of obedience was that he had deceived the participants on two counts:

→ He had led them to believe they were taking part in a study of the effects of punishment on learning.
→ He had then led them to believe they were actually delivering electric shocks.

Take note

Critics of Milgram's study did not believe that the deception had worked. Milgram provided compelling evidence that it had.

In order to understand why deception is such an important issue in psychological research we need to examine, from the participants' point of view, the impact of such practices.

→ Deception may make participants suspicious about a research investigation, or they may develop negative feelings about any future research participation.
→ It may reduce support for psychological research in general.
→ It may undermine the commitment of researchers to always telling the truth.

Probably the most serious consequence of deception is that it removes the ability of research participants to give their full informed consent to take part in an investigation. This does create dilemmas for the researcher, especially since complete openness may decrease the effectiveness of the investigation. In Milgram's research complete honesty would have made the research untenable.

Checkpoint 1

In what way would complete honesty have made Milgram's research 'untenable'?

Informed consent

The essence of the principle of informed consent is that research participants should be allowed to agree or refuse to participate in the light of comprehensive information concerning the nature and purpose of the research. Homan (1991) suggests that there are two elements implied in being 'informed', and two that constitute 'consent':

→ 'Informed' suggests that all relevant aspects of what is to happen and what might happen are disclosed to the participant and that they should be able to understand this information.

Checkpoint 2

Can you think of situations where consent might not be 'voluntary' or free from 'undue influence'?

→ 'Consent' suggests that the participant is competent to make a rational and mature judgement and that their agreement to participate should be voluntary, free from coercion and from undue influence.

Even if researchers have sought and obtained informed consent, that does not guarantee that participants really do understand what they have let themselves in for. Another problem is the requirement for the researcher to point out any likely benefits and risks of participation. Researchers are not always able accurately to predict the risks of taking part in a study. Milgram claimed that he could not have foreseen the severity of the stress experienced by his subjects (Milgram 1974).

Take note

Only a minority of research participants appear fully to understand what they have volunteered to do when they agree to take part in an experiment.

Protection of participants from harm

A further concern is that participants should be protected from undue risk during psychological research. The definition of undue risk is based on the risks that individuals might be expected to encounter in their normal lifestyle. Thus, the risks that an individual may be exposed to during a psychological investigation should not be greater than the risks they might already be expected to face in their everyday life.

One of Baumrind's main criticisms of Milgram's research was that participants would suffer permanent psychological harm from the study, including a loss of self-esteem and distrust of authority (Baumrind 1964). Milgram responded by providing evidence that, in psychiatric examinations one year after the study, there was no sign of psychological damage that was attributable to the experiment.

Was Milgram's research really so unethical?

Diana Baumrind claimed that the benefit to humanity of Milgram's work was not sufficient to justify the anxiety and distress felt by those who took part. Baumrind also claimed that Milgram violated the basic human rights of his participants by exposing them to a potentially harmful experience without first getting their informed consent to do so.

Milgram's response to these criticisms provided a powerful defence of his actions, showing that although most participants did indeed suffer distress during the experiment, a follow-up survey showed that the vast majority were glad to have taken part and some actually volunteered to take part in further research. Erikson (1968) wrote of the 'momentous contribution' that Milgram had made, and suggested that the ethical criticisms arose simply because Milgram had 'opened our eyes' to the possibility that such blind destructive obedience may be possible in all of us.

"Milgram, in exploring the external conditions that produce such destructive obedience ...seems to me to have done some of the most morally significant research in modern psychology."

Elms (1986)

Exam practice   answer: page 87

Using **one** research study into social influence as an example, consider the extent to which this study might have been seen as unethical. (12 marks)

Dealing with ethical issues

Take note

Ethical codes of conduct and guidelines for research are ways of dealing with difficult dilemmas faced by psychologists in their work.

Ethical codes are standards of conduct or rules of behaviour adopted by various professions. Ethical codes help to guide conduct within that profession and establish guidelines for standard practice and competence. Ethical codes are quasi-legal documents that have specific functions within professions; they are not abstract ideas or theories.

Ethical guidelines for research with human participants

→ Ethical guidelines tend to be based on a 'cost-benefit' approach – scientific ends are sometimes seen as justifying the use of methods that sometimes sacrifice individual participants' welfare, particularly when the research promises 'the greatest good for the greatest number'.

The jargon

BPS. The British Psychological Society, the professional body for British psychologists.

→ The BPS Code of Conduct (1995) is unique in that it gives primary attention to research. It recognises that psychologists owe a debt to the individuals who participate in research, and that in return those 'participants' should expect to be treated with the highest standards of consideration and respect.

→ Each section consists of a series of statements clarifying appropriate conduct (e.g. deception, consent). It is acknowledged that many people view the use of research deception as unacceptable conduct. However, it is recognised that many psychological processes could not be studied if individuals were fully aware of the research hypothesis in advance. Therefore, a distinction is made between withholding some details of the research hypothesis and deliberately providing false information to participants.

Dealing with specific ethical issues

Deception

Checkpoint 1

In what way were Milgram's participants deceived?

Withholding information or misleading participants is unacceptable if the participants are typically likely to show unease once debriefed. Where this is in any doubt, appropriate consultation must precede the investigation. Intentional deception of the participants over the purpose and general nature of the investigation should be avoided whenever possible, although it may be impossible to study some psychological processes without withholding information about the true object of the study or without deliberately misleading the participants.

Informed consent

Checkpoint 2

In what way was the principle of informed consent compromised in Milgram's research?

Whenever possible, the investigators should inform all participants of the objectives of the investigation. The investigators should inform the participants of all aspects of the research that might reasonably be expected to influence their willingness to participate. Research with children or with other vulnerable participants requires special safeguarding procedures.

Protection of participants

Investigators have a primary responsibility to protect participants from physical and mental harm during the investigation. Normally the risk of harm must be no greater than in ordinary life. Where research may involve behaviour or experiences that participants may regard as personal and private, the participants must be protected from stress by all appropriate measures, including the assurance that answers to personal questions need not be given.

Limitations of ethical codes for resolving ethical issues

→ All codes imply an obligation to behave in a particular way, which in turn implies that a professional group is definable and that there is a clear dividing line between members and outsiders (Homan 1991). A number of researchers (e.g. A-level and university students) do not belong to a professional organisation such as the BPS and are therefore not professionally bound by its codes.

→ Most professional codes, particularly those in the social sciences, have very little power of censure over their members. Exclusion from a professional body does not exclude social scientists from continuing to carry out research. The BPS has introduced a professional 'qualification' – Chartered Psychologist status. This is a further way in which the BPS can assure good practice among its members.

→ Some researchers have argued that the ethical decision-making should also involve a consideration of the costs and benefits of not doing the study. Social psychologists such as the late Stanley Milgram have an ethical responsibility to society as a whole, and we might argue that they would not be fulfilling that responsibility if they did not carry out such important research to the best of their ability.

→ Elliot Aronson (1995) suggests that psychologists face a particularly difficult dilemma when their wider responsibility to society conflicts with their more specific responsibilities to each individual research participant. This would include 'socially sensitive' research where the results of the research (e.g. on drug-taking behaviour) have far-reaching implications for many people. The conflict is greatest when the issues under investigation are issues of great social importance.

Take note

In a study of ethical codes across nine countries, Shuler (1982) found that 'protection' was of primary importance in all of them.

Watch out!

Ethical codes are not foolproof and may not always deal adequately with the ethical issues faced in research.

Checkpoint 3

What would have been the costs of *not* carrying out Milgram's research?

Exam practice   answer: page 88

Consider how effective psychologists have been in dealing with ethical issues in psychological research. (12 marks)

Quantitative research methods

Quantitative methods of research involve measurement and the collection of numerical data. Such data can be treated descriptively in the form of statistics, such as averages, or in the form of visuals, such as graphs and charts. They can also be treated inferentially by the application of statistical tests.

Watch out!

Qualitative (non-numerical) data can sometimes be converted to quantitative data.

Experiments

An experiment is a research method in which the experimenter changes some influence on the participants (an **independent variable** or **IV**) and observes and measures the effects of the changes on some aspect of their behaviour (the **dependent variable** or **DV**) while keeping all other sources of influence (**extraneous variables**) constant. Uncontrolled extraneous variables which interfere systematically with the influence of the IV on the DV are called **confounding variables**.

Checkpoint 1

Some people argue that we can only call some of these true experiments. Why is that?

	The experimental environment is controlled by the experimenter	The experimental environment is not controlled by the experimenter
The IV is directly manipulated by the experimenter	Laboratory experiment	Field experiment
The IV varies naturally (or fortuitously)	Quasi-experiment	Natural experiment

Strengths of experiments

→ The amount of control possible in some experiments makes it possible for the experimenter to make causal statements about behaviour. Understanding cause is one of the key aims of science. This cannot be done so readily with other methods.

→ Knowing what causes behaviour to change puts the experimenter in the position of being able to control it.

Problems with experiments

→ There is a lack of realism in certain kinds of experiment, especially the laboratory experiment, so that findings do not apply to real life.

→ The loss of control in the more 'true to life' experiments, such as the natural experiment, means it is more difficult to be confident about what causes what.

→ In spite of rigorous control, there is always the chance that behaviour is not affected by the IV but by a confounding variable.

→ Ethical considerations are as relevant here as in any other form of psychological research.

Link

See Ethical issues and Dealing with ethical issues on pages 70–73.

Correlation

Correlation is used to detect linear relationships between samples of paired data. It can be expressed pictorially as a scattergram, or numerically as a correlation coefficient which will range from +1 through 0 to –1. The sign (+ or –) gives the direction of the relationship and the number (0 to 1) gives the strength of the relationship (e.g. a correlation of +0.6 is weaker than a correlation of –0.7). Correlation coefficients have to be tested for statistical significance.

Watch out!

Correlation is not a research method. It is a method of data analysis.

Patterns of correlation

Correlation analysis will reveal one of the following patterns:

→ perfect positive correlation (+1.0)
→ imperfect positive correlation (e.g. +0.6)
→ no correlation (0)
→ imperfect negative correlation (e.g. –0.7)
→ perfect negative correlation (–1.0).

Action point

Sketch scattergrams to show an imperfect positive and a perfect negative relationship. Identify variables that might correlate in these ways.

Scattergrams

These scattergrams show a perfect positive, a zero and an imperfect negative relationship.

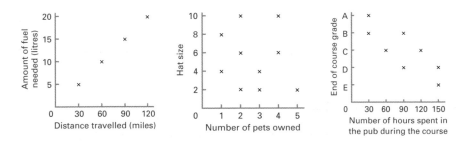

Strengths of correlation

→ It allows us to see how two variables relate to each other.
→ It allows us to predict the likely value of one variable when we only have information about the other one.
→ It is useful in checking certain kinds of reliability and validity.

Checkpoint 2

Give a real-life example of one variable being predicted from another.

Limitation of correlation

→ It is purely a description of relationships between variables. It does not allow us to say one variable causes changes in another.

Exam practice   answer: page 88

Give **one** advantage and **one** disadvantage of each of the following research methods:
- laboratory experiment (4 marks)
- field experiment (4 marks)
- natural experiment. (4 marks)

Qualitative research methods

Qualitative methods of research are less concerned with objective measurement than are quantitative methods. Their emphasis is on systematically observing, describing, exploring, interpreting and making sense of an issue or problem.

Watch out!

Qualitative and quantitative methods should be seen as complementary and equally valuable.

Naturalistic observation

→ 'Naturalistic' means that the researcher studies participant(s) in a setting which is familiar to them; e.g. home, classroom, playground.
→ 'Observation' means that the researcher systematically watches and records behaviour. Manipulation of an IV does not occur.
→ The researcher may observe from the outside (non-participant observation) or from within a group (participant observation).
→ The method of data collection can vary from simple note-taking to sophisticated recording techniques.

Action point

In your own words, write a definition of naturalistic and observation.

Strengths of naturalistic observation

→ It produces rich and detailed descriptive accounts of behaviour.
→ It often provides ideas for further research.
→ It can be used when other methods might be unethical.

Problems with naturalistic observation

→ The presence of the observer may influence participants' behaviour in unwanted ways.
→ The observer must be able to identify and acknowledge possible personal biases.
→ There are many uncontrolled influences, which may affect participants' behaviour, making it hard to know which aspects are the important ones.

Checkpoint 1

Find two actual examples of psychological research that used naturalistic observation.

Questionnaire surveys

Questionnaires usually comprise a standard set of questions about an issue and are presented to participants in exactly the same way.

→ Questions can be open or closed and be answered face-to-face, by post or by telephone.
→ A survey is usually a large-scale study of a representative sample of a relevant population.
→ This method can produce quantitative data when a Likert scale is used to record the answers. The participant ticks along a line from 1 to 5 to show how much they agree with a particular statement.

Link

See Selecting participants in Research planning on page 78.

Strengths of questionnaire surveys

→ They are useful for gathering data from large numbers of people.
→ Anonymity or lack of face-to-face contact with the researcher can encourage more honest responses.

Problems with questionnaire surveys

→ There can be difficulties with devising unambiguous questions that avoid bias, 'leading' the respondent or cause offence.
→ Respondents may answer to give a socially favourable impression (though guaranteeing anonymity might help avoid this).
→ There may be low rates of return.
→ Respondents may participate because they have a special interest in the issues being surveyed, thus the sample becomes 'self-selected'.

Interviews

Interviews usually involve one-to-one, face-to-face contact between researcher and interviewee. Types of interview include:

→ structured – fixed questions and fixed answers for the participant to choose from
→ semi-structured – specific questions are asked but flexibility is allowed in responses
→ clinical – often used in therapeutic settings where the participant and interviewer may explore an issue with a view to helping the participant understand their problems
→ open and closed questions – open questions can allow for a full range of answers while closed questions allow for fixed answers such as yes or no (closed questions can therefore allow the data to be analysed quantitatively).

Link

Some of the strengths and problems with using questionnaires apply here also.

Strengths of interviews

→ Interviews can provide detailed information about the individual's subjective view.
→ They can permit the exploration of complex ideas and issues which do not readily lend themselves to measurement.
→ They can be more flexible than other methods.

Checkpoint 2

Identify an actual example of psychological research that used the questionnaire survey and another that used interviewing.

Problems with interviews

→ Interviews can yield information which is open to misinterpretation, over-interpretation or partial interpretation (Banister et al 1994).
→ The interviewee may feel unable to be totally open and honest, particularly if the issue of interest is sensitive.
→ Certain kinds of interview might exclude people who have difficulty articulating their thoughts.

Take note

In a case study, a single person's behaviour is researched in considerable depth. Case studies are far more detailed than other methods and give more of a personal insight into the individual. They also focus on the individual and therefore account for individual differences. However, it is hard to generalise the findings to a wider population and the method is highly subjective and liable to researcher bias.

Exam practice   answers: page 80

A researcher decided to join a religious cult to investigate the particular form of social influence that it had over its members. She was able to observe members in their daily behaviours and then wrote up her notes in the evening.
(a) What specific form of investigative method is being used here? (4 marks)
(b) Give **one** advantage and **one** disadvantage of this method. (4 marks)
(c) Explain **two** ethical problems with this method. (4 marks)

Research planning

This section covers preliminary considerations when designing research, i.e. formulation of research aims and hypotheses, selection of participants and the importance of the relationship between researchers and participants.

Aims and hypotheses

Experimental research usually begins with a question, e.g. 'Do boys and girls differ in their ability to spell?' This gives rise to:

→ an **aim** (e.g. to devise research to help answer the question)
→ a **hypothesis** – a testable statement, based on theorising and/or research, that predicts the outcome of a study, e.g. boys and girls differ in spelling ability. Correlational hypotheses predict a relationship. Experimental hypotheses predict a difference. These become **alternative hypotheses** when the terms in them are precisely defined (operationalised) and can be statistically tested, e.g. age of boys/girls and the spelling test specified
→ a **null hypothesis** which predicts that a difference or relationship will be zero.

Directional hypotheses predict the direction of a difference (e.g. girls' spelling is superior to that of boys) or correlation (e.g. there is a positive relationship between weight and height). Non-directional hypotheses allow for differences or correlation in either direction (also known as one- or two-tailed hypotheses). Hypotheses are retained or rejected on the basis of research findings.

Selecting participants

Psychologists begin research with a particular target population in mind. **Population** refers to the total number of individuals who qualify to participate because they have the certain characteristics, e.g. all the couples marrying at a particular town in a given year. If it is possible to test all members of a population, the study constitutes a **census**. If not, a representative group called a **sample** is selected. The sample should be large enough adequately to represent the population.

Reasons for sampling

→ It is usually only practical to study a selection of the population.
→ It helps to ensure that the sample is representative of the population.
→ Findings from a representative sample can be generalised to the population from which it was drawn.

Sampling techniques

→ **Random sampling** – each member of the population has an equal chance of being chosen. Population members are assigned a number and the required number of participants selected using random number tables or computer-generated random numbers. This is the best way to obtain a representative sample from a population but it fails to produce a truly representative sample.

Action point

Distinguish between a research question, aim, alternative hypothesis and null hypothesis.

Watch out!

Note that certain kinds of qualitative research, such as naturalistic observation, may only have aims and no quantitatively testable hypotheses.

Checkpoint 1

Write out a directional, a non-directional and a null hypothesis for either an experimental study or a correlational study.

Action point

Write your own definitions of population, sample and census.

- **Stratified random sampling** – the population is organised into sub-groups (strata) and random samples are taken from each stratum in the same proportions that appear in the population.
- **Opportunity sampling** – the researcher decides on the type of participant needed and approaches anyone who appears suitable. It is the easiest method to use but the sample may not be representative.
- **Quota sampling** – the population is organised into sub-groups (strata) and opportunity samples are taken from each stratum in the same proportions that appear in the population.
- **Systematic sampling** – the researcher has a list of population names and every 10th, 15th or 100th name is picked depending on the ratio of people to be included in the study. This avoids bias but means that it may not be possible to identify those chosen.
- **Volunteer sample** – participants volunteer to take part in a research study. It is a simple and easy method but the sample may not be truly representative as volunteers represent a specific group of people with particular traits.

The relationship between researchers and participants

Weber and Cook (1972) identified four roles which participants being studied might adopt:

- The **faithful** participant tries to react to the situation as naturally as possible.
- The **co-operative participant** tries to discover the hypothesis being tested so that they can do their best to help support it.
- The **negativistic** participant tries to discover the hypothesis in order to disprove it.
- The **evaluatively apprehensive** participant is concerned about the impression they are creating or that the experimenter might discover something about them.

Rosenthal (1969) discovered three key influences, which could affect participants' behaviour in experiments and other kinds of research:

- **biosocial or physical characteristics** of the experimenter, such as age, sex, race and appearance
- **psychosocial factors**, which have to do with the experimenter's social skills in dealing with participants
- **experimenter expectancy effects**. Experimenters who have a hypothesis in mind may end up validating it simply because of their belief about how the results will turn out. It then becomes a self-fulfilling prophecy.

> *"...science is a social business..."*
>
> Richardson (1991)

Action point

Name and define the four kinds of participant identified by Weber and Cook (1972).

Take note

Human participants are often affected by the knowledge that they are being observed. Orne (1962) said that they are influenced by **demand characteristics** by which he meant that cues in the experimental situation (e.g. the physical set-up of the experiment or the experimenter's behaviour) might alert the participants to the hypothesis being tested.

Watch out!

The importance of participant, investigator, and situational influence varies according to the research method being used.

Exam practice answers: page 89

Without using your book, suggest two ways that:
(a) the participants might affect the outcome of an experiment (other than their reaction to the IV)
(b) the experimenter might affect the outcome of an experiment. (12 marks)

Checkpoint 2

What classic research study claimed to demonstrate the operation of teacher expectancy effects?

Research design

This topic covers some of the technicalities of good research design, concentrating on experimental research design and techniques of control.

Link

Good research design always takes ethical considerations into account. See Ethical issues and Dealing with ethical issues on pages 70–73.

Variables

Researchers sometimes need to define precisely (operationalise) what they mean by the terms they use in hypotheses and put them into a measurable, or quantifiable, form. This is a problem for psychologists who often deal with concepts such as aggression, fatigue or anxiety. In a study investigating the hypothesis that fatigue impairs driving ability, fatigue may be operationalised as a numerical measure of sleep quality and driving ability as a score in a standardised test of driving skill.

Checkpoint 1

How might you operationalise aggression?

Experimental designs

Simple experiments involve collecting scores from participants under two different conditions to see if there are differences between them. In a laboratory or field experiment, it is usual to have a **control group**, which lacks the influence of the IV and provides baseline data, and an **experimental group**, which is influenced by the IV.

All **extraneous variables** need to be controlled so that the only systematic difference between groups is the presence or absence of the IV. A systematic difference that interferes with the effect of the IV on the DV is called a **confounding variable**. In a natural or quasi-experiment the researcher compares two levels of the IV. There are three ways of collecting the two sets of data. These help to control variation due to participants.

Take note

The **single blind procedure** is when participants do not know the research aim or hypothesis. This helps to guard against participant reactivity.

The repeated measures design

Participants take part in both conditions. Advantages include:
→ It is economical in the number of participants used.
→ There are fewer individual differences affecting the DV.

Problems with it include:
→ Participants may become used to being tested and carry over the effects of practice or fatigue from one condition to the other. These are called **order effects**. **Randomised presentation** can guard against them, as can **counterbalancing**, i.e. half the participants do condition A first and half do B first (ABBA design).
→ Participants may not return to be tested a second time.

Take note

The **double blind procedure** helps to guard against researcher and participant influences – the researcher instructs someone else to collect the data but neither that person nor the participants know the hypothesis.

Take note

Standardised instructions are the same for all participants in a particular condition and are given in the same way. This should avoid favouring some over others.

The matched pairs design

Participants are put into pairs on the basis of variables relevant to the investigation. One member of the pair is then randomly assigned to condition A and the other to condition B. Advantages include:
→ There are no order effects.
→ There are fewer individual differences between conditions.

Watch out!

If order effects are a real possibility, counterbalancing is not the solution. In such cases, a different design should be used.

Problems with it include:
→ Good matching can be difficult to achieve.
→ Some individual differences will remain uncontrolled.

The independent groups design

Participants are divided randomly between conditions, or the groups are arranged on the basis of a naturally occurring IV. Advantages include:

→ It is relatively quick and easy to set up.
→ It avoids order effects.

Problems with it include:

→ It takes more participants than the repeated measures design.
→ Differences between the two groups are likely to be greater at the outset than in the other two designs.

Checkpoint 2

How would you match drivers into pairs for a test of driving ability?

Reliability

For any research to be reliable you must be able to repeat it and get the same findings. When collecting research you can check the reliability of the tests used to collect data by two methods:

→ the test-retest method – where the same test is given to participants at different times to see if scores remain similar
→ the split-half technique – the test is divided into two, e.g. all odd or all even questions. The scores are then compared on both tests in the same way as for the test-retest method.

Take note

Reliability is important when carrying out observations, especially when an observer is trying to accurately report some specific behaviour. Two or more observers can be used and then compared to provide a measure of inter-rater reliability.

Validity

Two kinds of validity are important – internal (are the results caused by the IV?) and external (can the results be generalised to the outside world?). True internal validity is hard to achieve but methods include:

→ controlling all confounding variables
→ having clear standardised instructions
→ using a representative sample of participants
→ where possible, controlling for experimenter effects, demand characteristics and participant reactivity.

Watch out!

Single and double blind procedures raise particular ethical problems because participants are not fully informed about the study before they take part in it.

It is important to make sure that the test measures what was intended. This may be via concurrent validity (comparing the tests used against an existing measure) or via content validity (looking to see if the questions asked are appropriate to test the behaviour being measured). True external validity is also hard, if not impossible, to achieve. Four aspects need to be considered:

Link

See Obedience to authority on pages 66–67.

→ **populations** – do the sample findings apply to the larger population?
→ **locations** – do the findings apply to other settings and/or situations, not just the laboratory?
→ **measures** (or constructs) – do the findings generalise to other measures used? e.g. if self-esteem is measured using two different self-esteem questionnaires, would the results be the same?
→ **times** – can the findings be generalised to the past or the future?

Exam practice   answers: page 89

A researcher was interested in whether students revised better when listening to music than when revising in silence. He randomly split a class into two groups – and played music to one group only, whilst they revised.

(a) What type of experimental design has been used here? (4 marks)

(b) Give **one** advantage and **one** disadvantage of this design. (4 marks)

(c) Suggest **two** extraneous variables that should be controlled. (4 marks)

Analysing quantitative data

This topic concerns simple descriptive analysis of quantitative data. Such data can be described in the form of summary statistics and in the form of 'visuals' such as graphs. The correct use of these requires an understanding of how the data have been measured.

Types of measurement

Measurement differs in its level of sophistication:
→ nominal measurement – frequency counts into named categories
→ ordinal measurement – values on this scale represent rankings, ratings or placings
→ interval and ratio measurement – these scales are more sophisticated and measure quantities or numbers of fixed units with equal distances between all the points on the scale.

Measurement scales can also be:
→ discrete – i.e. whole units such as numbers of children
→ continuous – values can be subdivided ad infinitum, e.g. a timescale.

Checkpoint 1

Give an example of nominal, ordinal, interval and ratio measurement scales.

Measures of central tendency

These are used to summarise a sample of data using one typical score.
→ **mean** – the arithmetic average. Its sensitivity is a strength and a weakness (an extreme score can distort the mean).
→ **median** – the central value found when scores have been arranged in order of size. It is immune to extremes but affected by small changes in the number of scores.
→ **mode** – the most frequently occurring value. It is immune to extremes and good for relatively large amounts of homogenous data.

Choosing between them depends both on the measurement scale:
→ interval or ratio – mean preferred if appropriate
→ ordinal – median preferred but means are sometimes used
→ nominal – mode can be used;

and on the shape of the frequency distribution:
→ normal – mean preferred
→ skewed – median preferred
→ bi- or multimodal – mode preferred.

Checkpoint 2

When might a mean be inappropriate for interval/ratio data?

Measures of dispersion
These indicate how varied scores are around the measure of central tendency.
→ **range** – the difference between the largest and smallest score.
→ **standard deviation** – a more complex measure which takes into account every score and its deviation from the mean. It is useful with interval and ratio data.

Watch out!

Measures of dispersion are sometimes called measures of variability or spread.

Frequency diagrams

Choice of the appropriate type of frequency diagram depends on knowing whether data are:

→ shown on a nominal, ordinal, interval or ratio scale: nominal are qualitative, interval and ratio are quantitative and ordinal fall in between
→ discrete or continuous.

The diagrams below provide some illustrative examples.

Link

Correlation can be presented in the form of scattergrams. See Quantitative research methods on pages 75.

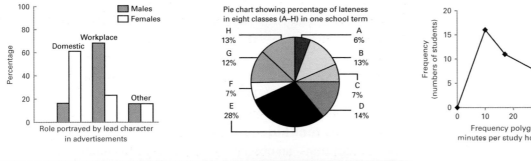

Inferential statistics

This kind of data allows the researcher to draw conclusions about the wider population from which a particular sample has been drawn.

A significant level must be stated to see whether we can reject or retain the experimental hypothesis. With any results we cannot be 100% sure that they are accurate. The minimum level which is seen as acceptable is 5%, which basically means that there is a 5% or less chance that the results have been got by chance: $p = 0.05$ or 5%.

Choosing an incorrect significance level can lead to type 1 or 2 errors. Type 1 error is when the null hypothesis is rejected mistakenly because the significance level is too high, e.g. 10%. A type 2 error occurs when the null hypothesis is rejected mistakenly because the significance level is too stringent, e.g. 1%.

In order to choose the correct statistical test, we need to know if the data is being tested for differences, relationships or associations. We also need to know the level of measurement and the design of the study. Below is a table of non-parametric tests that are used when you have ordinal level data (if in doubt about what tests to use it is better to stick with non-parametric tests).

Level of measurement	Test of difference	Test of difference	Correlation
Nominal	Independent data (experimental design) Chi-squared test for independent samples	Related data (experimental design) Sign data	
Ordinal, interval or ratio	Mann Whitney U test	Wilcoxon matched pairs signed ranks test	Spearman's rank order correlation coefficient

Tests that are more powerful, such as t tests and Pearson's Product Moment Correlation Coefficient can also be used when the data is measured on an interval or ratio scale and the data in the population from which you have drawn your sample are normally distributed.

Exam practice answers: page 89

(a) When would a median be preferable to a mean?
(b) What extra information is achieved by using a measure of dispersion?
   (12 marks)

Analysing qualitative data

Link

See Analysing quantitative data on pages 82–83.

Qualitative methods yield a wide variety of data. These may be quantitative or in the form of written accounts which can sometimes be converted to quantitative data and treated with descriptive and inferential statistical techniques. Researchers use the method that suits their purpose best.

Observations

In both participant and non-participant observation, the observer may choose to make a written record of events or take video or tape recordings for more detailed analysis later.

Observation techniques

Diary description – an observer who is in regular contact with a participant makes a written account of any changes in behaviour as they occur. Piaget (1896–1980) made diary descriptions of the development of his own three children and, from these, was able to identify developmental changes. Diary descriptions:

Checkpoint 1

What other advantage do you think diarists might have?

→ give a rich and full account of behaviour on all levels
→ are a fertile source of hypotheses for further research
→ are limited in their generalisability to other cases
→ may lack objectivity if the observer is closely involved with the subject.

Specimen description – the observer makes as full an account as possible of behaviour in a chosen segment of the subject's life, e.g. Barker and Wright (1951) who made a record of an American boy's day. Specimen descriptions:

→ can be very time-consuming
→ require special attention to the reliability of the observations
→ can be a useful starting point for more detailed research.

Event sampling – a specific type of behaviour is identified and the number of times it occurs, its context and events surrounding it are recorded, e.g. Bell and Ainsworth's (1972) study of infant crying. Event sampling is:

→ particularly time-saving where the type of behaviour to be recorded occurs infrequently
→ is good for preserving the context in which the event occurs.

Time sampling – useful when the behaviour of interest occurs relatively frequently. The researcher observes for a specified time and then records for a specified time. The presence or absence of the behaviour during each observation interval can be recorded to give an idea of how frequently it occurs. This method:

"Two heads are better than one."

Proverb

→ is quick and efficient
→ tends to lose the continuity of behaviour
→ may give a fragmented picture, not the full context.

In all these methods, it is good policy to have more than one observer watching and recording the same thing or analysing the same written account. This leads to greater inter-observer reliability and helps to guard against biased or subjective interpretation.

Interviews

The type of data gathered by interview depends on the type of interview conducted and its purpose:

→ Structured interviews tend to yield responses which can be treated quantitatively using descriptive and inferential statistics.
→ Semi-structured interviews may also yield some quantifiable information but generally generate a great deal of verbal information. The analysis of this 'discourse' or 'text' can be for a number of things including meanings or recurring themes.
→ Clinical interviews can be sharply focused or wide-ranging depending on the context and may include, amongst many other things, clinical notes, recordings and test results.

Triangulation

Triangulation in qualitative research involves checking the reliability of findings by scrutinising them from different vantage points:
→ method triangulation – use of two or more methods
→ data triangulation – data collection from different sources
→ investigator triangulation – use of two or more researchers
→ theory triangulation – use of two or more theoretical viewpoints.

Content analysis

One way to analyse written data is with content analysis. This is a way of observing, not people directly, but the communications that they have produced. Shneidman (1963) analysed the speeches of Nixon and Kennedy during their presidential debates. It is possible to decipher such works and obtain an understanding of a person's psychological state or gain some insight into general behaviour within a culture. Analysing TV programmes could give us an insight into levels of increased violence in society.

Watch out!

Case studies are not always of people with problems.

Checkpoint 2

What is the general meaning of the term 'reliability'?

Link

See Qualitative research methods on page 77 for more details about interviews.

Exam practice answer: page 89

Describe **two** advantages that qualitative data might have over quantitative data. (12 marks)

Answers
Social psychology and research methods

Interpersonal relationships

Exam practice

The only experimental design you could use would be independent, two different groups compare, because it is a study looking at the difference between men and women (gender). Problems with this design are individual differences but it does remove the issue of order effects.

The formation, maintenance and dissolution of relationships

Checkpoints

1 Through argument and negotiation, or perhaps through changing partner. In many cases, individuals may play down the importance of an attitude to minimise any perceived imbalance.

2 Because the selection of mates is seen as a way in which the individual can ensure that their genes stand a 'good chance' in the next generation. Evolutionary explanations of homosexuality might stress the role of inclusive fitness, i.e. helping those with whom we share genes.

Exam practice

This question requires an outline description and an evaluation of two explanations of interpersonal attraction. It is important, therefore, to plan your response carefully. In a 30-minute answer, you would give 15 minutes to the first explanation, and 15 minutes to the second. This means about four paragraphs, each of about 150 words:

- outline description of interpersonal balance theory – we are attracted to those who share our attitudes; this makes a balanced cognitive world
- evaluation of this theory – people are able to put up with inconsistency; balance can be achieved in a number of other ways, and the theory ignores other important factors
- outline description of the repulsion hypothesis – we are attracted to everyone but then discount those who are dissimilar
- evaluation of this hypothesis – including the use of the false consensus effect, and the contrary research findings which challenge its claims.

Cultural and sub-cultural differences in relationships

Checkpoints

1 Individualist cultures include the USA, Australia and the UK. Collectivist cultures include China, Russia and Guatemala.

2 According to Buss's research, males typically chose females who symbolised youth and health (important for childbearing), whereas females typically chose males who were ambitious and hardworking (important for the provision of resources).

Exam practice

Discuss requires both an evaluation and an evaluation of research into differences between relationships in Western and non-Western cultures. It is tempting to fill your answer with examples and anecdotes, but you should keep this answer as psychological as possible. You might include the following:

- differences between individualist (commonly Western) and collectivist (commonly non-Western) cultures and their relevance here
- research relating to voluntary and involuntary relationships (e.g. arranged marriages)
- research relating to permanent and impermanent relationships (e.g. attitudes to divorce in different cultures)
- evaluation of cross-cultural research including the problem of equivalence (i.e. accepting that research questions and responses have the same meaning in different cultures).

The causes of aggression

Checkpoints

1 Children would be most likely to imitate behaviour of models when they see the model being reinforced for their aggressive behaviour.

2 It does not explore aggression in a real-life setting. The Bobo dolls were designed to be hit and, unlike in real-life, the children could strike out without fear of retaliation from the victim of their aggression (i.e. the Bobo doll).

Exam practice

Describe is the AO1 part of the question. With most exam boards this will usually be worth 10 or 12 marks, and in this question it is worth 10 marks. The candidate would be expected to describe Bandura's theory and refer to his research. The *evaluate* part of this question is worth 15 marks and the candidate would be expected to evaluate the theory by referring to studies that either support or criticise this theory. The theory has also been criticised for the methods it used. Biological factors can also be brought in as another way of explaining aggression.

Conformity

Checkpoints

1 The former is known as 'informational influence' and the latter as 'normative influence'.
2 This suggests that many people engage in public compliance rather than private acceptance. Conformity, therefore, does not necessarily mean agreement.
3 In an individualist culture, self-interest and individual rights are promoted rather than the rights and interests of the community (as in a collectivist culture).

Exam practice

The two most obvious reasons why people conform are because of 'normative influence' and 'informational influence'. An alternative explanation is 'referential social influence'.

You should begin your answer by explaining each of your chosen reasons, then perhaps show how each of these might have contributed to the conformity found in (for example) Asch's research.

Remember this is only an outline injunction, so requires a concise, highly focused description of the two reasons.

Obedience to authority

Checkpoints

1 If the learner is physically removed from the teacher, the latter is psychologically 'buffered' from the consequences of their actions. As this distance decreases, buffers are removed, the consequences become more obvious and obedience levels drop.
2 Milgram did, in fact, point out that most of his participants felt they had learned something valuable about themselves. Distrust of an authority figure who ordered them to engage in destructive acts would be socially desirable.

Exam practice

Twelve minutes to answer this question gives you about 200 words (or about 100 words per study).

This might involve Milgram *and* Hofling's studies, or two studies carried out by Milgram. You should only describe, not evaluate either of these studies.

Explaining and resisting obedience

Checkpoints

1 'Foot-in-the-door' refers to the gradual commitment to a course of action. By initially agreeing to give a low level of shock it was more difficult for participants to refuse to deliver subsequent higher levels of shock.
2 The use of cruise missiles does not require visual contact with the victim; attacks at night; the dropping of bombs from high altitudes; or the use of landmines where victims are harmed at some later date.

Exam practice

This question is not asking you to *defend* Milgram's research, but to consider whether it was 'worthwhile'. This might be achieved by examining the ethical problems of the work and balancing these against any lessons learned from this research (i.e. the *legacy*).

If such research was not *valid*, this would make it less worthwhile (see page 66). Milgram has challenged such claims.

Finally, there is the view that knowledge of Milgram's research may enhance people's ability to resist destructive obedience.

Ethical issues

Checkpoints

1 This research relied on a deception (that participants believed they were delivering shocks). Without this, Milgram would not have been able to explore the power of obedience with any degree of realism.
2 These might include situations where participants are paid or where participation in research is seen as compulsory in some way (e.g. schools or prisons).

Exam practice

This appears to be quite a challenging question, but really isn't that difficult. A number of the studies that you have considered in this area might be seen as unethical nowadays (although perhaps not at the time). Milgram's study is the most obvious example. This might be addressed on three fronts.
• Baumrind's objections to Milgram's work (e.g. deception, lack of informed consent).
• Milgram's response to these criticisms.
• Valuable lessons learned as a result of Milgram's research (i.e. the legacy of the research, which offers some ethical justification of it).

Dealing with ethical issues

Checkpoints

1 Milgram's participants were led to believe that they were delivering real electric shocks as part of a study on the effects of punishment on learning.
2 Although they had *consented* to take part in the research, participants were not fully informed of the fact that they would be pressurised to continue.
3 It has been argued that Milgram's research has taught us valuable lessons concerning the power of situational factors in destructive obedience. This finding, that destructive obedience is common (rather than being a personality flaw in some people) is an important discovery that has clear social implications.

Exam practice

It is important to remember that you are being asked to do more than simply *describe* how psychologists have attempted to deal with ethical issues, but to *consider* how effective these attempts have been. There is scope for *some* descriptive content here (e.g. describing the nature and purpose of ethical guidelines) but it is vital that you *engage* with this material in some way.

You may begin by describing the purpose of ethical guidelines (primarily to protect the well-being of those who take part in research) and then show how these are applied to specific ethical issues.

You can then move on to a critical consideration of whether these are actually *effective* given the nature and aims of psychological research. The limitations of ethical codes for resolving ethical issues are covered on page 73.

One technique for answering these critical questions is to think of yourself as a courtroom lawyer, presenting arguments and then showing their strengths and weaknesses to an uninformed audience. For example, you may state that within ethical codes, clear guidelines are given concerning what is unacceptable conduct *but*, as Elliot Aronson points out, sometimes psychologists' wider responsibilities to society may conflict with their specific responsibilities to individual research participants.

Quantitative research methods

Checkpoints

1 Strictly speaking, an investigation only qualifies as an experiment if the IV is directly manipulable by the experimenter. By this definition, laboratory and field experiments are true experiments, but quasi- and natural experiments are not.
2 Places at university are often offered on the basis of predicted A-level grades because A-level performance is usually a reliable indication of how well an individual would cope with degree level work.

Exam practice

Laboratory experiment:
Advantage – the experimenter has full control over the independent variable and other variables therefore causal statements are more certain.
Disadvantage – participants know they are in an experiment and may adjust their behaviour.

Field experiment:
Advantage – behaviour occurs in a naturalistic setting therefore is more true to life.
Disadvantage – because participants are not aware they are taking part in a research study, there may be some ethical problems, such as invasion of privacy.

Natural experiment:
Advantage – as the IV is manipulated by outside agencies, this enables psychologists to study issues that are of high natural interest (such as the effects of two types of child-rearing technique).
Disadvantage – experimenter lacks control over other variables that might affect the behaviour being studied.

Qualitative research methods

Checkpoints

1 Piaget used naturalistic observation to provide material for his diary descriptions of his own children's intellectual development. Sylva et al (1980) used naturalistic observation in a time-sampling framework to study the patterns of play in children in Oxfordshire playgroups and nursery schools.
2 Shere Hite (1971) conducted an extensive survey of female sexuality using postal questionnaires. Sears, Maccoby and Levni (1957) carried out a classic study on child-rearing styles using interviews.

Exam practice

(a) Participant observation.
(b) Advantage – enables a more in-depth study of the group in question. Disadvantage – impossible to write up notes 'in situ' therefore relies on memory.
(c) Invasion of privacy as people 'open up' without knowing of the researcher's other role. Deception, by the researcher as she deceives the group as to her true reason for being there.

Research planning

Checkpoints

1 A non-directional experimental hypothesis:
There is a difference in the mathematical abilities of boys and girls.

A directional experimental hypothesis:
Girls' mathematical ability is superior to that of boys.
A null hypothesis for an experiment:
There is no difference in the mathematical abilities of boys and girls.
A non-directional correlational hypothesis:
There is a relationship between variable A and B.
A directional correlational hypothesis:
There is a positive (or negative) relationship between variable A and B.
A null hypothesis for a correlational study:
There is no relationship between variable A and B.

2 Rosenthal and Jacobson's (1968) study called 'Pygmalion in the Classroom' claimed to show the effects of positive teacher expectations on the behaviour and educational attainment of elementary school children.

Exam practice

Turn to page 79 for some suggestions about how participants and investigators can affect the outcome of an experiment. Check your answers against the information there.

Research design

Checkpoints

1 Aggression is notoriously difficult to define. It can be verbal or physical, direct or indirect, directed towards people or objects. Some researchers use acts of physical violence as an indication of aggression and count the number of times they occur within set time periods.

2 To match drivers into pairs, a researcher might take into account bodyweight, sex, usual drinking pattern, previous driving experience, type of vehicle typically driven, timing of most recent meal and many other variables besides.

Exam practice

(a) Independent groups design.
(b) See page 77.
(c) Possible extraneous variables include the nature and loudness of the music, the material being revised, the motivation of the students, and so on.

Analysing quantitative data

Checkpoints

1 Most physical measurements of weight, time, speed, etc. qualify as ratio measurement. Interval measurement scales are similar in that they involve quantities of things but these scales do not have absolute zero so °C and °F scales are good examples. Rank positions in a race are an example of ordinal measurement. Frequencies of male and female newsreaders on TV constitute nominal data.

2 Although the mean is preferred for interval or ratio data, it might not give an accurate impression of central tendency in a skewed sample of data. In this case, the median would be preferable.

Exam practice

(a) When there are extreme scores that might distort the mean or where the data is ordinal.
(b) It measures the degree of spread around the mean (i.e. how varied are scores in the sample).

Analysing qualitative data

Checkpoints

1 Diary descriptions of the kind carried out by Piaget are unlikely to be distorted by participant reactivity to being observed. Piaget was a familiar figure to his children so they were unlikely to be affected by being observed by him.

2 Another word for reliability is 'consistency'. There are several kinds of reliability. The example given here is of inter-observer reliability, which is used to minimise bias in observations. To establish this, two or more observers would record their observations independently of each other and then crosscheck them to ensure that they matched.

Exam practice

- Qualitative methods tend to give a rich and full account of behaviour at all levels rather than a 'snapshot' of behaviour at only one level.
- They can generate data that can be explored for meaning and underlying themes.

Revision checklist
Social psychology and research methods

By the end of this chapter you should be able to:

1	Understand why we form a relationship and the reason why some relationships are maintained while others dissolve.	Confident	Not confident **Revise** page 58
2	Understand how culture can have an effect on relationships.	Confident	Not confident **Revise** pages 60–61
3	Understand what causes aggressive behaviour.	Confident	Not confident **Revise** pages 62–63
4	Understand the different types of conformity and the reasons why some of us obey and some of us don't.	Confident	Not confident **Revise** pages 64–69
5	Know about the ethical issues within psychology and how they are dealt with.	Confident	Not confident **Revise** pages 70–73
6	Design a study using a research method producing qualitative data and then be able to analyse this data.	Confident	Not confident **Revise** pages 76–81, 84–85
7	Design a study using a research method producing quantitative data and then be able to analyse this data.	Confident	Not confident **Revise** pages 74–75, 78–83

Cognitive and developmental psychology

Cognitive psychology focuses on the operation of information processing in the brain. Its major topics are perception, attention, language, thinking and memory. It proceeds largely through the construction of models of parts of a process (e.g. a model of short-term memory operation). Models are not descriptions of the actual biological processes, but of the information flows in those organs; these generate testable hypotheses. There is always a tension between genetic factors and the influence of environments in the development of that genetic potential, and nowhere is that more evident than in the topic of intelligence.

Developmental psychology is no longer a matter of childhood development, but of the whole human lifecycle. This holistic viewpoint is, however, not reflected in the balance of the material – almost all research is focused on the initial development in childhood, with little research on subsequent stages in the lifecycle.

Exam themes

- Memory
- Cognition and Perception
- Attachment and daycare
- Gender
- Moral understanding
- Intelligence
- Lifecycle

Topic checklist

	Edexcel		AQA/A		AQA/B		OCR		WJEC	
	AS	A2	AS	A2	AS	A2	AS	A2	AS	A2
Remembering and forgetting	○		○		○			●		●
Models of memory	○		○		○					●
The role of emotion in memory					○					●
Eyewitness testimony	○	●	○				○	●	○	●
Cognition and the law	○	●	○			●	○	●	○	●
Perceptual organisation				●	○					
Perceptual development				●						
Cognitive development			●	●		●		●		●
The development of social cognition				●		●				
Attachment			●	○	●					
Daycare			●	○	●					
Sex and gender	○			●	○	●		●		
Theories of gender development				●	○	●				
Development of moral understanding						●		●		●
Theories of the nature of intelligence				●						●
Genetic and environmental effects on intelligence				●						●
Erikson and lifespan theories										●
Adolescence										●
Middle and late adulthood										●

Remembering
and forgetting

Memory is a process which is vital to our survival. For psychologists, memory processes are called:

- **encoding**, whereby incoming information is changed into a form that the system can cope with
- **storage** for a particular length of time, in a particular form, in a store with a certain capacity
- **retrieval,** i.e. getting information out of a memory store.

Take note

From an evolutionary perspective, survival information is remembered and other information forgotten as the normal course of events. Humans are forgetting machines.

Concepts in memory

Sensory Information Store (SIS)

Sperling (1960) believed that information in the SIS is held as a sensation, e.g. a visual stimulus is held as a visual image. To demonstrate this he showed participants three rows of four mixed numbers and consonants for a very brief time, then played them a tone (high, medium or low) to prompt them to recall the top, middle or bottom line. Participants could do this easily if they recalled immediately but the image faded rapidly, lasting for no more than one-quarter of a second. In this way, Sperling was also able to show that SIS holds 5 to 9 items.

Short Term Memory (STM)

Information selected for further processing passes from the SIS into the STM. It is thought that STM holds information in the form of images, sounds or meanings. Early researchers thought that information in STM was kept 'alive' by rehearsing (repeating) items or chunks. Miller (1956) asked participants to listen to strings of numbers or consonants of varying length and recall them in order. The average recall was 7 ± 2 items (Miller's **magical number seven**). Our STM is, therefore, capable of holding between 5 and 9 items or chunks.

The jargon

Procedural memory. Doing things.
Semantic. General factual knowledge.
Episodic. Personal autobiographical events.

Long Term Memory (LTM)

LTM consists of many different systems – knowledge, imagery, music, language, etc. LTM appears to have unlimited capacity and an indefinite lifespan.

Link

See Models of memory on pages 94–95 for some theories about these processes.

Forgetting

SIS forgetting

SIS has a life span of only about one-quarter of second and a capacity of 5 to 9 items (Sperling 1960). Inability to recall items is due to the sensation in the sensory system rapidly fading away.

Take note

SIS, STM and LTM are convenient names for processes but are too easily conceptualised as single structures in the brain. STM, for example, is a property of many sensory systems in some form. Early research used letters and numbers perceived visually or acoustically, and this may not generalise to other systems and stimuli.

STM forgetting

→ **Trace decay theory** says we lose items because they fade away. As Peterson and Peterson (1959) showed, STM traces have a maximum life span of 18 to 30 seconds if unrehearsed.

→ **Displacement (interference) theory** says items are lost because when we exceed STM's capacity, something has to go to make room. This is in line with Miller's (1956) magical number seven.

→ The **central executive** decides how to share out the limited resources of STM and deals with both auditory and visual stimuli. It has a limited capacity and deals with tasks that are cognitively demanding.
→ An **articulatory loop** deals with verbal information and is essentially a rehearsal system. It is likely that the capacity of this system is limited to that which can be read aloud in approximately two seconds (Baddeley et al 1975).
→ A **visuo-spatial sketchpad** can hold and rehearse visual and spatial information.

Evaluation of the working memory model

→ In line with research findings that have cast doubt over the importance of verbal rehearsal, its role in memory is reduced to the articulatory loop only.
→ The working memory model can explain how, in brain-damaged patients, selective deficits may occur in short-term memory.
→ It is now the current 'modal model' and the base theory for modern research, and accounts for most current research findings – the test of a good model!

Craik and Lockhart's levels of processing theory

Craik and Lockhart (1972) disagreed with Atkinson and Shiffrin's idea that memory consisted of separate stores. Instead, they suggested that memory depends on how we process information when it comes in.

→ **Shallow processing** takes two forms. Structural (or iconic) processing is when we encode only the physical qualities (appearance) of something. Phonemic (or acoustic) processing is when we encode its sound. Shallow processing only involves maintenance rehearsal and leads to fairly short-term retention of information.
→ **Deep processing** involves semantic processing which happens when we encode the meaning of a word and relate it to similar words with similar meaning. Such elaborative rehearsal leads to longer-term retention.

Evaluation of the levels of processing approach

→ The levels model seems to describe what is happening rather than explaining why deeper processing leads to longer lasting memories (Eysenck and Keane 1990).
→ It is very difficult to test the model by controlling what kind of processing people use.

Grade booster

A very high evaluation level is that Baddeley (2000) has modified the model several times, but he still cannot account for the 'binding problem': how do all the different inputs bind together to present an integrated 'picture' in our consciousness?

Take note

The definition of level of processing is circular in that depth is both defined and measured by success of recall, but is not measurable by any other independent means. This is a serious scientific flaw in the theory.

Exam practice   answers: page 130

(a) (i) Outline key features of the working memory model. (6 marks)
    (ii) Explain one strength of the working memory model. (4 marks)
(b) Describe and evaluate the working memory model. (10 marks)
(c) Discuss alternatives to the multistore model of memory. (30 marks)

The role of emotion in memory

According to evolutionary perspectives, all perceptual inputs have an emotional component attached, as they are assessed for their threat status. This is shown to be the case in memory via evidence such as Capgras Syndrome (Ramachandran 2005). Mood-dependent memory is a well-known but controversial phenomenon (Yiend and Mackintosh 2005) and one which is difficult to experimentally investigate, especially as mood manipulation (as an IV) is problematic.

Repression

Sometimes called motivated forgetting, repression is the purposeful suppression of memories. Freud (1901) suggested that memories that are too threatening or laden with anxiety are hidden in the unconscious mind and that it is necessary to expend psychic energy to keep them there. The implication of this is that such memories could be retrieved accidentally because of a precipitating event or deliberately through psychoanalysis.

→ Abundant clinical evidence for repression exists in conditions such as fugue states where, following a stressful event, an individual loses personal identity and is often found wandering miles from home.
→ It has been difficult to demonstrate repression unambiguously in the laboratory, not least because of ethical problems in deliberately attempting to induce it.
→ Holmes (1990) reviewed 30 years of studies and concluded there was no convincing experimental evidence for repression.

Flashbulb memories

Flashbulb memories are of events that were outstanding in some way. People in their 50s and older often recall where they were when they heard of US President J. F. Kennedy's assassination. Younger people are likely to carry a similar memory of when they heard of Princess Diana's death in 1997 or the 9/11 terrorist attack in 2001.

→ Brown and Kulik (1977) analysed people's recall of similar national events and found that such memories carried a high element of surprise, emotional arousal and a sense of the event's importance.
→ Williams (1993) studied the Hillsborough football disaster and found that so-called flashbulb memories decayed over time just like ordinary memories. This conclusion was also reached by Schmolck (2000) over the O. J. Simpson trial in the USA in 1995.
→ It is highly likely that people rehearse these memories, either with peers and family or via media reminders (e.g. the death of Princess Diana).

The jargon

Capgras Syndrome. A condition in which sufferers have had part of their **limbic system** damaged and have lost their emotional response when recognising people.

Check the net

Look up the famous case of Agatha Christie's fugue on the Internet. View different accounts, and decide whether she was faking or not!

Action point

What were you doing when the war in Iraq started? When Hurricane Katrina struck New Orleans? When the London bombings occurred (the 7/7 attacks)?

Checkpoint

On balance, does the evidence support either repression or flashbulb memory?

Post-traumatic stress disorder (PTSD)

One of the major symptoms of PTSD is the flashback, where a major traumatic incident is spontaneously and overwhelmingly recalled, in an immersive experience (McNally 2003).

In evaluation:

→ There is much clinical evidence for the phenomenon (Brewin and Holmes 2003).

→ However, it may be **cue-dependent recall** as PTSD sufferers have big attentional biases towards anxiety-raising stimuli (Mathews and MacLeod 2002).

Bower's network theory of affect

Bower (1981) and Bower and Gilligan (1984) proposed a theory which links mood and memory. Emotions are seen as nodes in a complex semantic network. A node can be activated by an internal or external stimulus. When this happens, activation spreads around the network in a selective rather than general manner.

In evaluation of the theory:

→ Bower et al (1978) tested mood state dependent recall. Participants learned two lists of words in a happy or sad mood and recalled them in the same or opposite mood. Recall was better when mood at learning and recall matched.

→ Bower et al (1981) tested the mood congruity hypothesis by inducing happy or sad mood in participants by hypnosis. Participants then read a story about Jack, who was depressed, and André, who was happy. Later, they were able to recall more about the character who matched their mood state.

→ Bower's theory best fits current evidence on mood dependent memory (Yield and Mackintosh 2005).

Action point

Can you summarise the four aspects outlined in this section, with one piece of evidence for and one against?

Grade booster

Have a prepared paragraph summarising the information on these pages and evaluating them in general. Does the simple evolutionary threat 'rule' account for all findings? Draw a strong scientific conclusion (i.e. largely, yes!).

Exam practice answer: page 130

Discuss the role of emotion in memory. (30 marks)

Eyewitness testimony

Eyewitness testimony (EWT) research is of particular interest in the investigation of crime. It is important to understand people's memories for events as well as their memory for the individuals involved.

Studies of EWT

Staged crimes

Buckhout (1979) staged a 'shooting' of a professor in front of 141 eyewitnesses (students and others). The eyewitnesses:

→ overestimated the time the crime lasted for
→ overestimated the weight of the gunman
→ underestimated the age of the gunman.

Seven weeks later, only 40% of the witnesses could identify the gunman from photographs. Even the 'shot' professor could not identify him, so victims are not necessarily better witnesses than bystanders. In similar research, Buckhout (1980) used a line-up of suspects and found only 14% of witnesses could pick out the right 'criminal'.

Leading the witness

Link

See page 45 for more about this study.

Checkpoint

How does Yuille and Cutshall's finding affect your perception of Loftus' research?

→ Loftus and Palmer (1974) showed participants in a study a film of a car crash. Later they were asked questions about the film. The wording of the questions was changed in certain ways. People who were asked 'How fast were the cars going when they smashed into each other?' estimated faster speeds than participants whose question included the word 'hit' instead. A week later, participants were asked if there had been any broken glass. The film showed none but 32% of the 'smashed into' group said yes compared to 14% of the 'hit' group.
→ In 1975, Loftus and Zanni showed participants a short film of a car accident. Later some participants were asked if they had seen a broken headlight and others whether they had seen the broken headlight. There was no broken headlight at all, but 15% of the 'the' group said there was one, compared with 7% of the 'a' group.
→ Yuille and Cutshall (1986) studied witnesses who had seen a real violent crime. They were impressively accurate in recalling main events but could be misled by questions about peripheral incidents.

Emotion can affect recall

In violent events, the high levels of arousal generated may shut down (focus) attention to anxiety-arousing objects like weapons or personal injuries. Loftus (1979) found significant reductions in identification of a weapon-carrying individual in a staged field experiment.

Age and EWT

Children are far more easily affected by leading questions (Goodman and Reed 1986) but are as accurate as adults when given factual questions.

Evaluation of EWT

→ There is a major distinction between real-life and staged studies, in terms of both ecological validity and results. Real-life studies suggest that adults are far more accurate than staged studies suggest.

→ The work on leading questions, principally by Elizabeth Loftus, has had a massive impact on legal proceedings in the USA, by undermining the assumption that the eyewitness is reliable.

Watch out!

Don't get tied up in long lists of studies when you need to evaluate your descriptive material as well. Be brief and accurate!

Check the net

Look up Loftus' work on 'False Memory' on the Internet. Remember that she received death threats for her scientific testimony in courts. (This is especially relevant for AQA B.)

Action point

Test yourself! Write a list of studies and their descriptions in brief in one column of a sheet of paper. In the other column give specific or general critical points relating to each study.

Grade booster

Make two major points in final evaluation:
→ The difficulty in conducting ecologically valid studies, especially for ethical reasons
→ Court proceedings are not always rational decision-making theatres, and even strong eyewitness testimony sometimes has no impact on a verdict in the real world.

Exam practice answers: page 130

(a) Explain why studies of eyewitness testimony have been criticised as lacking validity. (5 marks)

(b) Discuss factors affecting the accuracy of eyewitness testimony. (30 marks)

(c) Describe the debate surrounding false and recovered memories. Evaluate this debate with reference to psychological evidence. (12 marks)

Cognition and the law

Cognitive psychology has several interfaces with the legal system, most notably in eyewitness testimony. Others include the memory enhancement of the cognitive interview technique and the debate about the existence of criminal modes of thinking.

The false memory debate

Link

See Eyewitness testimony on pages 98–99.

→ Loftus has shown conclusively that is possible to create false memories – even under experimental conditions (Loftus1974) and far more easily under real-life conditions – often to devastating effect (e.g. Loftus 1979).

→ Supposedly repressed memories recovered via hypnotherapy have subsequently been shown to be false in many cases, usually due to cueing by the therapist (Brown 1998).

→ Holmes (1990) has reviewed 30 years of research into repression and concluded its existence is unproven scientifically.

→ On both moral and scientific grounds, most psychologists have taken a sceptical position in testimony to courts about recovered memories.

Cognitive interview technique (CIT)

Devised by Fisher and Geiselman (1987), the CIT has been used as a technique by trained officers in the UK from the late 1990s. It has four main components:

→ recreating the context (often by describing seeming irrelevant aspects)
→ focusing concentration (asking questions around specific memories)
→ multiple attempts to retrieve memories (without leading questions)
→ varied retrieval (different order of recall in different retrieval attempts).

Evaluation

Action point

Why might the police be resistant to use of a successful technique such as CIT?

→ CIT was generally found to provide more information than standard interview (Kohnken 1999).

→ Clarke and Milne (2001) reviewed police interviewing practice in England and found little implementation, with overall interviewing standards being poor.

Action point

Do you know other research relating to interviews? (Hints: eyewitness testimony, leading questions)

Criminal thinking patterns

Yochelson and Samenow (1976) proposed that all criminal behaviour is the result of rational thinking and forms a criminal personality. This was based on interviews with 240 male offenders. They identified forty 'thinking errors', which included:

→ need for power and control
→ failure to assume responsibility
→ fantasy about anti-social and violent behaviour.

Evaluation of the research

→ The sample was unrepresentative.
→ There was no control group.
→ Many errors appear to be psychological defence mechanisms (Wulach 1988).

Rational choice theory (RCT)

This was proposed by Cornish and Clarke in 1987. Rational Choice Theory states that criminals make rational decisions based on a cost/benefit analysis.

Evaluation

→ RCT has been useful in analysing property crimes such as burglary and also drug dealing (Hollin 1989).
→ Bennett and Wright (1984) found that convicted burglars made rational decisions based on a risk analysis.
→ RCT is not applicable to any interpersonal crime except perhaps armed robbery (Ainsworth 2002).

Moral thought in criminals

Kohlberg's theory of moral development (1976) has been applied to criminality, on the assumption that criminals may be 'moral defectives'.

Evaluation of Kohlberg's theory

→ Arbuthnot (1987) in a meta-analysis found that, in 12 out of 15 studies, young offenders functioned at a lower moral level than comparable non-offenders.
→ The relationship seems only to apply to convicted offenders – is it a reflection of general intelligence or ability levels? (Do only stupid criminals get caught?)
→ Criminals convicted of property crime show higher moral levels than violent criminals.

Grade booster

The focus on rational thinking means that there are no mitigating circumstances in defence, and this has been advised to US President Bush by Samenow. This is politically good 'science' for the pro-capital punishment government –'they made their choices and must take their punishment'. Use 'real world' information such as this as often as you can in evaluations – it scores well!

The jargon

Cost/benefit analysis. This is when someone contrasts the benefits of an action with its possible costs (what might go wrong) and acts according to the results of the analysis.

Action point

Can you summarise the evidence for and against rational thinking theories, with three points for and three against?

The jargon

Meta-analysis. When a researcher looks at several studies of the same topic and comes to some general conclusions about them.

Examiner's secret

The thinking patterns of criminals is a key topic in 'theories of crime' for WJEC A2 students.

Link

See Kohlberg's theory summarised om p106-107.

Exam practice   answer: page 130

Outline any relevant research which can inform us about how a witness should be interviewed. (10 marks)

Perceptual organisation

An important aspect of perception is that we organise and make sense of the information conveyed to us through our senses.

Direct theories

The direct, stimulus-driven, Bottom-up (BU) approach was most notably taken up by James Gibson (1979). Gibson rejected the laboratory theories of constructivists (see below). He argued that sensory information that the retina receives is underestimated, and that the information we receive is all that we need to make sense of our perceptions.

While making pilot training films during the Second World War, Gibson described optic flow patterns: a flow of data past the viewer (pilot) which provides unambiguous information about direction, speed and altitude. Also important are texture gradients (systematic changes in the pattern of light), affordance (the potentiality of objects) and resonance (we receive visual data, just as a radio receiver picks up sound waves).

Another element in Gibson's theory is motion parallax (movement): as we move around our environment, the patterns of light we receive will change, so changing the patterns in the optic array, giving direct and unambiguous perceptual information. Contrary to constructivist theorists, Gibson rejects the need for processes to transform incoming information into internal representation or to enrich it with memory.

Constructivist theories

Constructivist or Top-down (TD) theorists regard perception as an active, constructive process, not entirely determined by stimulus information arriving at the sense organs. For Richard Gregory (1972), visual material received by the retina is ambiguous 'floating scraps of data'. He believes we go beyond simply decoding information, that we form a hypothesis (make inferences), which is then tested by sensory data. Gregory has made use of visual illusions to demonstrate his theories of constructive perception. He argues that previous knowledge which we acquire for the perception of three-dimensional objects is sometimes inappropriately applied to the perception of a two-dimensional figure.

Organisational cues in perception

The visual system gathers and processes sensory information into meaningful patterns. The ability to perceive depth depends on cues provided by incoming stimulation. Some examples of monocular cues:

→ linear perspective – parallel lines converge into distance (see Ponzo illusion)
→ relative size – distant objects produce a smaller image on the retina
→ motion parallax – objects closer to the eye move quickly, further objects appear to move more slowly.

Movement cues include motion parallax (see opposite) and retinal image movement – induced by an object moving across the retina. However, when we move our eyes and heads we do not perceive everything around us as moving, because the brain also receives information about the movement of the eye and head and compensates. Sensations of head and eye movements also compensate for external motion. Gibson (1966)

Watch out!

Don't get tied up in the difficult terminology. Show understanding rather than grinding out detail.

Take note

BU theorists have no answer to visual illusions. Gibson argues that they are an unfair test of perception. However, Gregory argues that they are vital to exposing the TD biases inherent in the perceptual systems.

Checkpoint

Can you write out a paragraph summarising both BU and TD approaches? Test yourself now!

proposed that the information we need to perceive movement occurs in the visual stimulus itself.

Constancies

Constancies refer to the ability to see objects as being the same, regardless of orientation (shape constancy), lighting conditions (colour and brightness constancy) and distance (size constancy).

The size of the image of an object on the retina depends on the distance of the object from the eye: the further away, the smaller the image. However, known objects do not appear to 'shrink' or 'grow' as they move away or towards us.

Holway and Boring (1941) demonstrated the importance of distance and background in size constancy. They found that size constancy decreases as distance and background information decreased. Participants perceived an ambiguous object in accordance with the retinal image when they lacked information about distance and background. This experiment can be interpreted in different ways by constructivists and direct theorists. Gregory (1970) argues that constancy scaling is important. We use information about distance and background to correct the size of the retinal image, keeping perception relatively constant. Gibson (1976) maintains that size constancy occurs because both objects and background change together, e.g. the retinal size and textural change of the background change with the retinal size and textural change of the object.

Face recognition

Face recognition is an area of research in which both BU and TD theorists are actively engaged. That face-processing is in many ways different from the processing of objects comes from the study of patients with **prosopagnosia**, who cannot recognise familiar faces but can recognise familiar objects. The patient studied by DeRenzie (1986) could discriminate between many types of object, but could not recognise his family and friends by sight (though he could by their names and voices).

Sergent et al (1992) discovered that several regions in the right hemisphere of the brain (in non-brain-damaged people) were more active in face identification than object identification.

Bruce and Young's model on face recognition (1986) proposed that familiar and unfamiliar faces are processed in different ways. Familiar faces activated face recognition units and person identity nodes in the brain, which were located separately from view-centred analysis units. Malone et al (1982) provided evidence for this theory with their study of brain-damaged patients: one had good recognition of familiar faces and poor recognition of unfamiliar faces, while another was the opposite, indicating that the processes involved in recognising unfamiliar and familiar faces are different.

Face recognition also suffers from decay, as do other memories (Bahrick 1984), except when **familiarity** is established, when recognition seems to persist despite ageing changes (Bahrick 1975).

> **The jargon**
>
> **Prosopagnosia** is normally caused by gross damage to the right cerebral hemisphere, usually through traffic accidents, falls or tumours.

Exam practice	answers: page 130

(a) Describe and evaluate Gibson's bottom-up/direct theory of perception.

(25 marks)

(b) Describe and evaluate Gregory's theory of visual perception. (10 marks)

Perceptual development

Nativist (or direct) theorists argue that perceptual abilities are inborn. They believe that neonate abilities are immature and develop through maturation. Empiricists (or constructivists) argue that perceptual abilities are learned through experience.

Pattern perception

Neonates have very restricted visual abilities:

→ Very poor visual acuity – they cannot distinguish detail as well as adults (Hainline 1998).
→ Tracking objects is very jerky and uncoordinated (Aslin 1981).
→ Colour discrimination is very limited (Teller 1978).

Research on the perceptual development of neonates has included:

→ There is an early preference for patterned shapes (Fantz 1961), with complexity preferred as the infant's age increases (Fantz and Fagan 1975).
→ Faces are preferred, when measured by gaze tracking, even when newborn (Goren 1975) but not after three months (Johnson 1991).
→ Children may be born with face-specific processing abilities but this system gives way to a rapidly-developing face recognition system after three months (Simion 2001).
→ Face recognition probably starts with the primary carer's face in the first few weeks of life (Walton 1992).

Perceptual constancies

Perceptual constancy means seeing an object as the same despite changes in size, shape or colour. Research has included:

→ Bower (1965) conducted a set of experiments using responses to different-sized cubes and concluded that 6 to 8 week-old infants had size constancy.
→ Slater et al (1990) demonstrated possible size constancy in neonates.
→ Slater and Morrison (1985) also demonstrated shape constancy.

Depth perception

→ One of the famous early studies was by Gibson and Walk (1960) using a 'visual cliff' apparatus. This clearly demonstrated depth perception in infants who could crawl.
→ Schwartz et al (1973) used heart rate as a measure with five- and nine-month-old infants, and suggested that they could see a difference but that they did not show a heart rate suggesting they feared a fall.

The jargon

Neonate. Newly born.

Checkpoint 1

What problems will the visual abilities of neonates create for researchers?

Checkpoint 2

What does Schwartz et al's 1973 study tell us about infant depth perception?

Auditory perception

Head-turning towards the source of a sound appears soon after birth, but Lecanuet (1998) showed auditory responses from the foetus in the womb. Researchers used teat-sucking as a response to measure neonate preferences for voices.

The jargon

In utero. In the womb (uterus).

→ They found that 3-day-old infants would suck more to hear their mother's voice over that of a stranger.
→ DeCasper and Prescott (1980) found a lack of preference for the father's voice, suggesting *in utero* learning.
→ Moon and Fifer (1990) used a version of mother's voice altered to sound as it would in the womb and found this to be very highly preferred.
→ Moon (1993) showed neonates also prefer to listen to the mother's native language.

Evaluation of the nature-nurture debate

Early researchers tried to show what aspects of perception were genetically 'wired-in' to human brains. This was in contrast to the empiricist view.

Examiner's secrets

Always present evidence from both sides of an argument, and come to a considered conclusion using evidence – not just your belief or opinion.

→ The occurrence of *in utero* learning makes it very difficult to distinguish actual native abilities in auditory (and tactile) perception. Foetuses, like any living tissue from amoebas onwards, react to and learn from their environments.
→ It is likely that some visual abilities are native, but the extent of visual stimulation *in utero* complicates things a little. It is not possible to accurately guage the level of light stimulation to typical wombs, but there is some very diffuse illumination through the layers of tissues.
→ The most sensible conclusion is that the early, simple abilities are largely native but that experience builds on these, developing them very rapidly in the first few days after birth.

Exam practice   answers: page 131

(a) Discuss the nature-nurture debate in relation to explanations of perceptual development. (25 marks)
(b) Discuss the development of perceptual abilities in infants. (25 marks)

Cognitive development

Cognition refers to the mental processes that are needed to make sense of the world.

Piaget's theory of cognitive development

Key aspects of his theory are as follows:

→ Children's intelligence differs qualitatively from an adult's.
→ Children actively build up their knowledge about the world.
→ The best way to understand children's reasoning was to see things from their point of view.

Piaget viewed the intellect as a structured and organised mental system, which takes in and deals with information about the world. The structures are known as **schema** and their actions as **operations**. This system can absorb or change incoming information (**assimilation**) and be changed by it (**accommodation**). The intellect grows in **invariant stages** (steps in a set sequence).

Checkpoint 1

What is meant by 'qualitative' difference? How is that different from quantitative difference?

Applying Piagetian ideas in educational settings

The approach is based on the following ideas:

→ Maturational **readiness** is critical. Educational activities and materials should be fitted to the child's stage of development. The teacher's role is to arrange the curriculum to fit the child.
→ Children are naturally active and curious. They learn best by **discovering** things for themselves.

Evaluation of Piagetian ideas

Action point

Think about your own primary and secondary schooling. Was your primary education more exploratory, project and event-based?

→ Extremely influential, principally in primary school education in the UK.
→ Tends to underestimate the age progression in cognitive development.
→ The formal operational stage is not an invariant – many people in many cultures do not attain this stage.

Vygotsky's theory of cognitive development

Vygotsky died at the age of 34, leaving others such as Bruner (1983) and Wood et al (1976) to develop his ideas. His main objection to Piaget's ideas was that they played down the social context of learning. Rogoff (1990) suggested that Piaget saw the child as a scientist whereas Vygotsky saw the child as an apprentice. Other differences include:

→ **language** plays a key role in pushing the child forward.
→ teachers can **actively intervene** in learning rather than waiting for the child to be ready but they should still work within what the child can realistically achieve. Vygotsky (1967) called this working within the child's 'zone of proximal development' (ZPD).
→ knowledge develops **spirally**, so a child can understand anything at some level providing it is presented in an appropriate way.

Applying Vygotsky's ideas in educational settings

The work of Bruner (1986) helped to popularise and develop Vygotsky's ideas:

→ **Scaffolding** – A 'teacher', working within the child's ZPD, helps them to solve a problem through supporting them to a solution rather than giving the solution. The 'teacher 'constantly adjusts the level of guidance given to the needs and abilities of the child until the child's knowledge is ready to stand alone and the scaffolding can be taken away. Scaffolding also occurs in children learning about emotions (Dunn 1984) and ritual language games and rhymes (Butterworth 1987).

→ **Expert tutoring** – Any 'expert' could work with a child to help them learn, e.g. parents. In **peer tutoring** the tutor is another pupil who is a little ahead of the learner and so can work naturally in the learner's ZPD. **Co-operative group-work** is based on the same principle. Computer Assisted Learning (CAL) packages called **Intelligent Tutoring Systems**, using branching programs, are another kind of expert.

Evaluation of Vygotsky's ideas

→ Vygotsky left little direct prescription for education, so most of the work is interpretation and development by others

→ Very influential in individual and small group teaching, although Hedegaard (1996) showed use of ZPD in large class cross-curriculum teaching in Denmark.

The information-processing approach to cognitive development

Information-processing theorists (e.g. Sternberg 1990) view the mind as analogous to a computer. Like Piaget, they view the cognitive system as a structure that matures in an orderly way over time.

Differences between the processing abilities of individuals at different ages help theorists to map this development (e.g. Case's research into working memory, 1985). They are also concerned with individual differences in processing ability, e.g. Vernon and Mori (1992) linked speed of neural conduction to measured IQ, and in the strategies used to solve problems (Seigler 1978).

Applying the information-processing approach in educational settings

In mainstream schools, understanding the ways in which young children think, perceive, remember and attend can help in developing educational strategies across the curriculum, e.g. in teaching reading or problem-solving.

Studies of children with learning difficulties can also help teachers to take into account particular information-processing deficiencies when planning activities.

More recently, there has been interest in metacognition. Older children seem more able to consider their own cognitive strategies. Encouraging them in this leads to more active learning and greater flexibility in thinking (Davis 1984).

Checkpoint 2

How might differences in processing ability be connected to differences in measured IQ? Is the connection a valid or reliable one?

Watch out!

These theorists, like Piaget, largely ignore social influences on children's development.

The jargon

Metacognition. The ability to reflect upon one's own thinking.

Exam practice   answers: page 131

(a) Describe and evaluate theories of cognitive development. (30 marks)

(b) Describe and evaluate Piaget's theory of cognitive development. (12 marks)

The development of social cognition

Social cognition refers to the brain processes underlying our interactions with others, both the biological basis and the effects of their operations.

Biological explanations

The common ancestors of all primates – some 10 million years ago – must have possessed biological mechanisms that enabled co-operative living, and these are present today in all primates.

→ Co-operative living confers many survival benefits (as well as some costs).

→ Under severe selection pressure, good co-operators will be positively selected (those who band together and work well will survive).

→ Cultural preference, particularly sexual selection, is also likely to positively select for good co-operators on the grounds that they are more likely to mate (good chat-up routines, like physical or verbal grooming).

→ A brain mechanism that enables imitation (and therefore co-operative action) – the 'mirror' neurones – was discovered by Rizzolati (1999), and found to be common to primates.

→ Studies by Jeannerod (1999) and Ramachandran (2001) suggest that the same mechanisms are used to observe and control our own behaviour (Gray 2004).

This means that children use a developing brain mechanism both to recognise and control themselves and to develop interactions with others.

Development of a child's sense of self

Very young children simultaneously develop their self-recognition and the categorisation of other people.

→ The mirror test involves secretly placing a mark on a child's face, and seeing whether it recognises the mark is on itself when it looks in a mirror. Lewis and Brookes-Gunn (1979) showed that after 18 months consistent face-touching occurred, but not before 12 months.

→ Recognising oneself on video, with a secret sticker attached, did not emerge fully until children were nearly four years old (Povinelli 1996).

Categorising others

→ Infants discriminate between children and adult approaches when as young as 6 months old (Smith et al 2003).

→ Infants begin to behave differently towards adult strangers around 7 to 9 months old (Sroufe 1977).

→ Different responses to gender are detectable by 12 months old (Smith and Sloboda 1986).

→ Verbal labels to differentiate people (mummy, daddy) are used correctly between 18 and 24 months.

Action point

Identify how humans co-operate today to promote survival. Can you think of instances where co-operation is not occurring when it should?

Check the net

Look up the mirror test on the Internet. What other animals have passed it, apart from humans?

Evaluation of the explanations of social development

→ The evidence points clearly to a set of brain mechanisms that underpin the development of social understanding.
→ These mechanisms develop through interaction with the social environment partly in parallel (e.g. recognising oneself develops in parallel with categorising others).

The theory of mind (TOM)

→ TOM refers to behaviour that indicates another person's intention or state of mind has been understood – we act in this way because we know what the other person was thinking.
→ This has been tested by 'false belief tasks' (e.g. Baron-Cohen 1985).
→ Children under the age of four have difficulty in understanding that others might have a false belief (Smith et al 2003).
→ Two-year-old children understand that others have mental states that drive their behaviour (Wellman 1990).

Action point

Identify and count how many times in a morning at school or college you do something because you know what other people seem to be thinking.

Evaluation

→ Changing the 'false belief' task to make it more accessible enables 3-year-olds to pass it consistently (Freeman 1991).
→ Language skill is a key factor, with the more skilled children performing better (Jenkins and Astington 1996).
→ Family background and the quality of interaction is a major factor (Lewis et al 1996).
→ The quality of social interaction with peers also appears to be a factor (Dunn 1999).

Exam practice   answer: page 131

Describe and evaluate studies in the development of social cognition.

(25 marks)

Attachment

Maccoby (1980) defines attachment as 'a relatively enduring emotional tie to a specific other person'. Human infants seem to be born prepared to make attachments. However, this 'bonding' between an infant and its caregiver is usually a two-way process.

The jargon

'Prepared' means that the behaviour is genetically controlled, having been positively selected in evolution of the species, as it actively enables survival of the infant.

Theories of attachment

Behavioural theory (e.g. Sears 1963)

→ Feeding is reinforcing because it reduces unpleasant hunger and is associated with other rewarding experiences such as warmth, comfort and social stimulation. Such things are primary reinforcers because they directly satisfy needs. With time, the mother becomes a secondary reinforcer because she is regularly associated with the arrival of primary reinforcers.

→ Reinforcement is a two-way process – the infant becomes attached to the mother because she meets its needs. She becomes attached to the infant because it responds positively to her caregiving.

Research into learning theory and attachment

→ Harlow and Zimmerman's (1959) study of infant rhesus monkeys challenges the behavioural theory. Monkeys could feed from two surrogate models, one made of wire and the other of soft cloth. Tests showed that, although both surrogates provided food, the monkeys preferred the soft mother as a secure base and went to her when distressed.

→ Schaffer and Emerson (1964) also showed that, in 39% of cases, the main caregiver was not the primary attachment object.

Evolutionary explanations of attachment

Bowlby (1958) proposed that attachment had a biological and evolutionary basis in survival.

Take note

These responses are 'prepared' as noted above.

→ The infant's appearance and sociable behaviour are biologically designed to encourage closeness and caregiving in the parent

→ Attachment is a two-way process most likely to happen during a sensitive period in the infant's first months. This has some similarities with the imprinting process seen in some other animals.

→ The feeding situation is one of many opportunities for attachment to take place but is not necessarily the most important one.

Research into evolutionary explanations of attachment

→ Klaus and Kennel (1979) studied two groups of 14 mothers, one group having limited contact with their babies, and the other very close contact. The latter group behaved differently from the former: they soothed their babies more and had more physical contact with them.

→ Anisfield et al (1990) encouraged some mothers to carry their infants closely in soft baby pouches and others to use the harder, generally available baby seats. At three months, close contact mothers were more responsive to their infants' signals for attention and by

13 months the close contact infants were more likely to be securely attached to their mothers.

However, other research shows little or no effect and all studies show small or non-existent long-term effects.

Secure and insecure attachments

Ainsworth (1978) devised a test of attachment strength and security called 'the strange situation' and, after testing a group of one- to two-year-olds in this way, she identified three types of attachment:

→ **Type A: anxious-avoidant** – 20% of the infants tested seemed to be indifferent to the mother and were not obviously affected by her presence or absence. They were equally affected by the presence of a stranger.

→ **Type B: securely attached** – 70% of the infants liked to stay close to the mother when playing. They were distressed when she left but were quickly comforted when she returned. They were indifferent to strangers.

→ **Type C: anxious-resistant** – 10% of the infants seemed to have mixed (ambivalent) feelings towards the mother. They sought contact with her and then resisted it. They also resisted contact with strangers.

Cross-cultural variations in attachments

The percentages given above were taken from American studies. In seven other cultures, Van Ijzendoorn and Kroonenberg (1988) found that Type B attachment was the most common in the strange situation test. However, Japanese and Israeli kibbutzim children were much more likely to show Type C than Type A attachment, while West German, British, Dutch, Swedish and Chinese children showed the opposite.

Disruption of attachment

→ Robertson and Robertson (1968) detailed case studies of children separated from carers, who seemed to suffer damage to those relationships.

→ Bowlby (1969) summarised the damage that various kinds of disruption may cause both emotionally and in behaviour (e.g. criminality).

→ However, Rutter (1981) showed that the reason for separation is crucial to the effect caused (e.g. being away from an abusive relationship).

→ Many case studies (e.g. Koluchova 1976) show that damage can be repaired to a large extent with good substitute care; equally, some show that poor substitute care is linked to higher levels of hyperactivity and emotional disturbance in already damaged children (e.g. Roy 2000).

Examiners secrets

A key evaluation point is that Bar-Heim (2000) showed that attachment types are not stable after 24 months, and studies over 20 years show mixed results comparing attachment types to adult personality (e.g. Lewis 2000) – predictive validity is moderate at best.

Action point

Do *you* think that early attachment is important in making you who *you* are? Are you closer to mum or dad, or someone else, e.g. grandparents?

Checkpoint

Does separation cause lasting psychological damage?

Exam practice answers: page 131

(a) Explain how the behavioural theory of attachment differs from the evolutionary theory of attachment. (4 marks)

(b) Describe and evaluate research into infant attachments. (12 marks)

Daycare

Working parents in the UK will need to make their own arrangements for the care of their children while they are a work. Research has focused on the possible effects this may have on the child.

Child care possibilities

Working parents will probably use one or a combination of three common alternatives.

→ **Nurseries** can be private or run by the state. Some nurseries take children from babyhood until they start school; others specify a starting age. Children can attend part-time or full-time and are cared for alongside other children by trained nursery nurses.

→ **Child-minders** are most often mothers who care for up to two or three other children, often fitting the care around their own family life. In the UK they must be registered, which means that the home where a child will be cared for is checked for agreed standards of health, safety and facilities.

→ **Family members**, historically grandparents or similar, and increasingly fathers staying at home as mothers earn more, may take on the daycare.

Research into daycare

→ Belsky (1988) compared children in the USA who went into daycare for 20 hours or more per week with children who had no daycare or less than 20 hours before one year of age. Using the strange situation test, he concluded that 41% of the first group were insecurely attached compared with 26% of the second group.

→ Baydar and Brooks-Gunn (1991) found that daycare had negative effects on cognitive and emotional development.

→ However Clarke-Stewart (1989), with a similar sample, found better development in her daycare groups.

On child-minding there have been several UK studies. Mayall and Patrie (1983) studied minders in London, and Bryant et al (1980) studied minders in Oxfordshire. Both studies found that:

→ Children seemed less secure in the minder's home than in their own.

→ Minders did not feel it necessary to develop a close bond with the children.

→ Children scored lower than expected on tests of language and cognitive ability.

We cannot draw any firm conclusions from this because:

→ There were no matched controls of non-minded children for comparison. The standard of care in the child's own home could have been the same, better or worse.

→ Problems experienced by some children could have resulted from being minded or could have been already present.

Regarding home care by relatives, Falbo (1991) found that Chinese grandparent pre-school care was associated with better school performance than parent care.

Action point

Who took care of you when you were little? How might it have affected your life?

Watch out!

Research into daycare by fathers is very scarce as it is a new phenomenon in the UK and research has recently been more focused on single and alternatively-parented families.

The impact of daycare on cognitive development

In the UK, Melhuish (1990) compared the effects on children of care by relatives, child-minders and private nursery care. All the children had started the care arrangements before nine months of age. Results showed no differences in the type of attachment to the mother (an important control) but:

→ Communication abilities at 18 months were best in children cared for by relatives, followed by minded children, then nursery children. By three years of age the differences had all but disappeared.
→ There were no differences in other aspects of cognitive development.

Research into day care and aspects of cognitive development elsewhere has yielded very mixed results, for example:

→ Scarr and Eisenberg (1993) found that good quality care did not affect cognitive abilities in children from economically-advantaged American families but did affect disadvantaged children.
→ Andersson (1992) followed up 13-year-old middle-class children in Sweden who had begun daycare in infancy and found that they performed better in school than controls who had experienced little or no daycare.
→ Clarke-Stewart et al (1994) proposed that the setting for daycare mattered less than the level of 'cognitive enrichment' it provided in comparison to the home. Home and daycare settings could be very good for stimulating children's cognitive abilities just as they could be poor. Where children's home background is poor, a stimulating daycare environment is likely to be beneficial, but where home is good and daycare is poor, it could have the opposite effect.

The impact of daycare on social development

Again, the findings about daycare and social development are mixed.

→ Melhuish (1990) found that British nursery children showed more understanding of pro-social behaviour such as sharing and co-operation.
→ Andersson (1992) found that Swedish children with daycare experience were more socially skilled and played with others more harmoniously.
→ Bates et al (1994) found that children who had spent the most time in daycare from infancy through to pre-school, regardless of when care began, were more aggressive than children with little or no such experience. They were also less likely to take notice of adults in authority such as teachers and parents.

Checkpoint

Why might different societies provide different results for daycare research?

Exam practice   answers: page 131

(a) Discuss the impact of different forms of daycare on children's social development, including the effects on aggression and peer relations. (4 marks)
(b) Discuss the implications of research into attachment and daycare for child care practices. (4 marks)

Sex and gender

Nothing occupies our society more than the (presumed) different natures and behaviours of the sexes. Even the nature and its many variations is a matter of interest. 'Boys will be boys...'

Definitions

→ Sex – biological type, i.e. male or female.
→ Gender – psychological type, i.e. masculine, feminine or androgynous (Bem 1964).
→ Sex or gender-role – the attitudes and behaviour expected of males and females by society.
→ Sex/gender identity – being able to label yourself accurately as male or female/masculine or feminine.

Development of differentiation

→ Infants begin to behave differentially to males and females at about 12 months old (Smith and Sloboda 1986).
→ Perception of gender difference is established by three years of age (Thompson 1975).
→ Gender stability is established by four years but may be earlier if given specific education (Bem 1989).
→ Sex role stereotypes are well established in the Western world by five years of age (Best 1977).

Biological sex

There are four major dimensions:

→ chromosomal – genital growth is determined by genes on the appropriate sex chromosome (X for female, Y for male)
→ genitalia (female genitalia are the default structures)
→ reproductive organ type
→ hormone balance (between androgens and oestrogens).

Action point

Look up the cases of Daphne Went and the Batista family. Biological sex and behaviour are not as straightforward as you might think!

Abnormalities and atypical development

→ There can be chromosomal abnormalities not necessarily reflected in external appearance (e.g. Klinefelter's Syndrome where males have an extra female sex chromosome, or Turner's Syndrome where females only have a single sex chromosome).
→ Androgenital Syndrome is where a female foetus is subjected to excess androgens. The child is female, but has penis-like clitoral enlargements.
→ Hermaphroditism is where both sets of genitalia are present, and is very rare.

Evolution and gender

It is clear that biological sex and gender role are related:

→ Evolutionary psychologists would argue for a strong relationship.

→ Evidence is strong in behavioural areas such as aggression, sexual orientation and also 'rough and tumble' play (Collaer and Hines 1995).

→ Baron-Cohen (2003) argues that the female brain is wired for empathising, while the male brain is built for system-building, and that hormones dictate the type of brain.

→ Evolutionary psychologists point to the persistence of gender roles in most known societies through history as evidence that modern differences reflect enduring evolutionary differences (i.e. men go hunting and females tend the household).

Action point

Look at your behaviour and personality. Compare with your friends. Are there stereotypical male or female things you do? Some males love to cook and adore babies, while some women hate babies and won't cook. What's going on?

Evaluation

→ More recent evidence points to little support for gender differences in aggression (Schaffer 2004), spatial abilities (Durkin 1995) and verbal ability (Hyde and Linn 1988) – this is because earlier studies didn't include verbal aggression, for example.

→ The assertion of difference is more to do with political debate about the organisation of society (Gross 2005).

→ Baron-Cohen has demonstrated that the sex of a brain is not directly dictated by biological sex, so some females can have a more stereotypically male type of brain than some men, and vice versa (note that this is nothing to do with sexual orientation).

→ Cross-cultural studies show both similarities and differences (e.g. Whiting and Whiting 1975).

→ Although most societies today demonstrate gender role differences of a specific type, it is actually impossible to do more than speculate about past societies as there are no written or pictorial records of any kind older than about 5,000 years.

Action point

Are the males and females you know different in terms of aggression? Remember to count verbal aggression as well as physical! Who bullied most at school?

The biosocial approach

There is an interaction between biological factors and social ones, particularly the parental behaviour towards the child:

→ People behave towards children according to their perceived gender (Smith and Lloyd 1978).

→ Money and Erhardt (1972) published case study evidence that the raising and socialising of a child determines their gender identity.

Evaluation

→ Money built his career on these cases, and has been judged to have suppressed contradictory evidence (Usborne 2004).

→ There is no evidence that gender identity is shapeable for the majority of people (as opposed to their case studies who were individuals with rare conditions).

→ Their most famous case was a boy raised as a girl following loss of the penis during circumcision – in fact by age 14 he had decided to live as a male, and was clearly masculine (Usborne 2004).

Check the net

Look up the case of David Reimer on the Internet.

Exam practice   answer: page 131

Describe and evaluate biological influences on gender. (25 marks)

Theories of gender development

All the major approaches to psychology explain the development of gender in their own way. Many of them seem not to acknowledge undeniable biological differences between the sexes.

Psychodynamic theory

→ Freud (1923) believed that until the Oedipus Complex was resolved (at about 5 years) gender identity was not fixed. Girls had weaker identities than boys.
→ Evidence shows that gender identity is quite strong in both sexes by 5 years old, and earlier in some aspects, such as with the stereotyping of toys.
→ Single parent and homosexual parents don't produce insecure children, and there is no evidence of sexuality being influenced either (Golombok 2000).

Social learning theory (SLT)

→ Children are directly socialised by social agents such as parents, relatives and teachers (Bandura 1969).
→ Parents behave differently towards boys and girls (e.g. Fagot 1978).
→ Observational learning of particular role-models (indirect socialisation).

Evaluation

→ SLT is a parsimonious explanation of gender development.
→ Children do show same sex preferences in modelling behaviour (Bandura 1963).
→ SLT may crucially underplay the role of biological influences.
→ Few differences in parental behaviour are detectable (Golombok and Hines 2002), and all are explained by differing behaviour between boys and girls (i.e. the children are conditioning the parents!).
→ The child's own, already existing, understanding of its gender plays a crucial role in the effect of observational learning (Maccoby 2000).

Cognitive-developmental theory (CDT)

Kohlberg (1966) suggested that children need to develop an understanding of gender before they can take on a gender role. He suggested this happens in three stages:

Stage 1: Gender identity (two to five years) – correct identification of self as boy or girl.
Stage 2: Gender stability (four to six years) – child realises they always have been and always will be a particular sex.
Stage 3: Gender constancy (six to seven years) – child understands that changes in appearance do not change a person's sex.

Evaluation

→ It does seem to be the case that three-year-old children with gender constancy watch same sex models more (Weinraub 1984).

→ The developmental order suggested by Kohlberg seems to be constant across cultures (Munroe 1984).

→ However, children seem to show sex-typed behaviour long before this (e.g. Huston 1983).

Gender schema theory (GST)

A gender schema begins to develop as soon as the infant realises there are males and females. From then on, the child will sort all new knowledge about people, their objects and activities into the schema under the general headings of male or female. The schema helps them to organise and understand the world around them and acts like a magnet for new information (Bem 1985). The child's self-esteem becomes influenced by how well they measure up to their gender schema (Rathus 1990).

Evaluation

→ GST can explain how children start to show sex-typed behaviour and attitudes even before they have gender constancy. It is all part of the growth of their schema.

→ The theory sees the strong sex-role stereotypes that children hold as a natural stage in their developing understanding of gender. Children's attitudes are not fixed forever and will change depending on their experiences and the role models they encounter.

Cross-cultural comparisons

→ Gender division of labour differs considerably across the world (Hargreaves 1986).

→ Gender divisions differ away from dominant Western cultural influences. Some cultures recognise several variations (males who act as females, females as males, etc).

→ Global communication and the influence of religions tend to alter traditional gender patterns and substitute a different one.

The jargon

Schema. Any knowledge system that both influences behaviour and is changed by interactions with the environment. It is a form of shorthand for what must be very complex brain systems.

Action point

What to you is the most powerful influence on maintaining gender roles? Is it peer disapproval? Is it parents?

Checkpoint

Can you construct a general summary of the theories of gender development

Exam practice   answer: page 132

Describe and evaluate psychological theories of gender development.

(25 marks)

Development of moral understanding

This topic concerns some of the origins of morality and concentrates on theories arising from the cognitive developmental tradition. These focus on how understanding of moral issues develops. Other approaches have a different emphasis, e.g. psychodynamic theory can explain the origin of the conscience and moral feelings, whilst behaviourist theory can explain moral or immoral behaviour.

Checkpoint 1

When asked where rules come from, how might young and older children differ (e.g. 5 year-olds and 9 year-olds)?

Piaget's theory of moral development

Piaget (1932) proposed that the moral reasoning of children reflects their level of intellectual development (e.g. the ability to decentre or reason at the formal operational level). Younger children's reasoning is based on adult constraint; older children's is based on an understanding of the importance of co-operation, mutuality and rationality.

Piaget largely neglected the social environment in his theory, although his writings clearly show he had regard for the power of the peer group in his observations.

Kohlberg's theory of moral development

Kohlberg (1969) presented moral dilemmas to participants and explored their moral reasoning through semi-structured interviews. The stage of moral development reached by an individual is determined by the complexity of their reasoning, not by their age or by the actual judgement they reach. Some never reach the higher levels.

Level I Pre-conventional morality

The child is seen as responsive to the moral rules of others, either in terms of the power of other people to reward or punish, or the hedonistic consequences of their actions.

Level 2 Conventional morality

Moral reasoning is determined by an attitude of loyalty to interpersonal expectations and the social order (i.e. you do things because you're expected to by others).

Level 3 Post-conventional morality

Morality is based on universal ethical principles. These might include unconditional respect for individuals, the value of human life and an appreciation of justice based on the moral equality of individuals (i.e. doing things because they are right).

Examiner's secrets

Don't spend a huge amount of time describing Kohlberg's stages in great detail (AO1). The examiner wants you to demonstrate knowledge, but not at the expense of vital evaluation (AO2). Run out of time, run out of marks!

Evaluation of Kohlberg's theory

→ The theory has a limited database (approximately 50 American males) yet Kohlberg claimed cultural universality.
→ Cross-cultural studies (e.g. Vasudev and Hummel 1987) question the universality assumption. Indian participants were more likely to favour collective decisions.
→ People may reason at higher levels than they behave.

Gilligan's ethic of caring

Gilligan (1982) interviewed women facing real-life dilemmas and found that their moral reasoning centres more on care, whereas men's centres more on justice. Kohlberg's scoring places judgements based on care lower than judgements based on justice, thus favouring males. Gilligan suggested women go through three stages of moral reasoning:

→ caring for self
→ caring for others, perhaps sacrificing own needs to achieve this
→ balancing caring for self and others.

Evaluation of Gilligan's theory

→ Studies of sex differences in moral reasoning in children generally show no differences in care vs. justice judgements. However, women do seem to centre their judgements more on care than men do (Bee 1992).
→ Walker (1984) found no evidence that girls score lower on Kohlberg's scoring system.
→ Gilligan has alerted us to a possible bias in the way we think of moral issues, in that academic work often removes moral thought from its real-life context, and can neglect the experiences of at least half – if not almost all – the population of the world (as Kohlberg does!).

Eisenberg's model of pro-social reasoning

Eisenberg (1986) presented children with moral dilemmas in which they had to decide between self-interest and helping someone else. Five levels of pro-social reasoning were proposed. Lower levels concern consequences for self. More mature levels show increasing evidence of ideas about duty, empathy and personal responsibility.

Evaluation of Eisenberg's theory

→ Pro-social understanding develops by as early as four years old (Turiel 1998).
→ Eisenberg proposed that pro-social behaviour can be encouraged by example. Freidrich and Stein (1975) showed a pro-social children's programme to five- and six-year-olds. Children showed better understanding of pro-social behaviour and were more pro-social than children shown a neutral programme.
→ Rheingold (1982) found cross-cultural differences in pro-social development. Children who are encouraged to do domestic chores and care for other children develop pro-social reasoning faster than in cultures where this is all done for them.

Exam practice
answers: page 132

(a) Describe and evaluate theories of moral development. (25 marks)
(b) (i) Describe **one** theory of moral development. (10 marks)
   (ii) Discuss methodological problems in researching moral development in schools. (15 marks)

Checkpoint 2

Why might some people reason at a higher level than they behave?

Action point

Can you think of a real-life moral dilemma?

Examiner's secrets

There are profound cultural differences, even in northern Europe, in the social construction of moral debate. In the UK the killing of five-year-old Jamie Bulger provoked demands for life sentences for the two 10-year-old boys who did it. A similar case in Norway only provoked great sadness and recognition that children have limited moral understanding (Asquith 1996). Moral debate is culturally relative and claims for universality in a theory should be greeted with scepticism.

Theories of the nature of intelligence

One of the most contentious concepts in psychology is that of intelligence. Its nature, its measurements, and even whether it exists at all, are all still areas for argument over 150 years after Galton's first formulations.

Definitions of intelligence

→ **Biological** – behaviour is intelligent when a living organism alters itself or its environment in response to an environmental change (e.g. Piaget).
→ **Psychometric** – innate general cognitive ability (Burt 1955), 'what intelligence tests measure' (Boring 1923).
→ **Information processing** – problem-solving steps or processes (e.g. Sternberg 1979).
→ **Multiple intelligences** – the potential to solve problems or create products appropriate to cultural contexts (Gardner 1983).

Psychometric theories

Spearman's two-factor theory

→ Proposed an innate general factor (g) that accounts for people who do well in different types of test items (and a specific factor (s) that covers differences).
→ Spearman was ideologically inclined to interpret any data in this way however!

Burt and Vernon's hierarchical model

→ This extended Spearman's model with **g** as the major factor but with many group factors which particular tests measure.
→ It led to educational tests like the 11 plus, which purported to divide children into groups sent to different types of school from 11 years old onwards.

Thurstone's factors

→ Using multiple correlation techniques Thurstone identified seven distinct factors underlying intelligence test results.
→ **G** was an average of different test results, although he wobbled towards the Spearman position a little in later life.

Evaluation of psychometric theories

→ Different factor analysis techniques give different results.
→ Clusters of correlations are named by the researchers, and are at best guesswork about what they represent (Gould 1981).
→ The mainspring of these theories was an elitist, sexist and racist view of humanity, which originated with Galton and other Victorians who saw the lower classes, women and foreigners as genetically inferior. An echo of this view resonated through all 19th and early 20th century psychometric approaches.

The jargon

Innate. Literally 'present at birth', but used by most early theorists to mean 'genetic'.

Checkpoint 1

What is 'g'? Explain in one sentence.

Multiple intelligences

Gardner (1983) observed in brain trauma patients that injury affected some abilities but not others. He noted that different cultures have different definitions of intelligence and argued that the academically dominant Western concepts are extremely ethnocentric (see Galton on p.120). He defined eight different types or domains of intelligence, some testable (e.g. spatial), some not (e.g interpersonal).

Gardner was criticised for confusing intelligence with talent (e.g. Scarr 1989), but critics had no answer for the very valid cultural differences (e.g. Diamond 1997).

Information processing

Sternberg (1988) proposed a triarchic theory:

→ that intelligence had three major aspects – **analytic**, **creative** and **practical**
→ that intelligence was totally contextualised within a particular culture (as Gardner also believed)
→ that intelligence is what information processing parts of the brain do, not a general ability (g) or some sort of unexplained factor.

Evaluation of non-psychometric theories

→ They are based firmly in both physiology and social observations.
→ The remove the racist and sexist elements from early formulations.
→ They highlight different cultures and the shifting definition of intelligence within them.

Evolution of intelligence

Factors include:

→ Environmental pressures ruthlessly select those intelligent or lucky enough to survive to reproduce.
→ Group co-operation and the development of brain systems to deal with group living, combine in a positive feedback spiral – each drives the other.
→ Relative brain size may not be fully correlated with abilities – earlier humans such as the Neanderthals had bigger relative brain size – although it is clear there is a weak general trend for brain size to correlate with the complexity of tools through the last three million years.
→ Anatomically modern humans (AMHs) seem to be no more than 250,000 years old and left Africa only about 80,000 years ago, yet are the only humans now left. This may be due to intelligence (e.g. creativity) or culture (e.g. inclination to genocide). The jury is out on this.
→ AMHs may have a broader behavioural flexibility due to language abilities (Mithen 2005).

Checkpoint 2

How different is Gardner's theory from previous ones?

The jargon

Triarchic: three things above all others.

Grade booster

For the final paragraph, make an over-arching evaluative point such as 'There is a massive genetic similarity of all humans, since we all originated from a tiny founder population in Africa (less than 10,000 individuals). Compared with other animals, we are clones! This casts huge doubts on genetic theories and highlights the role of culture'.

Exam practice   answers: page 132

(a) Describe and evaluate theories of the nature of intelligence. (30 marks)
(b) Describe **one** theory of intelligence. (9 marks)

Genetic and environmental effects on intelligence

The jargon

Monozygotic (MZ) twins are genetically identical (more or less!) but **dizygotic** (DZ) twins are non-identical siblings born at the same time. Multiple births can be mixtures of MZ and DZ siblings.

Checkpoint 1

How could MZ twins reared apart come to have similar environments?

Checkpoint 2

What do correlation coefficients show? What is the main limitation of correlation studies?

Early debates about intelligence asked how much was inherited and how much learned. These days we tend to ask how heredity and environment interact with each other to affect intelligence. This raises questions about the inherited inferiority of certain groups of people on the grounds of class, race or gender. Beliefs in such inferiority have been used to excuse all kinds of discrimination.

Research into intelligence test performance

Genetic concordance studies

→ There are lots of studies that show that genetic similarity correlates with IQ similarity (e.g. Bouchard and McGue 1981).
→ The strongest correlations are for MZ twins.
→ However, MZ twins have a different family environment than DZ twins and others.
→ Twins reared apart also show some concordance (e.g. Shields 1962 found MZ twins reared apart to have 0.77 correlation).
→ However, they have shared prenatal experiences (Howe 1997).
→ Where environments are very different, so are the IQ scores (Newman 1937).

Adoption studies

If intelligence has more to do with heredity than environment, children's IQs should correlate more highly with their natural parents' IQs than with their adoptive parents' IQs.

→ Burks (1928) found correlations between adopted children and their adoptive parents of only +0.13.
→ Skodak and Skeels (1949) found a higher correlation of +0.44 between the IQs of adopted children and that of their natural parents, suggesting a genetic basis to intelligence.
→ Kamin (1974) argued that, in the 1920s, children were generally placed with better-off families. In the 1940s, children were placed in homes similar to the natural parents' home.
→ Schiff (1978) showed that socio-economic difference between adoptive and biological parents accounted for a 15-point gap between adopted and unadopted siblings, on average.

Studies of social class differences

Statistics repeatedly show that children from lower social classes score lower on IQ tests than children from higher social classes. Broman et al (1975) plotted 50,000 four-year-olds' IQs against social class. IQ rose with social class and with the mother's level of education.

Enrichment studies

If intelligence is largely inherited, attempts to improve it should not work. However, interventions such as Project Headstart, which began in the USA in 1965, were designed to give children a boost before they start school.

→ Most programmes resulted in IQ gains of up to 10 points in the short term but the gains did not last long (Rutter 1992).
→ Follow-up studies, however, have shown lasting gains in things other than IQ, e.g. in behaviour in school, in academic achievement and in later employment (e.g. Bee 2000). This 'sleeper effect' may occur because enrichment improves children's self-esteem and confidence or because the child's family becomes more supportive and positive about schooling (Collins 1983).

Race and intelligence

Jensen (1969) and Eysenck (1971) have argued that differences in IQ scores between black and white Americans, and between British whites and West Indians, are due to genetic differences between races.

→ There is very little genetic difference between members of different races, and indeed in the USA the genetic interpenetration of superficially white or black persons is profound (President Thomas Jefferson was genetically partly African, yet superficially white).
→ The role of environment, especially poverty, is largely ignored (Bee 2000). Studies of children who are black, white or of mixed race and raised in similar environments show that the children's IQs are very similar (Price 1999).

Watch out!

Examiners dislike expressions of racial or cultural stereotypes (e.g. Africans live in huts), which show ignorance at best. Avoid them!

Evaluative comments

→ It is impossible to separate the effects of environment and heredity. Genes are expressed through environments, not independently.
→ For ethical reasons, we cannot do controlled breeding experiments with humans or bring them up in controlled environments.
→ There is debate about the worth of IQ tests as a measure of intelligence. There are many intellectual qualities that IQ tests do not tap.
→ In evolutionary terms the debate is nonsense (Diamond 1997). Modern hunter-gatherer groups (largely non-European and non-white) have been ruthlessly selected for intelligence by their unprotected lifestyle, whereas those in modern agricultural societies (e.g. UK, Europe, China, USA) keep their less intelligent members alive (via medicine and protected lifestyles) and reproducing! This gene pool is therefore less intelligent!

Exam practice
answers: page 132

(a) Discuss the role of genetic factors in the development of intelligence.
   (30 marks)
(b) Evaluate the role of genetic factors in intelligence test performance.
   (16 marks)

Erikson and lifespan theories

Lifespan theories owe much historically to the recapitulation theories of growth and Freudian theory, where children develop through stages that they must 'resolve' to progress further, and where failure to resolve creates problems for adult personality.

Erikson

→ Each stage is a struggle between positive and negative forces in the personality.

→ Resolution occurs when the positive forces outweigh and overwhelm the negative.

→ Social forces influence the resolution of stages (e.g. Western societies allow adolescents to delay adulthood – this is called a 'moratorium').

→ Most societies have norms for different stages, and **ceremonies** for the key transition to adulthood.

→ Failure to resolve the conflicts of a stage leads to **identity crisis**.

→ Failure to integrate self-perceptions into a single 'self' is known as **role confusion**.

→ These are most common in adolescence, but can occur in any stage.

Action point

Can you think of stages and transitions in your life so far?

Action point

Who in your life has had key roles in guiding, supporting and advising? Has someone helped you through a life transition or change?

Levinson

Levison (1978) in his 'Seasons of a man's life' described a 'life-structure' theory:

→ A series of adult 'eras' are connected by extended 'transitions' named early adult, mid-life and late adult.

→ Each transition involves processes of changing ourselves and experiencing the different 'worlds' available to us.

→ Others in our social world have key roles in guiding, supporting and advising.

Gould

Gould (1980) proposed the evolution of adult consciousness.

→ A key task is to lose the security of childhood, and develop a sense of self-sufficiency or **autonomy**.

→ A person's **sense of time** changes, from unlimited time in their early 20s to time running out from their early 40s onwards.

→ In any societies there are **critical life events** that mark transitions – these are normative events such as forming partnerships, marriage, becoming a parent, etc.

Evaluation

All lifespan theories tend to:

→ be very culture-bound
→ reflect very conservative and normative assumptions about the nature of a society
→ be based on relatively small samples.

Cultural relativity

→ There were different findings in South Africa between genders and racial groups (Ochse and Plug 1986).
→ Male and female identity formation appear to have different paths even in the same culture (e.g. Gilligan 1982).
→ In Western culture, the highly normative nature of appropriate stage behaviour has been challenged by people (often called Baby Boomers) who carry stereotypical adolescent behaviours through into late adulthood.
→ Negative commentary on this phenomenon (e.g. Beaumont 1996) is as much a reflection of the inadequacy of life-span descriptions as it is 'failure to grow up'.

The jargon

Normative. Sticking to the socially-acceptable ideas about how people should behave in a particular situation (e.g. assuming people in UK will get married mostly in their 20s).

The jargon

Baby Boomer. A person born during the period at the end of and after the Second World War (1945-50), when there was a large increase in births in the Western world.

Action point

Ask people you know who were born between 1945 and 1950 to see if they agree that they still have some adolescent interests and attitudes.

Checkpoint

What is the major difference between Erikson's theory and the others?

Exam practice   answer: page 132

Describe and evaluate life-span theories of development. (30 marks)

Adolescence

In Western culture, adolescence is often viewed as a distinct phase of development characterised by 'storm and stress' and identity crisis. The stereotypical teenager is rebellious, at odds with mainstream society in general, and parents in particular. Is this view typical of all adolescents?

Identity crisis

Following from Erikson's (1968) psychosocial stage theory of lifespan personality development, Marcia (1980) argues that adolescent identity formation involves:

→ **crisis** – having to re-evaluate old choices and values, trying out new ones
→ **commitment** – after 'crisis' the individual takes on a new set of roles and ideologies.

There are four main identity statuses:

→ moratorium – crisis ongoing; no commitment made
→ foreclosure – crisis not gone through but commitment made
→ identity achievement – crisis fully dealt with
→ identity diffusion – neither in crisis nor committed.

Action point

Look up in a good dictionary the meanings of the terms 'moratorium', 'foreclosure' and 'diffusion'.

Waterman (1985) found a decrease in diffusion status and an increase in identity achievement with age. Moratorium was uncommon but one-third at all ages were in foreclosure. Identity achievement was later than Erikson predicted but this may have been because most of the participants were college students postponing adult status. Munro and Adams (1977) found that 45% of non-college individuals in work had achieved identity status compared to 38% of college students. This is more in line with Erikson's prediction.

Checkpoint 1

How might foreclosure occur? Give an example

Smith and Cowie (1993) query the theoretical validity of Erikson and Marcia's work, especially regarding the idea of 'crisis'. They say that:

→ moratorium could operate in different areas of life at any one time
→ identity achievement is not confined to adolescence.

Coleman suggests that Erikson's view of disturbance in adolescence was affected by the use of atypical and disturbed individuals.

Storm and stress

Rutter et al (1976) looked for evidence of conflict in 2,303 adolescents aged 14 to 15 living on the Isle of Wight. Parents and teachers answered questionnaires about the teenagers' behaviour and teenagers were selected for interviews and psychiatric assessment. A randomly-selected and a high deviancy group were compared in terms of conflict between themselves and their parents.

The teenagers perceived a higher frequency of conflict than parents did but rarely reported serious disagreements or criticised their parents. For the 'deviant' group conflict in communications with, and in behaviour towards, their parents was generally three times more common. Evidence for inner turmoil (expressed as behaviour psychiatric problems) was also examined but little support was found for it. The general picture was one of good relationships between parents and their teenage children.

Coleman's focal theory of adolescence

Coleman (1974) suggests that, during adolescence, individuals focus on different aspects of change (e.g. biological, cognitive and social) at different times. Coleman and Hendry (1990) tested this by examining issues important to 800 boys and girls aged 11, 13, 15 or 17 years:

→ Each issue seemed to have a different distribution curve, peaking in importance over a particular age.
→ The coincidence of a number of important issues could cause problems but, generally, adolescents choose when to engage with particular issues, mixing stability with adjustment.

Adolescence across cultures

Coleman's recent research has been borne out in New Zealand and North America. Is the pattern universal in other cultures?

→ Margaret Mead (1928) studied Samoan adolescents and suggested that, compared with North American culture, adolescence was tranquil and sexually permissive. She implicated Samoan extended family life and a less repressive child-rearing style than in North American families. Mead's work seemed to suggest that adolescent turmoil was a cultural, rather than universal, phenomenon.
→ Freeman (2000) questioned the methods of Mead's studies and her own conflicts revealed in diaries, to conclude that her findings were more a personal wish-fulfilment than a reality.
→ Chinese Hong Kong culture places more responsibility on adolescents than American society. However, Yau and Smetana (1996) showed a very similar pattern of conflicts to African-American households in the USA (Smetana and Gaines 1999).
→ In modern global society it is likely that behavioural patterns would converge across cultures, with only more socially-isolated subcultures differing.

> **Checkpoint 2**
>
> In what ways are British adolescents segregated and discouraged from entering adulthood?

Exam practice   answer: page 133

Discuss conflict in adolescence including theories of 'storm and stress' and alternatives. (30 marks)

Middle and late adulthood

Later periods in the lifecycle have been studied relatively little until recently, with stereotypes of decline and dementia being prevalent. The survival into old age of more Western Europeans has stimulated research, not least by academics who are themselves entering these stages!

Mid-life

Many people refer loosely to the idea of a mid-life crisis, where people enter a phase of conflict between attachment and independence, and where existential questioning surfaces.

→ Levinson (1978) saw people as having a soul-searching crisis between about 45 and 50 years old. Radical changes in lifestyle could occur.

→ In Western societies it is possible for people to radically change lifestyle, often moving out of highly-paid high-pressured jobs and expensive living into cheaper, rural and less stressed existences (Tredre 1996).

→ Women in particular can make big changes, especially if the child-nurturing phase is over and the children are relatively independent (Levinson 1997).

→ Marcia (1998) suggests that often adolescent ideas and behaviours can re-emerge in transitions or mid-life crises (e.g. over 40s women going clubbing – now very common in the UK).

→ The second peak of divorce in the UK occurs in mid-life after 15 or more years of marriage (Turnbull 1995).

Evaluation

→ These findings are highly **ethnocentric** as in many societies the struggle for existence means no possible change – indeed shorter life-spans mean midlife is in a person's 30s, not near 50.

→ Samples used for primary data may be very small and **unrepresentative** (e.g. Levinson 1978 and 1997).

→ There are massive individual differences in life changes in this period, making it questionable to **generalise**.

→ The research is based on heterosexual data, and the assumption that homosexual life paths are similar may not be justified – however research is still in its infancy here.

Late adulthood and old age

The later parts of a lifespan may often be stereotyped negatively as a failure of body and mind (ageism). This can in itself have a detrimental effect. Research has shown:

Differing ages

The following effects are felt:

→ chronological (how many years old)
→ biological (actual age of bits of your body)

- → psychological (the subjective feel of how old you are)
- → functional (what you are able to do)

Effects of ageist stereotyping

These include:

- → Affects social attitudes directly (Adler 2000).
- → May trigger stress and illness (Adler 2000).
- → May directly affect memory performance (Levy and Langer 1994).

Action point

What is 'old'? Ask other people. Does what they say differ depending on their age?

Cognitive changes

These include:

- → Fluid intelligence decreases for all age groups over time from 30 onwards (Schaie and Herzog 1983).
- → Cognitive processes in general get slower in a very small but measurable way (Stuart-Hamilton 2003).
- → People who have intellectually demanding work or recreation have a lower incidence of dementia (Snowdon 2000).

Evaluation

- → There are massive individual differences within all cultures.
- → Cross-sectional research falls foul of the cohort effect.
- → Many people perform better than young people, especially where crystallised intelligence can be used (e.g. Maylor 1994).

The jargon

Fluid intelligence is the ability to solve problems you have never experienced before. Using your experience is called **crystallised intelligence**.

Social disengagement or re-engagement?

Some researchers believe that the elderly withdraw slowly from society (disengagement). Others believe that society withdraws from them, which they try to manage (re-engagement).

- → Disengagement involves fewer interactions with others, and a dignified acceptance of this.
- → Manthorpe (1994) sees this as an inevitable move towards death.
- → Retirement is seen as a significant marker of disengagement (Atchley 1982).

Action point

Think about the way you are with older people. Do you think they're all losing their memory? Do you treat them as doddery slow old duffers? Are you ageist?

Evaluation

- → Havinghurst (1968) showed that those who disengage least are the most psychologically healthy.
- → The elderly have control removed from many areas of their life except friendship (Rainey 1998). Loss of control is a major factor in withdrawal and decline, so social arrangements (e.g. moving to a nursing home, becoming chair-bound) may be a factor in hastening decline.
- → Focusing on the emotional aspects of the present experiences in life is common to all near the end of their lives and not just the elderly (Carstensen 1996).

Exam practice   answer: page 133

Discuss the effects of events during late adulthood. (30 marks)

Answers
Cognitive and developmental psychology

Remembering and forgetting

Exam practice

(a)

	Short-term memory	Long-term memory
Capacity	7+/– 2 items	Unlimited
Duration	Seconds	Up to a lifetime
Encoding	Mainly acoustic	Mainly semantic

(b) This is a question with a large potential range. For top band, most of the below would need a mention, with evaluatory studies or contexts:
- Decay and displacement in STM, with evidence
- Interference with evidence
- Decay in LTM
- Cue, state and context dependency, with evidence for and against
- Repression, with evidence for and against
- Slips and omissions (e.g. strong habit intrusion, tip of the tongue)
- Biological evidence such as temperature, change, etc.
- Evolutionary priorities – the forgetting brain

Models of memory

Exam practice

Covering the same descriptive ground (AO1), questions (a) and (b) are asking for a brief description – don't forget that a diagram with accompanying text is fine – plus positive and negative evaluations. Don't forget the positive strengths! Question (c) requires a detailed description of at least two alternatives (working memory and levels of processing) plus the strengths and weaknesses of both. Don't forget to compare with the multistore model and also mention further developments of the working memory model.

The role of emotion in memory

Checkpoint

There is a lot of case-study evidence for repression, but no real experimental evidence. The jury remains out on this one. Flashbulb memory, however, has considerable counter-evidence and a simple theoretical explanation – communal or individual rehearsal of material.

Exam practice

A long answer is needed, requiring a good range of the following:
- Evolutionary reasons for threats to survival being prioritised in memory
- High arousal and forgetting including weapon focus (studies on both sides)
- High arousal and repression (evidence for and against)
- High arousal and remembering including PTSD flashbacks
- Flashbulb memory (studies for and against)

Eyewitness testimony

Checkpoint

You should question the ecological validity of much of Loftus' laboratory-based work. Real incidents differ on most crucial dimensions from artificial set-ups.

Exam practice

(a) Short answer needed, covering poor ecological validity (many studies using video, etc.) or lacking key features such as high arousal, rehearsal effects, delay in questioning, etc.

(b) Long answer needed, covering personal, situational and post-situational variables. Extensive use of studies needed with big questions asked about the ecological validity and actual utility of many studies. Don't forget the cognitive interview either.

(c) Use the leading question material, as well as cognitive interview material, to enter the false memory debate. Loftus's work and the reconstructive nature of memory is central. False memory should be shown to be a natural occurrence, but a dangerous one in the 'recovered abuse' epidemic of the 1980s and 90s.

Cognition and the law

Exam practice

This answer should cover the moral thinking and the rational cognitive theories, with a highly critical stance in evaluation – the rational cost/benefit analysis in property crime should be noted, as against the less rational motivations of interpersonal violent crime.

Perceptual organisation

Checkpoint

BU processing implies that the information received by the sensory processes is all the brain needs to perceive an organised and systematic world. In contrast, the TD theorists say that the brain itself imposes templates and hypotheses formed by genetic processes or by experience onto incoming data. This is revealed when templates and hypotheses are applied inappropriately, creating illusions and distortions.

Exam practice

Question (a) requires a deep detailed reading of Gibson's theory, with the material in the revision chapter. In a good answer, evaluation will include contrast with Gregory's theory. Question (b) requires a brief account and evaluation (contrast with Gibson as well as positive evidence) using the material in the revision chapter. Avoid over-describing and make sure plenty of space is given to evaluation.

Perceptual development

Checkpoints

1 It makes it extremely difficult:
   - to create a viable dependent variable in experiments, as there is little to measure!
   - to determine what is unintended or undetermined movement as opposed to deliberate tracking.
2 This study suggests that the visual abilities to perceive depth are present but the experience that indicates a threat is not, i.e. has not yet been learnt.

Exam practice

Both of these variations on the same theme can be answered by detailing perceptual development:
- The genetic basis for development should be clearly noted along with the environmental inputs.
- By placing nature-type results in contrast to nurture-type, and in both cases using strengths and weaknesses, a very substantial amount of AO2 material can be generated – which is vital for a good mark!

Cognitive development

Checkpoints

1 'Qualitative' refers to a quality or characteristic of something that is not directly measurable using numbers (e.g. beauty of a person, their sense of humour) whereas quantitative refers to something that can be directly measured or described numerically (e.g. a person's age, height, weight, etc).
2 It is argued by some cognitive psychologists that processing speed is the basic factor in intelligence (the so-called factor g). Since there is actually no agreed way of measuring this variable (not valid), nor any definition of what it actually is (an average of different nerve conduction speeds in the brain?) then researchers have no standards to judge overall research by (lacks reliability).

Exam practice

Question (a) requires some depth in dealing with:
- Piaget, making both positive and negative criticism
- Vygotsky, showing the development by Bruner and others.
- Information processing approach, with its applications in school.

Question (b) requires a basic description of Piaget's theory but with extensive evaluation emphasised – it is a usual mistake for students to overdo the descriptive detail and run out of time.

The development of social cognition

Exam practice

- It is important to emphasise the biological explanation as the well-established mechanism! Evaluation can be largely positive, on how the various pieces of this jigsaw fit together.

- The central area of study should be TOM coupled with the 'sense of self' material.
- The question marks raised about TOM provides some critical evaluation.

Attachment

Checkpoint

The bulk of the evidence suggests that it is the way you are cared for, rather than any separation from carers, that causes problems. Children who understand the reasons for separation and are secure in their relationships with their carers, should be relatively unharmed. Living constantly in disturbed or abusive relationships is far more damaging psychologically.

Exam practice

The short question (a) essentially counterposes the preparedness material from the evolutionary account (i.e. setting up the conditions for attachment) with the behavioural material, which focuses on the development and strengthening of these prepared emotional ties. They are not exclusive, but one follows on from the other. This theme can be used to start the longer second question – the evolutionary material can be followed by the Ainsworth research. Behavioural material should then follow, with disruption studies to finish off. Keep it short and remember to evaluate or link after each part.

Daycare

Checkpoint

Even amongst superficially similar societies, like the UK and Sweden, almost any social variable is different. For example, the regulation of daycare to provide a standard experience is more stringent in Sweden, children in the UK may start daycare earlier, and so on. Many extraneous variables exist, ensuring different results.

Exam practice

For question (a), a short set of three or four points (cognitive, emotional, aggression, social) will be sufficient, with two forms of daycare contrasted. Question (b) requires the shortcomings and good practices to be noted and linked to how parenting and general child care should be carried out.

Sex and gender

Exam practice

- Use the biological sex and evolutionary material.
- Follow with the five evaluation points.
- Point to the general stability of sexual differentiation.
- Note the reinforcements of parent/adult responses to 'correct' gender behaviour.
- Note the historically diverse gender roles in world-wide cultures.
- Conclude – most influence biological, but with significant socialisation.

Theories of gender development

Checkpoint

It would seem than no one theory fully accounts for gender construction in modern society. Psychodynamic theory has the least research foundation. Gender schema theory seems most plausible, but generates less testable hypotheses than either social learning theory or CDT.

Exam practice

- Start off with Freud, short description and critical demolition.
- Go on to CDT, then use GST as an evaluation (to gain the AO2 marks).
- Introduce SLT and then use the evaluation points.

Development of moral understanding

Checkpoints

1 Younger children are likely to give 'magical' answers (from God), fail to understand, or suggest 'Mummy and Daddy'. Older children will give far more complex explanations, will be conscious that rules can be made up, but may still invoke the agency of some authority figure (e.g. teacher).
2 Inevitably, people asked to reason out a moral dilemma will use the highest levels of moral reasoning available to them. There are no consequences, no real life immediacy to the situation. When behaviour is evoked in a more ecologically valid situation, people tend to react with more habitual behaviours. An example is when people say they are unlikely to obey authority, yet psychology has shown how easily ordinary people can be made to behave appallingly (e.g. Milgram's obedience experiments).

Exam practice

Question (a) requires coverage of at least two areas of theory for a pass or better, and Kohlberg's work should always be one of them. If possible, all the theories in the chapter should be briefly described, with a clear emphasis on evaluation to give it equal weight. Don't forget methodological criticism! Question (b) should use Kohlberg for the descriptive part (i) and the focus in (ii) should firstly cover the use of dilemmas, and then alternatives, bearing in mind the ethnocentric nature of the material.

Theories of the nature of intelligence

Checkpoint

1 The factor named 'g' was thought to be the single underlying mental quality that powered all intellectual abilities.
2 Gardner rejected the notion of a single factor of intelligence, or even a single definition.

Exam practice

When undertaking the first question:
- Put the theories into categories (single vs. multiple intelligences).
- Criticise the single theories individually, then criticise the whole 'g' idea, both positively and negatively – especially noting the impetus from political interests.
- Move on to the multiple theories, using cross-cultural evaluations.
- Come to an overall summary, questioning the whole idea of 'intelligence' if time allows.

The second question requires exactly the same descriptive job doing to one theory – it is suggested to use the category of 'g' as a single theory, as there is a lot of descriptive material available.

Genetic and environmental effects on intelligence

Checkpoints

1 Many were, and are, cared for in the extended family or with neighbours. In many studies some of the twins were found to have had considerable contact!
2 The mathematical relationship between two ordinal or numerical variables, both strength and direction. Correlation does not imply a causal relationship, no matter how strong. Other evidence is needed to establish a causal relationship (e.g. experiment).

Exam practice

- The concordance and adoption study materials should be used first, with evaluations.
- Don't forget to hit the whole idea of twin and adoption studies with a criticism!
- The race material could then follow.
- The evaluation given in the chapter includes effective critical evaluation of the whole field from an evolutionary viewpoint.

The second question requires the naming of the various factors with a very brief description – the whole in one sentence per factor. Each pertinent evaluation should then follow – remember that this is an AO2 question, so descriptive material should be minimal.

Erikson and lifespan theories

Checkpoint

Erikson's retains the Freudian idea of each stage being a crisis that needs to be resolved, with the implication that some people may get stuck or fixated at a certain stage, and not progress.

Exam practice

Examiners will look for the full range of studies, with the relevant evaluations and also making 'compare and contrast' points between the three. The best candidates will discuss the validity of the whole concept, especially in the light of the ethnocentrism criticism.

Adolescence

Checkpoints

1 An adolescent escapes a crisis by adopting an identity that effectively 'blanks out' the previous crisis. An example would be someone struggling with family break-up issues who suddenly 'finds Jesus' and re-centres their life on a sectarian church, refusing to acknowledge family members. This is common, especially in religious societies such as the USA.

2 Points include the raising of the school leaving age, age restrictions on alcohol, tobacco, wage discrimination by age, etc. Note that many ethnic minority children make transitions to adulthood much sooner within their communities (e.g. Muslims, Hassidic Jews).

Exam practice

The question revolves around the evidence for the 'storm and stress' thesis, and its rejection through the use of later, extensive investigations. The better candidate will note the differences in the concept of transition between different cultures, hence the ethnocentrism of some ideas.

A good over-arching point is the development of theory through the use of well-conducted large-sample scientific evidence, as opposed to early stereotypical formulations.

Middle and late adulthood

Checkpoints

Child-nurturing is over and those responsibilities and obligations have ceased. People re-evaluate their lives and often find they no longer wish to live with their previous partners or arrangements.

Exam practice

'Empty nest', divorce and subsequent remarriage, grandparenthood, retirement, deaths and subsequent bereavement, facing the inevitability of death – it's all cheerful stuff! The evaluation of the material should be focused around the disengagement hypothesis, judging whether it is accurate or not. Cross-cultural material may be necessary to show that disengagement may not occur in some cultures.

Revision checklist
Cognitive and developmental psychology

By the end of this chapter you should be able to:

1	Recall basic concepts in memory.	Confident	Not confident **Revise** page 92
2	Itemise the different theories of forgetting.	Confident	Not confident **Revise** page 92
3	Describe and evaluate three models of memory.	Confident	Not confident **Revise** pages 94–95
4	Explain the role of emotion in memory.	Confident	Not confident **Revise** pages 96–97
5	Recall basic facts and evaluations of eyewitness testimony.	Confident	Not confident **Revise** pages 98–99
6	Itemise key points relating to the cognitive interview.	Confident	Not confident **Revise** page 100
7	Discuss three aspects of criminal thinking patterns.	Confident	Not confident **Revise** pages 101, 118
8	Summarise top-down and bottom-up theories of perception.	Confident	Not confident **Revise** page 102
9	Understand cues and constancies in perception.	Confident	Not confident **Revise** page 102
10	Recall basic findings in face recognition.	Confident	Not confident **Revise** page 103
11	Describe and evaluate the nature-nurture debate in perceptual development.	Confident	Not confident **Revise** pages 104–105
12	Describe and evaluate three approaches to cognitive development.	Confident	Not confident **Revise** pages 106-107
13	Discuss aspects of the development of social cognition.	Confident	Not confident **Revise** pages 108–109
14	Critically assess theories of attachment using scientific evidence.	Confident	Not confident **Revise** pages 110-111
15	Examine the impact of daycare on children's development.	Confident	Not confident **Revise** pages 112-113
16	Critically discuss the formation and differentiation of gender.	Confident	Not confident **Revise** pages 114-115
17	Compare and contrast four theories of gender development.	Confident	Not confident **Revise** pages 116-117
18	Describe and evaluate four theories of moral development.	Confident	Not confident **Revise** pages 118-119
19	Compare and contrast single intelligence theories with multiple intelligence theories.	Confident	Not confident **Revise** pages 120-121
20	Critically discuss genetic and environmental effects on intelligence.	Confident	Not confident **Revise** pages 122-123
21	Describe and evaluate three lifespan theories.	Confident	Not confident **Revise** pages 124-125
22	Critically assess the ideas of 'crisis' and 'storm and stress' in adolescence.	Confident	Not confident **Revise** pages 126-127
23	Describe and evaluate findings relating to mid-life.	Confident	Not confident **Revise** page 128
24	Discuss the theory of social disengagement in late adulthood.	Confident	Not confident **Revise** page 129

Health, clinical and sport psychology

This section looks in depth at health psychology with theories that could explain health behaviours in humans. These models of health behaviour and the problems with stress relate to our everyday life. Clinical psychology considers abnormality and how society might diagnose and misdiagnose disorders. It also looks at how abnormality is defined, and the explanations and treatments of a range of disorders. In sport psychology the topics are concerned with an individual sportsperson's performance, and the internal and external factors that might influence their performance.

Exam themes

- Stress
- Healthy living
- Dysfunctional behaviour
- Disorders
- Sport performance and motivation
- Social psychology of sport
- Exercise psychology

Topic checklist

	Edexcel		AQA/ A		AQA/ B		OCR		WJEC	
	AS	A2	AS	A2	AS	A2	AS	A2	AS	A2
Stress as a biological response, factors affecting stress			○			●		●	○	
Measuring and managing stress			○			●		●		●
Healthy living								●		●
Definitions of abnormality		●	○					●		●
Models of abnormality – assumptions		●	○					●	○	
Models of abnormality – treatments		●	○					●	○	
Psychotic disorders – schizophrenia		●		●		●		●		●
Mood disorders – depression		●		●		●		●		●
Anxiety disorders – phobias		●		●	○			●		
Eating disorders		●		●						
Autism		●			○					●
Substance abuse		●		●		●				●
Sport and the individual		●						●		●
Sport performance		●						●		●
Social psychology of sport		●						●		●
Exercise psychology								●		●

Stress as a biological response, factors affecting stress

Stress is a natural response to a stimulus, and we all need to be slightly stressed to ensure that we avoid danger. If we weren't stressed we would stroll across the road, not worrying about oncoming traffic. Psychologists are interested in what causes stress, how we react to stressors and how stress can be managed, to avoid damage to our physical and psychological health.

Physical responses to stress

Selye (1936) believed that the body reacts to psychological and physical stressors with the same physiological activation, which he called The General Adaptation Syndrome (GAS). Stimulation by the sympathetic division of the ANS causes the adrenal medulla to release the hormones adrenaline and noradrenaline into the bloodstream. These stimulate heart rate and blood pressure and mobilise energy reserves. The GAS has three stages:

→ **alarm**, which is when the presence of a stressful event is registered and the body goes into a state of shock
→ **resistance**, which is when the physiological systems in the body try to maintain normal functioning
→ **exhaustion**, if the stress is intense or prolonged, the body is no longer able to deal with it and physiological symptoms such as gastric ulcers start to appear.

Stress can damage the body in different ways (Green 2000)

1. The body's stress response **increases heart rate**, pumping blood around the body faster and at higher pressure. This increased mechanical pressure may lead to damage and a shorter life.

2. **Energy mobilisation** is part of the stress response, where corticosteroids, adrenaline and noradrenaline release stored carbohydrates and fats into the bloodstream. When the stressful situation passes, these are reabsorbed. However, if the stress is prolonged, reabsorption cannot cope and they remain in the bloodstream, where they fur up the cardiovascular system.

3. The **immune system** protects the body from infection by harmful viruses and bacteria (the immune response), and helps in the repair of tissue damage. Short-term stress leads to the suppression of the immune system. Kiecolt-Glaser (1984) believed that, although many people exposed to prolonged stress may not display obvious illness, they may have lowered immune functions (known as immunosuppression) caused by stress, making them more vulnerable to illness. She measured the activity of the immune system from blood samples taken from volunteers. Her results showed significant immunosuppression in the groups under chronic stress. These included: unhappily-married women, long-term carers for Alzheimers patients and students taking examinations.

The jargon

ANS. Automatic Nervous System.

Grade booster

Make detailed notes of the effect of adrenalin on the Autonomic Nervous System. This will help you understand the effect of the physiological response to stress and write a detailed answer to gain full marks.

The jargon

The immune response. The reaction of the body to the introduction of harmful toxins.

The jargon

Immunosuppression. The partial or complete suppression of the immune response of an individual.

Checkpoint 1

Make a list of some of the different ways in which stress might damage the body.

Sources of stress

Life events are events that necessitate a significant transition or adjustment in various aspects of a person's life. This classification would include events such as widowhood, divorce, retirement, etc. Holmes and Rahe (1967) were able to construct an index of the recent life stress of their respondents. They used the scale retrospectively (using people who already had stress-related illnesses) and prospectively (assessing life stress and following respondents over the following 18 months). They found that the higher the score the more likely that the person would develop, or had developed, stress-related illness.

Workplace stress can affect psychological and physical health. Johansson et al (1978) investigated employees in a Swedish timber mill. One type of worker was highlighted as being especially vulnerable to stress – the 'finishers', who were the workers at the end of the assembly line responsible for the final stages of the timber preparation process. Johansson et al measured levels of stress hormones during work days and rest days, as well as looking at other measures such as sickness and absenteeism. What they found was that these workers had raised levels of stress hormones on work days, they had a higher incidence of stress-related health problems and there was a higher rate of absenteeism for this group than for a control group of cleaners in the sawmill.

Friedman and Rosenman (1974) studied the behaviour and personality of patients who were suffering from coronary heart disease (CHD) and discovered that they displayed a particular type of behaviour pattern, characterised by: constantly being under time-pressure, being intensely competitive at work and in social situations and being easily frustrated by the efforts of others.

They called this pattern of behaviour the 'Type A' behaviour pattern. A number of studies have investigated the link between Type A behaviour and coronary heart disease. Significant correlations have been found, but these tend not to be very high. Some studies have also reported negative findings, with people displaying the Type A behaviour pattern being less vulnerable to stress.

A key aspect of our experience of stress and our ability to manage it is our sense of control. Geer and Meisel (1972) set up an experiment to see if perceived control over something aversive (unpleasant) reduces stress. They showed participants photographs of dead car crash victims; those who knew what was coming and had control over the photographs showed less stress.

Action point

Make a note of which aspects of your school, college or workplace you find most stressful.

Check the net

www.stress.org.uk
This site is full of useful information about the occupational effects of stress.

Check the net

Take an online personality test to see if you display Type A behaviour:
www.queendom.com/jff_access/the_type_a_test.htm

Checkpoint 2

What evidence is there that the factors described here do cause stress?

Exam practice   answer: page 168

Describe and evaluate research into causes of stress. (25 marks)

Measuring and managing stress

Psychologists need valid ways of measuring stress, so that the effects of stress and stress management techniques can be identified. The potentially harmful effects of stress mean that effective techniques for stress management are essential. Some techniques are physical (such as the use of drugs) whilst others are psychological (such as meditation).

Measuring stress

Physiological measures of stress can overcome the subjectivity of the self-report by relying on scientific measurements of hormones, chemicals, heart rate, blood pressure, etc. Geer and Maisels's study measured the stress in their participants using a polygraph to collect psychophysiological data.

Self-report methods can include questionnaires, interviews and diary-keeping. Holmes and Rahe used a self-report measure with their Self-Readjustment Rating Scale (SRRS). They felt that readjustment needed to cope with such an event causes stress. The more adjustment you have to make the more stressed you are. Each life event was given a score and a score of 300 would predict a strong risk of physical or psychological illness.

It is possible to **combine methods** of measuring stress, as in Johansson's study on work stressors. They used a combined method of physical tests of cortisol and self-reports of mood, plus statistics of absenteeism. Increases in cortisol levels indicate a higher stress level in the person and, as there is a link between stress and illness, more stress could cause a person to have more time off work. Using a combined method should increase the validity of their measures.

Managing stress

Physical approaches include using drugs such as Benzodiazepine (BZ) and anti-anxiety drugs such as Librium and Valium. These drugs work by reducing the activity of the neurotransmitter serotonin. This has an inhibitory effect on the brain, producing muscle relaxation and an overall calming effect. Beta-blockers such as Inderal work by reducing activity in the pathways of the sympathetic nervous system and are therefore effective against raised heart rate and blood pressure.

Biofeedback is a technique for controlling physiological responses by receiving information about the body's stress response as it occurs. Monitoring devices track responses such as heart rate and blood pressure. These provide the person with feedback in the form of a light or audible tone whenever they change the response in the desired direction. The aim of this technique is to find a strategy to reduce a particular stress-related response (such as increased heart rate) which can then be transferred to the outside world and used regularly to relieve stress.

Budzynski's (1970) study compared patients with tension headaches and found that biofeedback reduced the amount of headaches, their severity and the amount of medication people had to take. These effects were still noticeable three months after the treatment.

Link

See Geer and Meisel's study showing a cause of stress on page 137.

Checkpoint 1

What are the ways of measuring stress?

Grade booster

What are the strengths and weaknesses of each method of measuring stress? At least 2 of each are needed to gain full marks in an evaluation essay.

Check the net

For advice on understanding, recognising and managing stress:
www.mindtools.com/smpage.html

The jargon

Beta-blocker. A drug that prevents the stimulation of increased cardiac action.

Psychological approaches to stress management can be either general, such as using relaxation techniques or meditation to reduce the body's state of arousal, or specific, using cognitive and behavioural training. Progressive muscle relaxation is an active approach to reducing bodily arousal. In a typical relaxation session a client would be trained to progressively tense and relax muscles, working up the body from the legs to the facial muscles. Eventually the person can use the technique as a way of reducing bodily arousal. During the relaxation state, stress response mechanisms are inactive and the parasympathetic nervous system is dominant.

A **cognitive approach** to stress management is Meichenbaum's (1972) stress-inoculation training. This technique has three phases:

→ **Conceptualisation** – the cognitive element, in which the client is encouraged to relive stressful situations, analysing what was stressful about them and how they attempted to deal with them.
→ **Skills training and practice** – the client is taught a variety of techniques (e.g. relaxation, social skills and time management) in the therapeutic setting.
→ **Real-life application** – following training, the client can put what they have learned into practice in the real world. Reinforcement of techniques learned in therapy makes the practices self-sustaining.

Social support networks have also been seen to decrease illness associated with stress. Waxler Morrison's (1993) projective study of women with breast cancer found that women with larger social networks tended to have better survival rates and, as there is a link between stress and cancer, it is logical to believe that if the reduction of the disease is found in women with stronger social support, then this could indicate less stress in these women.

The concept of 'hardiness' is taken to mean resistance to illness, or ability to deal with stress. From studies of highly stressed executives, Kobasa and Maddi (1977) were able to identify the characteristics of those who handled stress well from those who did not. Those who reported the fewest illnesses showed three kinds of hardiness.

They showed an openness to change, a sense of purpose in their activities and a sense of control over their lives. Kobasa proposed three ways in which people's hardiness could be improved – by recognising stressful events then reliving stressful encounters and identifying whether their techniques were effective. This is followed by self-improvement and being encouraged to take on challenges that they can cope with.

Folkman (1984) identified problem-focused and emotion-focused coping strategies for managing stress. Problem-focused coping means behaving in such a way that the stressful situation is reduced or eliminated. With emotion-focused coping, the behaviours will simply reduce the negativity of the emotions by avoidance, distraction or rethinking the situation, i.e. the situation doesn't change but the person's feelings do.

The jargon

Meditation. Concentrating on one thing, or emptying the mind of thoughts to aid relaxation.

Action point

Summarise the assumptions of the cognitive approach to human behaviour.

Checkpoint 2

What advice would you give to someone who was suffering from stress, based on Waxler Morrison's research?

Watch out!

Kobasa's original studies were of highly-stressed executives. This may not generalise easily to other occupational groups.

Grade booster

Compare and contrast these techniques, looking for similarities and differences. This type of analysis should attract high marks if done effectively.

Exam practice   answers: page 168

(a) Describe research into managing stress. (10 marks)
(b) Evaluate the effectiveness of measurements of stress. (15 marks)

Healthy living

An important aspect of health psychology involves identifying what causes people to adopt (or not) the health behaviours that will increase their well-being. If psychologists can identify this, then they can effectively use health promotion to ensure that people change their behaviours and become healthier.

Models of health behaviour

The **health belief model** is a cognitive model which identifies factors linked with adopting health behaviours. These are the perceived threat of not adopting the health behaviour, and this is made up of perceived seriousness (will it actually kill me?) and perceived susceptibility (am I likely to get it?).

A costs-benefits analysis ensures the costs of adopting a behaviour are balanced against the benefits of doing so. Demographic variables such as gender and social class influence this process. We need to be reminded of the health behaviours and their consequences by external cues such as media programmes; internal cues such as illness can also remind us. Becker (1978) found, when he researched mothers' use of an inhaler with their children, they were more likely to comply with the prescribed dose if they believed that their child was susceptible to asthma attacks and if they thought it was a serious condition. The costs and benefits included how much using the inhaler interfered with the mothers' routine, compared with the disruption to their own activities if they didn't. As for demographic variables, married mothers and more educated mothers were more likely to comply.

Rotter's (1966) **locus of control** theory considers where someone places the responsibility for their health – internally, i.e. with them, or externally, i.e. with someone else. Rotter reviewed research and found that, if people felt they had control over a situation, they were more likely to show behaviours that would enable them to cope with potential threats.

Bandura (1997) thought a person's belief in whether they could adopt health behaviours (**self-efficacy**) would convince them to engage in such behaviours. The key features which influence a person's self-efficacy are:

→ vicarious experiences, where you see other people do something successfully
→ verbal persuasion, where someone tells you that you can do something
→ emotional arousal which means too much or too little anxiety might reduce a person's self-efficacy.

Health promotion

There are many different methods used to promote healthy behaviours. Each has some effectiveness, but the individual differences of the target population will affect their impact.

Cowpe's (1989) research into chip-pan fires looked at **advertising** in 10

The jargon

Costs-benefits analysis. Judging a behaviour in terms of its value in relation to its cost, to choose the behaviour with the greatest benefit.

Link

Self-efficacy is also a factor influence sport performance – see pages 162–163.

The jargon

Vicarious. Something which is experienced through someone else, not at first hand.

Action point

Use these theories to explain why people might or might not give up smoking.

Take note

The health belief model may account for some of these differences.

regional television areas of the UK from 1976 to 1884. He analysed the data for reported chip pan fires and used a survey of the populations in the TV areas. The two adverts involved showed the initial cause of the fire and the actions required to put it out. He found that reported chip pan fires declined in each. The surveys reported an increase in the awareness of chip pan fire adverts and in the knowledge of how dangerous they are.

Some activities can be **legislated** against. Dannenberg (1993) looked at cycle helmet use, when a law was passed which made it illegal for children under 16 not to wear a cycle helmet whilst they were riding a bike. When asked, participants in the county where the law had been passed reported increased use from 11.4% to 37.5%. This was compared with other counties which had no legislation where the increases were much less, for example from 6.7% to 11.1% in Baltimore County.

Many health promotion campaigns use **fear arousal** in order to get the message across. Janis and Feshbeck's (1953) study on dental hygiene found that students exposed to high levels of fear with regard to dental hygiene had less behavioural change than those exposed to mild fear arousal. It might be that something too unpleasant can cause denial. It is important that fear arousal is mild enough not to cause denial but strong enough to arouse some anxiety which will promote behaviour change. They concluded that relatively low fear arousal is likely to be the optimal level for promoting health.

Checkpoint 1

What are the main methods of health promotion? Describe one example of research for each method.

Action point

Take a contemporary health promotion campaign and identify the psychology behind it. Don't forget the health belief model.

Adherence

Rational non-adherence is the logical decision not to adhere to medical advice. Bulpitt's (1988) study on males with hypertension found that the cost of the side-effects of taking anti-hypertension drugs to lower blood pressure outweighed the benefits of having lower blood pressure. There are numerous ways of measuring adherence and, as in all psychological research, no perfect research method. A **physiological measure** could be used, which is how Lustman (2000) measured adherence in his research into diabetes and depression. He found that people being treated with an anti-depressant called Fluoxetine were more likely to have less depression, measured by psychometric tests, but also better glycemic control, indicating a better adherence to the regime required by their diabetes.

A study by Chung and Naya (2000) monitored patient drug use with a TrackCap® **device**, which registered when the tablet bottle was opened. They found high adherence rates, although this might be due to the patients knowing they were being tracked. To improve adherence, behaviourism uses the idea of **reinforcement** as being instrumental in behavioural change. Watt's (2003) study on children with asthma using a 'Funhaler®' found that mothers were more likely to have administered the inhaler than when using a normal inhaler. This shows that reinforcing adherence by making it fun can improve the adherence, at least of children.

The jargon

Funhaler®. An inhaler with a whistle and spinner to reward children for using it correctly.

Checkpoint 2

What factors influence adherence to medical regimes?

Exam practice   answer: page 168

Discuss factors affecting health behaviours. (25 marks)

Definitions of abnormality

How do we decide that somebody has a mental disorder? There are currently a number of different approaches to abnormality which manage to co-exist. The model to which a psychologist subscribes has an important part to play in both the explanation and treatment of a mental disorder.

Deviation from statistical norms

Action point

Sketch a curve of normal distribution.

Many human characteristics fall into a frequency pattern known as a normal distribution. In a normal distribution, scores cluster around the central point, or mean. The further away from this point a score is, the rarer it is. If we could measure the characteristic in question, e.g. frequency of hand-washing, most people would be placed in the middle section of this distribution and very few at the extremes. Statistically, then, abnormality is defined as those behaviours or personality traits that are extremely rare. For the statistical model to be useful we must be able to: measure the behaviour in question on a continuum, establish norms against which comparisons can be made and decide on cut-off values for abnormality at both ends of the scale.

Deviation from social norms

Action point

Think of an example of behaviour that is not necessarily statistically rare but that violates social norms.

In this view, abnormal behaviour is not a large deviation from a statistical norm but deviation from a social one. Social norms are implicit rules about how one 'ought' to behave and anything that violates these is abnormal. Having a child when unmarried, for example, is not statistically rare, but acceptance in the current climate is not total because some may see it as immoral or undesirable. This model overcomes the problem of desirable extremes which dog the statistical model, since it is implicit that normal is desirable and deviation is wrong or undesirable. It allows for value judgements where the statistical model does not.

Failure to function adequately

In judging our own or someone else's mental state we often use practical criteria of adequate functioning and see mentally healthy people as being able to operate within certain acceptable limits. This model is the one most lay-people and some mental health professionals use in the initial stages of judging abnormality. Sue, Sue and Sue (1994) suggest that the presence of one or more of the following may impair our ability to function adequately:

Link

These are symptoms of schizophrenia, see pages 148–149.

→ Discomfort – this can be psychological (e.g. depressed mood) or physiological (e.g. fatigue) or both, and may be intense, prolonged or exaggerated.

→ Bizarreness – vivid or unusual behaviour or experiences that grab the attention, e.g. hallucinations, delusions, inappropriate exposure of the body.

→ Inefficiency – difficulty in adequately fulfilling one's everyday duties and roles and/or failure to reach one's potential.

Deviation from ideal mental health

This approach takes us one step further than the failure to function adequately model and asks what characteristics mentally healthy people possess. Abnormality, then, is judged as deviating from this ideal picture. Jahoda (1958) suggests that to have ideal mental health you should:

→ have a positive view of yourself
→ be capable of some personal growth
→ be independent and self-regulating
→ have an accurate view of reality
→ be resistant to stress
→ be able to adapt to your environment.

Cultural and gender bias

All the approaches described so far share one key problem, which is how to take account of the undeniable influence of culture in defining abnormality. Berry et al (1992) noted that abnormal conditions can be:

→ absolute (same nature and incidence in all cultures)
→ universal (found everywhere but with varying frequency)
→ relative (unique and meaningful only to certain cultures).

Culturally absolute conditions may or may not be organically caused. The others, especially culturally relative disorders, call into question the role of socio-cultural factors in determining abnormality. These highlight how culturally set norms or ideals not only lack objectivity but should not be applied universally.

Some conditions seem to appear only in particular cultures. These are known as **culture bound syndromes** (CBSs). They are recognised as illnesses but do not fit any recognised Western category. An often-cited example of a culture bound syndrome is that of dhat, which is an illness found on the Indian continent. Men believe that their fatigue and depression are caused by too much semen in their blood. Chadda and Ahuja (1990) found that the men actually seem to be suffering from depression, and it is this that is causing their lethargy, so perhaps this was a cultural explanation for a global disorder.

Some diagnoses are biased by the characteristics of the patient, such as **gender**. For example, women receive more diagnoses than men of anxiety and depression and much more attention has been paid to PMS than to the role of males' hormones in mental health (Sampson 1993). Ford and Widiger (1989) found that when consultants were given the same symptoms for male or female patients, they diagnosed the women incorrectly more often.

Race can also cause a bias. In the UK, Cochrane (1977) noted higher rates of diagnosis of schizophrenia in Afro-Caribbean immigrants than in whites. The 'Count Me In' Census (Mental Health Act Commission 2005) looked at the rate of diagnosis in cultures within Britain and found that black-white mixed race patients were over three times more likely to be admitted to hospital than white or Indian patients.

Checkpoint 1

What are the four different definitions of abnormality?

The jargon

Objectivity. Lacking involvement or opinion.

Action point

Think up one example of:
→ behaviour that is acceptable in one culture but not in another
→ behaviour that was once unacceptable but is now acceptable.

Action point

Look at research into cultural and gender differences that can illustrate lack of validity.

Checkpoint 2

What do you think are the main problems with diagnosing disorders?

Exam practice

answers: page 169

(a) Describe **one** definition of abnormality. (4 marks)
(b) Evaluate the definition of abnormality you have described. (4 marks)

Models of abnormality – assumptions

Psychologists draw on a number of different ways of explaining abnormality and their ideas about causes will influence how it is dealt with. Here we look at contrasting explanations: the biological (medical) model, behavioural model, cognitive model and psychodynamic model.

Assumptions of the biological model

The biological model of abnormality proposes that psychological disorders have underlying biological or biochemical causes. Psychological disorders are referred to as mental illnesses. These are thought to arise from one of four main causes:

→ **Infection** by germs or viruses leading to a cluster of symptoms or a syndrome. Very early work on general muscle weakness established that this condition could be brought about by an untreated syphilis infection.

→ **Inherited** systemic defect. A number of mental disorders run in families and may be transmitted down the generations.

→ **Neurochemical** factors. Some disorders may be caused by the action of neurochemicals in the brain. Schizophrenics, for example, show a characteristically high level of dopamine (a brain neurotransmitter).

→ Effects of trauma can be physical (e.g. brain damage or poisoning) or psychological (e.g. bereavement, rape). Korsakov's Syndrome is an alcohol-related condition that can lead to memory disturbances, confusion and apathy.

Assumptions of the behavioural model

The behavioural model of abnormality makes two major assumptions:

→ that all behaviour is the product of **learning**, even if it is maladaptive
→ that what has been learned can be unlearned.

It follows that symptoms (abnormal behaviour patterns) are the whole problem. There is no need to look for deeper causes. Abnormal behaviour is mainly attributed to the following types of learning:

→ In the **classical conditioning** process, a neutral stimulus is paired with one that naturally evokes anxiety and thus also becomes capable of eliciting anxiety.

→ **Operant conditioning** models emphasise the role of reinforcement, punishment and extinction in shaping and maintaining behaviour. Behaviours that have pleasant consequences are more likely to be repeated than those that do not, e.g. a person who displays a phobia is reinforced by welcome attention from others.

→ The work of Bandura in the 1960s demonstrated that we can learn by **observing** significant others (models). He also showed that we sometimes imitate that behaviour if we perceive that the consequences have been desirable for the model. Bandura argued that behaviour could thus arise without any direct need for reinforcement.

The jargon

Somatic or **biomedical** are sometimes used in place of medical.

Watch out!

'Systemic' means 'to do with a system'. Be careful not to confuse it with 'systematic'.

Link

See biological therapies on page 146.

Link

These theories of learning are applied in education. See page 176.

Assumptions of the cognitive model

The cognitive approach to abnormality has a number of forms, for example:

→ The **information processing approach**, which views the person as similar to a computer and abnormality as a malfunction in processing at one or more of the stages of input, storage, manipulation or output.

→ The '**faulty cognitions**' approach, e.g. Beck (1976) talked of cognitive errors, Meichenbaum (1976) of counterproductive self-statements and Ellis (1962) of irrational thoughts. Such cognitions are distortions of reality and can lead to people feeling worthless, unhealthy or unhappy and being unrealistic about the future.

The jargon

Cognitions are thought processes – in this case, ways of construing the world and ourselves.

Assumption of the psychodynamic approach

To illustrate the psychodynamic approach, the psychoanalytic theory of Sigmund Freud (1856–1939) is used here. Freud's followers (e.g. Jung, Erikson, Klein) developed his theory and changed some of its emphases but continued to share some of the original assumptions.

→ Much of our behaviour is biologically determined by the **unconscious** operation of instinctive forces.

→ **Early experiences** are also important and can have a profound effect on later behaviour. Personality develops in stages. The sequence is universal but the individual's early experiences result in a unique personality. The fully-developed personality consists of an id, ego and superego. Psychological problems can arise from a number of sources.

→ Psychic energy may be **fixated** at an early stage of development and unbalance the adult personality.

→ The concept of **anxiety** is central. This can be anxiety about real dangers, moral anxiety (the result of conflict between the ego and superego) or neurotic anxiety (the result of conflict between the id and ego).

Anxiety that threatens to go out of control could be **traumatic**. The ego can employ a number of **defence mechanisms,** such as repression or displacement, to protect itself. Repressions usually form in childhood when the ego is weak but may not show themselves until later, perhaps during adolescence when sexual maturation is occurring or as a result of a personal crisis. Symptoms are often symbolic of internal conflicts.

Link

The case study of Little Haus shows Freud's theory. See the case study on page 46.

Checkpoint

What are the key assumptions of each of the approaches?

Action point

Evaluate each model of abnormality, using evaluation issues such as reductionism that are on your specification.

Exam practice   answer: page 169

Drawing on your knowledge and understanding of approaches in psychology, assess how appropriate it is to assume dysfuctional behaviour appears to be a biologically-based problem. (12 marks)

Models of abnormality – treatments

The aim of therapies is either to reduce symptoms to a more manageable level so that a person's lifestyle is not compromised, or to remove the cause of the behaviour so that a person has a healthier psyche, which might also constitute a cure.

Biological therapies

Biological, or biomedical, treatments of mental disorder aim to reduce symptoms by addressing their underlying biological or biochemical cause. **Chemotherapy** involves the use of therapeutic drugs. Their general function is to alter the action of the chemical messengers in the brain, known as neurotransmitters. They fall into three major groups:

→ **anti-anxiety** drugs which relieve tension and nervousness
→ **anti-psychotic** drugs which are used to reduce psychotic symptoms such as mental confusion and delusions
→ **anti-depressant** drugs which are used to elevate mood.

Electroconvulsive therapy (ECT) is a treatment where a sub-lethal electric shock is passed through the temporal lobes of the brain to produce a cortical seizure and convulsions. Muscle relaxants and a short-acting anaesthetic are given beforehand and other medical procedures followed. Treatment may be given a number of times over several weeks, depending on the individual's progress.

The use of ECT has declined since the 1960s and 1970s but is still used today for certain conditions. Its mode of action is uncertain but it seems likely that it produces neurochemical changes in the brain. ECT is thought to be highly effective for severe depression and bipolar disorder and it has an immediate effect, making it desirable for use on people who have suicidal feelings. However, ECT may cause death in 1 in 200 patients over 60, or irreversible cerebral damage (Breggin 1979). Small et al (1986) found that ECT produces some short-term intellectual impairment but that this is not inevitable and rarely permanent.

Behavioural therapies

Behaviourists emphasise the role of learning experiences provided by the environment in determining behaviour. Learned behaviour is usually useful or adaptive but sometimes it is not, in which case it may become so problematic that it is seen as a disorder. Abnormal behaviour is open to the same laws of learning as normal behaviour and can be shaped and changed using the same principles.

Therapies based on classical conditioning

These therapies are usually referred to as behaviour therapies and involve the application of classical conditioning principles. They tend to concern behaviours that are difficult to control voluntarily.

Flooding and **implosion** can be used to treat phobic disorders. Flooding involves immediate exposure to the actual feared stimulus, whereas implosion requires the phobic person to imagine their most feared situation. Both techniques work on the principle that, if the feared stimulus is repeatedly presented in a supportive setting, the fear of it will eventually be weakened.

Systematic desensitisation (SD) was successfully pioneered by Wolpe (1958) to treat phobias. SD has three stages: the client constructs a hierarchy of feared situations ranging from manageable to frightening, then they are trained in relaxation techniques and finally are exposed to the feared situations in their hierarchy, beginning with the least frightening. Once they can cope, the next stage is tried until desensitisation is achieved.

Aversion therapy involves training the client to associate sickness or pain with an undesirable aspect of their behaviour in order to discourage them from continuing with it. For example, a problem drinker may take an emetic which makes them vomit only when they drink alcohol. A variation on this is covert sensitisation, which involves the person being trained to imagine vividly the unpleasant consequences of their behaviour.

The jargon

Emetic. A drug that induces vomiting.

Therapies based on operant conditioning are often called **behaviour modification techniques**. They work well with behaviour that is more under voluntary control and which is reinforced by its consequences. Consequences can be changed in order to change the frequency of desirable and undesirable behaviour. This involves the use of: extinction – pleasant consequences of undesirable behaviour are removed, and desirable behaviour is shaped by giving punishment or rewards accordingly. Token economy systems, such as reward systems in clinics, use this principle. Biofeedback also uses reinforcement by feeding back to the individual their success in altering their physical state, e.g. heart rate

The jargon

A **token economy** uses a system of tokens such as stars, points or plastic counters which are given for good behaviour and can be saved and exchanged for reinforcers.

Cognitive therapies

Restructuring illogical thoughts is the key component to cognitive therapy. Ellis's **Rational Emotive Therapy**, has three key stages: ABC. The A stands for **activating events**, which are things that contribute to or initiate a disturbance in someone's psychological well-being. The B stands for the **beliefs**, which are what that person thinks about the event, such as believing themselves to be stupid if they fail an exam. The C stands for **consequences**, which is what can happen if that person has these faulty beliefs, leading them to illogically think they are worthless if they are so stupid they fail an exam.

Checkpoint 2

What are the aims of each therapy?

Psychodynamic therapies

Psychodynamic therapy covers all analytical therapies, which are usually based on the theories of Freud or his followers. In this type of therapy, the therapist keeps his own personality out of the picture. Most usually this 'talking cure' involves the therapist being a reflective blank canvas which patients can use to transfer their feelings onto. These are then reflected back to the patients who are able to deal with the deep feelings provoked. The emphasis is on the unconscious and the therapist tries to bring into the consciousness the feelings of conflict the patient has. The therapist usually has little input, and waits for the patient to come to their own conclusions.

Action point

Make an evaluation chart of each therapy with its strengths and weaknesses.

Exam practice   answers: page 169

(a) Describe how biological treatments can be used to treat any **one** psychological disorder. (10 marks)

(b) Evaluate the use of biological treatments for psychological disorders. (15 marks)

Psychotic disorders – schizophrenia

Schizophrenia is a serious mental disorder that is characterised by severe disruptions in psychological functioning. Schizophrenics may experience a variety of disturbing and frightening symptoms. Although the evidence in favour of the physical origins of the disorder is very strong, psychological factors are also important.

The characteristics of schizophrenia

→ Thought disturbances – a kind of reasoning that appears obscure and incoherent to others. Schizophrenics may suffer from delusions – interpretations of events that have no basis in reality.

→ Perceptual disturbances – including hallucinations and an inability to recognise the emotional states of others.

→ Emotional disturbances – displaying emotions or inappropriate emotional reactions.

→ Motor disturbances – unusual physical actions such as giggling, or standing immobile for long periods.

→ Disturbances in social functioning – an inability to maintain social relationships with others.

DSM-IV diagnoses a disorder as schizophrenia when the following criteria are met:

→ The person has shown continuous signs of schizophrenia for more than six months, including an active phase when at least two of the symptoms above are present.

→ The person has deteriorated from a previous level of functioning in such areas as work, social life and self-care.

→ Any manic or depressive episode, if present, occurred either before or after the psychotic symptoms or was brief in comparison.

→ The symptoms are not due to substance abuse or any other medical condition.

Explanations of schizophrenia

Biological explanations

→ Schizophrenia appears to be **heritable**, which is good evidence for it being a biological disorder. Both adoption studies and twin studies support a genetic link. However, schizophrenia does not appear to be caused by a single gene, as fewer than 50% of the children whose parents are both schizophrenic have the disorder. Gottesman and Shields (1996) found concordance rates of only 58% at best, so genetics can only play a part in explaining schizophrenia.

→ The **diathesis stress** model might emphasise the individual differences, as this suggests the environment will interact with a genetic predisposition.

→ Most schizophrenics show symptoms which suggest that they are suffering from **brain damage**. Evidence from CT scans shows

The jargon

Hallucinations. The experience of imagined sights, sounds or other sensory experiences as if they were real.

The jargon

DSM-IV. The Diagnostic and Statistical Manual, edition IV, is an American system for classifying psychological problems and disorders.

Link

See page 54 for Rosenhan's study looking at the validity of diagnosing schizophrenia.

Check the net

Read about the five types of schizophrenia – you will find an excellent site at: www.schizophrenia.com

Action point

Research the ICD-10 categories from the World Health Organisation. This will give you some comparison for the DSM.

that there can be damage to the frontal lobes, temporal lobes and hypothalamus. Frontal lobe damage may account for some of the negative symptoms.

Psychological explanations

Cognitive psychology, with its emphasis on logical thinking, might be thought to be less useful in explaining schizophrenia. Maher's (1974) theory proposes that delusional thinking is a result of a perceptual disorder. Maher argued elderly people who are deaf would logically think something is being hidden from them and experience paranoia.

Family explanations of schizophrenia suggest that the family environment contains such confusing elements as a schizophrenogenic mother and double-bind communications. Laing's (1965) existential theory claims that schizophrenia is a constructive process where people try to 'cure' themselves of the confusion and unhappiness that are a feature of their social and family environment.

Behaviourism could be considered to offer the least effective explanations for schizophrenia. With its emphasis on learning it wouldn't seem likely that people would learn psychotic behaviours but there is evidence that people with schizophrenia can learn less maladaptive behaviours (Paul and Lentz, 1977). This might lead to the assumption that the maladaptive behaviours were learned in the first place.

Treatment of schizophrenia

The biological explanation for psychotic disorders is probably the most common explanation. It reflects the medical treatments most often associated with controlling psychotic illnesses. If there is a biological problem as the cause of schizophrenia, the best form of treatment is biological. Traditional neuroleptic **drugs** (e.g. chlorpromazine) reduce positive symptoms. They block transmission of the neurotransmitter dopamine at the D2 dopamine receptors and shut down dopamine activity in the mesolimbic region of the brain.

Kane et al's (1982) research showed the effectiveness of Fluphenazine in treating schizophrenia, adding support to the biological theory of dysfunctional behaviour.

Recent studies in cognitive psychology have shown it is possible to restructure a person's perception to a more normal view. Sensky's (2000) research shows how **cognitive therapy** can be effective in treating patients with schizophrenia. By comparing Cognitive Behavioural Therapy (CBT) with non-cognitive interventions for patients, there was seen to be significantly fewer positive symptoms of schizophrenia in patients undergoing CBT.

Behaviourists Paul and Lentz show how patients with schizophrenia lack **reinforcement** for socially acceptable behaviour, so when they are taught this behaviour, and it is reinforced, they can have less psychotic episodes. Whether this is a cure or simply control of symptoms is debatable.

The jargon

Diathesis-stress model. A model that assumes individuals may have a predisposition (the diathesis) towards developing a particular disorder, which then makes them more vulnerable to later environmental events (the stress).

The jargon

CT scan – computed tomography. This involves building up a composite picture of the brain through an amalgamation of horizontal X-ray sections.

Checkpoint

What are the various explanations for schizophrenia?

Action point

What methods do you know of treating schizophrenia?

Exam practice   answer: page 169

Describe and evaluate **at least one** biological explanation of schizophrenia. (12 marks)

Mood disorders – depression

Depression is a type of mood disorder in which the person experiences feelings of great sadness, worthlessness and guilt, and finds the challenges of life overwhelming. Within DSM-IV, there are two categories of depression, major depression (or unipolar disorder) and bipolar disorder.

The characteristics of depression

→ Loss of interest or pleasure is nearly always present.
→ Appetite is usually reduced.
→ The most common sleep disturbance associated with a major depressive episode is insomnia.
→ Psychomotor changes include agitation or retardation.
→ Decreased energy, tiredness and fatigue are common.
→ The sense of worthlessness/guilt may include unrealistic negative self-evaluations or guilty preoccupations with minor past failings.
→ Many people report impaired ability to concentrate or make decisions, being easily distracted or having memory difficulties.
→ Frequently, there may be thoughts of death or even suicide.

DSM-IV diagnoses a disorder as depression when five or more of the following criteria are met:

→ Insomnia most nights.
→ Fidgeting or lethargy.
→ Tiredness.
→ Feelings of worthlessness or guilt.
→ Reduced ability to concentrate.
→ Recurrent thoughts of death.

Explanations of depression

Biological explanations

There is some evidence that mood disorders are **heritable**. Wender et al's research into adopted individuals with affective disorders found that biological relatives were eight times more likely to have unipolar depression and 15 times more likely to commit suicide than relatives of people without depression.

Serotonin depletion might also contribute to depression; serotonin-producing cells extend into many brain regions thought to participate in depressive symptoms. Cerebrospinal fluid in depressed, and especially in suicidal, patients contains reduced amounts of a major serotonin by-product (showing reduced levels of serotonin in the brain itself). Evidence comes from the effectiveness of drugs that inhibit the re-uptake of serotonin from the synaptic cleft. Prozac and other SSRIs are able to block serotonin re-uptake without affecting other neurotransmitters.

Psychological explanations

Cognitive theories emphasise the role of **irrational thoughts** and beliefs influencing the emotional state of the individual. Beck (1967) sees depression in adulthood as being caused by a bias towards negative interpretations of events. These are a legacy of childhood experiences such as the loss of a parent, social rejection by peers or the depressive attitude of a parent. These biases are activated whenever the individual encounters situations that are in some way similar. Studies have shown that cognitive therapies are better for preventing the recurrence of depression, although the combined advantages of cognitive therapy and drug therapies appear more helpful than either type of therapy alone.

According to the **learned helplessness** view of depression, people become depressed when they perceive a loss of control of the reinforcing aspects of their life. If this is attributed to internal, global and stable factors, they will feel helpless about preventing future negative outcomes and may experience unipolar depression. Seligman's original research on dogs found that they could quickly learn, through classical conditioning, to pair a light with an electric shock. For the first trials they could not escape the shock. Eventually, despite being able to escape, the dogs didn't bother to try. His theory of learned helplessness is used to explain depression in humans (Peterson and Seligman 1985).

Treatment of depression

Behaviourist treatments for depression are based on the assumption that depressed behaviours are learned and so can also be unlearned. The treatment therefore has to teach patients by **reinforcing** them for non-depressive behaviours. Lewinsohn's (1990) research showed how adolescents made some improvement in their depression if they were given cognitive therapy but that if their parents had been taught to reinforce the non-depressive behaviours their depression was lowered even further.

Biological treatments include **anti-depressants**, which vary in their mode of treatment, though they all act upon the neurological system of the body. Many will increase the neurotransmitter serotonin, as a reduction in this is linked with depression. Some prevent the serotonin that is released from being re-absorbed, so that the effect of the neurotransmitter is prolonged. This is thought to decrease the symptoms of depression. Karp and Frank's (1995) research reviewed evidence and the findings showed that drug treatments are as effective alone as they are when combined with psychological treatments such as cognitive therapy.

Cognitive treatments for depression try to restructure the faulty cognitions which are the assumption of the cognitive theory about depression. The aim of cognitive therapy is to restructure the thoughts from illogical thinking to rational thinking. It is believed that this will help the patient to perceive their world more accurately and so reduce the depression or hopelessness. Ellis (1962) in his research compared the effectiveness of **rational cognitive therapy** with psychoanalysis and psychoanalytically-orientated therapy – he found that cognitive therapy was more effective than both.

Checkpoint

What are the psychological explanations for depression?

Action point

Note down the similarities and differences between the psychological and biological explanations for depression.

The jargon

SSRIs (selective serotonin re-uptake inhibitors). A class of anti-depressant drugs that stop serotonin being taken back into the presynaptic cell, thus prolonging its action at that synapse.

Exam practice   answers: page 170

(a) Explain the use of **one** cognitive-behavioural therapy as applied to the treatment of depression. (10 marks)

(b) Outline and evaluate biological therapies as treatments of depression. (15 marks)

Anxiety disorders – phobias

Phobias are a persistent and unreasonable acute fear of a particular object or situation. The person with the phobia realises that these fears are irrational, the response far outweighing any realistic consequences of being in the situation.

Characteristics of phobias

The phobic stimulus causes an immediate response, which is characterised by physical symptoms of terror, which include shortness of breath, palpitations, and a feeling of losing control. The fear results in a person's everyday life being disrupted, for example not being able to go into a room if there is a spider in the room.

The **DSM-IV** classification specifies a phobia as:

→ marked and persistent fear that is excessive or unreasonable
→ when exposure to phobic stimulus provokes immediate anxiety response
→ the person recognises the fear as excessive
→ the phobic situation is avoided
→ the phobia disrupts the person's normal life
→ the phobia has lasted more than 6 months in people under 18 years of age.

Explanations of phobias

Behavioural explanation

One behaviourist explanation for phobias is that of **classical conditioning**. This suggests that a previously neutral stimulus, such as a dog, is paired with something unpleasant, such as the pain associated with being bitten by the dog. This pain produces a natural negative response which is paired with the dog and so the dog becomes a phobic stimulus.

Operant conditioning supposes that, if someone is rewarded for behaviour, these positive consequences will lead to the behaviour being repeated. For example, getting attention for being afraid of thunder will naturally lead a child to show that fear next time there is a storm.

The **social learning theory** can also explain the development of phobias. Bandura and Rosenthal (1966) researched phobias and their research discovered that someone would develop a phobia of buzzers if they saw an image of someone in pain which was paired with a buzzer sounding. The case study by Watson and Raynor (1920) on Little Albert showed how it was possible to condition a phobia of rats in a child when the rat was presented at the same time as a metal bar was hit with a hammer, causing a natural fright. The fear was also generalised to other white fluffy things like a rabbit and a Santa Claus mask.

The jargon

Palpitations. An irregular beating of the heart, often because of fear or anxiety.

Grade booster

Research the ICD-10 categories from the World Health Organisation. This will give you some comparison for the DSM and allow for detailed analysis which is needed for full marks.

Checkpoint 1

Explain the acquisition of a phobia using the terms from classical conditioning such as unconditioned and conditioned stimulus.

Biological explanation

It is considered that humans have a biological '**preparedness**' towards phobias of things that are more likely to be (or have been in the past) dangerous. This might explain why people more easily acquire phobias of snakes or darkness, than phobias of houses or flowers. It makes evolutionary sense that people with a fear of snakes would avoid them, and thus avoid being bitten and dying. These people would then survive to transfer their genetic predisposition to phobias. Ohman et al (1975) carried out research and found that it was easier to induce phobias of snakes than of faces or houses.

Cognitive explanation

Generalised anxiety disorders, which show much the same effect as phobias, are considered by the cognitive approach to be similar to phobias. A person with **faulty cognition** would have an excessive reaction, similar to phobias, which might include fainting, hyperventilating, etc. Worry about a situation that is out of proportion to the threat results in anxiety disorders. Beck's (1967) research found that 'excessive worry' was a common symptom in patients with general anxiety disorder.

Treatments for phobias

It is difficult to define a cure, especially for a disorder like phobias. One point of view might be that the cure is only when a person has no reaction to the stimulus, whilst another might say that it is enough to minimise the response to enable a normal lifestyle to be lived.

Behaviourists base their treatment on **relearning** a different response to the phobic stimulus. This might be by pairing the phobic stimulus with a non-threatening stimulus. Little Peter (Jones 1924) was desensitised from a phobia of rabbits by pairing the rabbit with food, until the feelings of pleasure associated with the food became paired with the rabbit. McGrath's (1990) study documented how systematic desensitisation was used on a girl with a noise phobia. She was shown the fear stimulus and it was paired with imagining her toys, and being taught to relax. These feelings of calm gradually became associated with the noisy objects such as balloons and her phobia was greatly reduced after 10 sessions.

Biological treatments assume that the problem is a 'medical' one and are usually based on **drug** treatment. Leibowitz's (1988) research found that, compared with a placebo group and a control group, an experimental group given a drug called phenelzine showed fewer social phobic responses.

Ost and Westling's (1995) cognitive research compared patients with panic attacks. One group was given muscle relaxation training and the other cognitive therapy. They found that **cognitive therapy** was as effective as relaxation, and that cognitive changes would probably also have taken place in the group with relaxation training.

Action point

What methods do you know of treating phobias?

Checkpoint 2

Explain the treatment of a phobia using the terms from classical conditioning such as unconditioned and conditioned stimulus.

The jargon

Placebo group. Participants are given a nopn-active substacne to make them think they have recieved treatment, **Control group.** Participants are given no therapy at all.

Exam practice   answer: page 170

Describe and evaluate research into **one** anxiety disorder. (25 marks)

Eating disorders

The two main classes of eating disorder – anorexia nervosa and bulimia nervosa – are described in ICD-10 (International Classification of Disorders) as behavioural conditions linked to both psychological and physiological factors.

Check the net

Two websites with lots of useful links to information about eating disorders are: www.edap.org and www.caringonline.com

Characteristics of eating disorders

Anorexia nervosa is 'nervous loss of appetite' and is characterised by:

→ prolonged refusal to eat
→ deliberate weight loss
→ distorted body-image
→ cessation of menstruation in women (amenorrhoea).

Some anorectic individuals are also **bulimic**, i.e. they binge eat then control their weight by causing themselves to vomit afterwards (purgers) or by vigorous exercise (non-purgers).

Most sufferers are young, white, Western, middle-class women, although there is evidence that more black women are becoming anorexic. Five to ten per cent of sufferers are men and half of these are homosexual (Petkova 1997). Onset of the condition is usually between 12 and 18 years of age. Anorexia is diagnosed when the sufferer reaches 85% of the weight clinically defined as normal for them. Anorexia nervosa and bulimia nervosa have much in common – a drive to be thin, a pre-occupation with food, depression, anxiety, a need to be perfect and difficulty with 'reading' internal states such as hunger or anxiety. However, some believe that there are also some important distinctions:

Checkpoint

What symptoms and problems are sufferers of eating disorders likely to have?

Anorexia nervosa	Bulimia nervosa
Refusal to maintain healthy body weight	Under- or overweight or in between
Hunger and disorder denied	Awareness of hunger and disorder
Less antisocial behaviour	More antisocial behaviour
Amenorrhoea common	Irregular menstruation common
Family conflict denied	Intense family conflict perceived

The jargon

Bulimarexia. A term introduced to cover those cases where the two conditions overlap.

Explanation for eating disorders

Psychological explanations have been applied to both anorexia and bulimia because of the way in which they can overlap. **Psychodynamic** explanations focus on the girl's relationship with her parents and the requirement that, during adolescence, she needs to develop her own identity and become separate from them. Three themes have emerged from this:

→ an unconscious desire to remain pre-pubescent
→ an unconscious fear of facing up to their sexuality in general and pregnancy in particular and
→ domineering parents who therefore foster dependence in their offspring (Bemis 1978).

Action point

List some of the ways in which idealised images of women's bodies and links between health and thinness are presented to the world at large.

Behavioural explanations focus on learning processes as the most important determinant of behaviour and see anorexia as weight phobia.

Western cultures tend to idealise images of slender women and link thinness with good health. A related idea is that of ineffective **parents**. Bruch 1973 found that many parents of anorexics control the child even to the point of deciding when, what and why they eat, so that the child never learns to respond appropriately to their own sensations of hunger and satisfaction.

Biological explanations for eating disorders are of two main types. These are explanations based on **genetic** inheritance and explanations based on **biochemical** dysfunction. There is no evidence, as yet, for the genes that cause anorexia nervosa or bulimia nervosa. Researchers have turned their attention to an investigation of the degree to which eating disorders run in families.

Results from family studies (APA 1994) have shown that there is an increased risk of eating disorders among first-degree relatives (parents, children, siblings) than among the general population. Results from twin studies by Holland et al (1984), involving comparing MZ twins with DZ twins, found a 55% concordance rate for MZ twins compared with only 7% for DZ twins. Wade et al (2000) found similar levels in their study of 2163 female twins. The authors of this study were unable to rule out the possibility that the greater concordance rate for MZ twins might have been caused, at least in part, by the contribution of a shared environment.

An alternative biological explanation for eating disorders focuses on the role of a **brain** region known as the hypothalamus, and the concept of a weight set point. Research with animals has shown that when the hypothalamus is damaged, it can lead to starvation.

There are two major areas of the hypothalamus that control eating. The lateral hypothalamus (LH) produces hunger when it is activated. If the LH of an animal is stimulated, it begins to eat. The ventromedial hypothalamus (VMH) depresses hunger when it is activated. If the VMH is stimulated an animal stops eating. If it is destroyed, the animal eats more often and becomes obese. It is believed that the LH and VMH work together to set up a 'weight thermostat' which maintains a set point for weight (the normal weight for that person, determined by genetic inheritance, early eating practices, etc.). If the 'thermostat' rises above this point, the VMH is activated; if weight falls below the weight set point, the LH is activated.

The action of the LH and VMH sends messages to other areas of the brain that in turn initiate thoughts and behaviours which will satisfy whichever is activated. It is possible that a malfunction in the hypothalamus might explain eating disorders.

Recent research (Walsh et al 1997) has implicated the neurotransmitter serotonin in patients with bulimia. Low levels of serotonin were found to be associated with binge eating. This association is supported by evidence that selective serotonin-active anti-depressants are effective in the treatment of binge eating.

> **The jargon**
>
> **MZ (monozygotic) twins**. Twins who develop from the same egg and therefore have 100% of their genes in common.
> **DZ (dizygotic) twins**. Twins who develop from two separate eggs and therefore share 50% of their genes – as do any other siblings

> **The jargon**
>
> **Hypothalamus**. A part of the brain that helps maintain various bodily functions, including hunger and eating.

> **Grade booster**
>
> Write a detailed description of the different explanations for eating disorders. Use this for your revision notes. It will help you write a detailed account which is necessary for full marks in an exam.

> **Exam practice**   answers: page 170
>
> (a) Outline factors influencing attitudes to food and eating behaviour.
>   (5 marks)
> (b) Outline and evaluate **one or more** psychological explanations of **one** eating disorder. (20 marks)

Autism

People affected by autism find difficulty in forming social relationships and often lack language skills. It is most often diagnosed in boys, and usually after the age of 30 months. It is now seen as a spectrum (or continuum) from slight to severe, or functional to non-functional.

Definition and symptoms

Kanner (1956) identified five areas which would lead to a diagnosis of autism. These are:

→ lack of affective contact with others, where children show little interest in other people
→ an obsession with keeping things the same, whether this is a routine or room – tantrums can result from any change
→ a fascination with particular objects – an autistic child may collect objects such as stones, or become obsessed with lifts, for example
→ communication difficulties, which may be profound, with many children being mute and most having some language restrictions and possibly using language inappropriately
→ often looking and behaving as if cognitive functions are normal.

These symptoms are present from early childhood. The **triad of impairments** which are prevalent in most children with autism are:

→ deficits in social interaction
→ deficits in communication
→ a restricted repertoire of activities and interests.

The DSM criteria for autism include:
→ qualitative impairment in social interaction
→ qualitative impairments in communication
→ restricted, repetitive and stereotyped patterns of behaviour, interests and activities
→ delays or abnormal functioning in at least one of the following areas:
  → social interaction
  → language as used in social communication
  → symbolic or imaginative play.

Explanations of autism

One of the first explanations for autism was offered by Bettelheim (1967), who claimed the cause was **inadequate parenting**. Rejecting parents, who did not respond to initiatives from the child, would cause hopelessness and apathy. This emotionless state is typical of children with autism. However, there is little evidence to support this, and more evidence which suggests normal parents can have a child with autism. A **genetic** link has been found in twin studies – Folstein and Rutter (1978) found that there was a higher concordance rate in MZ twins (83%) than in DZ twins (19%). A final biological explanation may lie in brain damage, where EEG measures of **brain activity** have found that many children with autism have abnormal brain patterns.

The jargon

Mute. Unable or unwilling to speak.

The jargon

Repertoire. Range.

Checkpoint 1

What are the characteristics of autism?

The jargon

Concordance rates. The number of pairs who have the same trait.

The jargon

EEG. Electroencephlogram.

Studying autism

A diagnosis of autism can sometimes be made on the basis of tests which have shown a difference in children with autism. One such study is the **Sally-Anne test**. In this test, a child is asked to see a situation from the point of view of a doll. The situation is set up so that the doll would not have the same point of view as the child so, if the child assumes the doll does have the same point of view, then the child doesn't have a theory of mind. Baron-Cohen (1985) used this test to compare children who had autism with children with Down's syndrome and normal children. The result was that only children with autism failed to display a theory of mind and this was seen as a core deficit of their condition.

Another simple test is the **Smartie Tube test**. A young child is shown a tube of Smarties and asked to guess what's inside. They will no doubt say 'Smarties'. But when the tube is opened they see they were wrong and it has got a pencil in it. The pencil is put back in, and the tube closed. The child is then asked, 'Your friend John is going to come in. What will he guess is inside the tube?' Up to the age of four, ordinary children will say, 'A pencil', because they assume John thinks the same as they do. However, from four onwards they realise that John would make the same mistake as they had. Children with autism don't develop this understanding of false belief.

A further core deficit is believed to be the **central coherence theory**, which suggests that children with autism have a limited ability to understand context or to 'see the big picture'.

A final cognitive explanation is **impaired executive functioning** (such as memory loss, lack of visual spatial skills and attention deficits) has been found to be common but not always associated with autism and so can not be the only explanation of autistic behaviour.

Therapeutic programmes for autism

Behaviour modification is based on behaviourist assumptions about learned behaviour. The **Lovaas technique** is applied behaviour analysis which consists of behavioural interventions breaking skills down into basic components and rewarding positive performance.

Harris and Handleman (1994) found that 50% of children with autism who were involved in this behavioural modification were re-integrated into mainstream school classrooms. However, there may be the need for much individual support to maintain this.

Lovaas' original technique also included aversive responses to stop unwanted behaviour, such as smacking children, shouting, or even using electrical shocks. Although these are no longer used by most institutions, the Judge Rotenberg Center in the US does still use electric shocks as aversives. This is the subject of ongoing legal challenges.

Some **drug treatments** are also used for autism. Studies have shown that some children with autism have higher than average levels of serotonin and so a drug to reduce this would appear to be a good treatment. Fenfluramine was used on 14 children with autism (Geller et al, 1984) and it was found that they showed increased social responsiveness, improved behaviour and increased IQ.

Exam practice   answer: page 171

Describe and evaluate the theory of mind explanation of autism. Refer to empirical evidence in your answer. (10 marks)

The jargon

Theory of mind. The ability to understand that someone else can think something different to our own thoughts.

Action point

Draw the Sally-Anne test in a storyboard, so that you really understand the procedure.

The jargon

Core deficits. The term used for the problems children with autism have in terms of their brain function.

Grade booster

Being able to evaluate issues such as the use of children in psychological research will help you to reach the top marks for analysis.

Checkpoint 2

What approach is the Lovaas technique based on?

Substance abuse

Substance abuse or addiction is a recognised disorder, with DSM criteria which suggest a maladaptive pattern of use, resulting in failures in social relationships, work and home. Hazardous and illegal acts are also indicative of substance abuse. The addiction can take the form of both psychological and physiological dependence.

Theories of substance abuse

The **social learning theory** encompasses the ideas of operant conditioning, classical conditioning and imitation of role models. Operant conditioning is where people are rewarded by the effects of the substance – this could be social acceptance or biological 'highs'. Classical conditioning is where the association is made between the feeling after the substance abuse, and the substance. It can start with feeling good after one glass of wine, caused by the dopamine reaction, and associating the wine with feeling good. Imitation of role models is also an important factor, which is why the media portrayal of celebrities can be so important.

The **biological theories** of substance abuse can include genetic explanations. There is some evidence (Comings, 1998) that a certain gene is found in 42% of people with alcoholism. However, a more obvious explanation is that the mode of action of drugs – for example alcohol, which releases the neurotransmitter dopamine, which make us feel good – is obviously rewarding and so we are more likely to repeat the behaviour. This is a **bio-behavioural** explanation. As the body gets used to the effect, it develops a tolerance and so to get the same level of response more and more of the substance has to be taken. If the substance is stopped then the physical and psychological response will be one which is so negative, the addict can be tempted to take the drug again, just to stop the withdrawal symptoms.

The theory of reasoned action, which can account for many health behaviours or lack of them, is one explanation of why individuals do or don't become addicted to a substance. It is a cognitive explanation which is divided into three parts:

→ their attitude towards the behaviour, which might include a person's own beliefs about the consequences
→ their subjective norm, which is social attitudes to the behaviour
→ their perceived locus of control,

A person's **attribution** is also important. Baumann (1982) compared the attributions of addicts who were just starting treatment and those who were nearly at the end of their treatment. Early-treatment alcoholics were more inclined towards situational attributions of alcoholics as opposed to dispositional attributions of non-alcoholics.

The jargon

Physiological dependence. When there are physical reactions if the addiction is stopped.
Psychological dependence. A dependency on a substance which doesn't give rise to physical symptoms but to psychological symptoms, such as anxiety, if stopped.

The jargon

Effect. A change which occurs as a result of an action.

The jargon

Mode of action. The biological interaction in the body which results in the effect of a substance.
Tolerance. When the reaction to a drug decreases so that larger doses are required in order to achieve the same effect.
Withdrawal. Discontinuing a drug or other substance, which results in negative symptoms.

Link

See Rotter's theory of locus of control in Healthy living on page 140.

The jargon

Attribution. How a person makes inferences about the causes of behaviour.

The jargon

Situational. Depending on the situation a person finds themselves in.
Dispositional. Because of something specific to the person, such as personality.

The self-esteem of young boys was an important factor identified by Taylor et al (2006). They studied 870 11-year-old boys for nine years to try to identify potential early warning signs for drug dependence. They asked the boys to rate themselves on measures of low self-esteem. The final follow-up interview took place when most of the boys were between 19 and 21 years old. They found that boys who had very low self-esteem in the sixth or seventh grade were 1.6 times more likely to meet the criteria for drug dependence nine years later than other children.

Treating substance abuse

Evans et al (1978) found three sources of **social pressure** which had a strong influence on seventh grade students. These were: peers, models of smoking parents, and media. When students were taught to resist these and shown the short-term effects of smoking, the onset of smoking in the groups who had the treatment was lower than in the control group.

Behavioural techniques, such as aversion therapy, need to ensure the addicts learn non-addicted behaviours. Danaher (1977) made smokers sit in a closed room and smoke a cigarette, taking one puff every six seconds. This continued until the smoker could not smoke anymore. The unpleasant feelings associated with smoking would have caused a relearning of behaviour. However, there are obviously ethical considerations in terms of damage to health.

Biological treatments have their basis in medication such as methadone, for individuals addicted to opiates. Nicotine patches, gum, and nasal sprays can help individuals addicted to nicotine.

Gomel et al (1993) investigated the effects on smoking of a **workplace ban**. By asking employees and by assessing breath and blood, they found that whilst employees reported less smoking, they were in fact smoking the same amount, just not at work.

Public health programmes on smoking are often advertisements which aim to prevent people from starting to smoke and also encourage smokers to quit. Pechman's (1998) research evaluated the strategies used in adverts to prevent adolescents smoking. They found that **fear arousal** was effective if it focused on the effects of smoking on the smoker's family. Peer pressure was also an influential factor and, if the adverts conveyed the message that most young people didn't smoke, and that smokers were perceived negatively by their peers, then adolescents showed less inclination to smoke.

Prochaska and DiClemente's Stages of Change model identified several stages in any behavioural change and these can be applied to the treatment of substance abuse. They are Pre-contemplation, Contemplation, Preparation, Action, Maintenance and Relapse.

Checkpoint 1

What explanations are there for substance abuse?

Grade booster

Being able to relate explanations to approaches and perspectives will help with top grade evaluation.

Checkpoint 2

What advice would you give to a person who is trying to give up smoking?

Link

Fear arousal is also discussed on page 140.

Action point

Look at a health promotion campaign and try to identify the psychology it is based on.

Exam practice   answer: page 171

Describe and evaluate **at least one** explanation for substance abuse. Refer to evidence in your answer. (12 marks)

Sport and the individual

Trying to identify what makes a successful sportsman or woman is key to sports psychology. If key attributes are isolated, these can be either fostered or instilled in people to improve their success. If those attributes are biologically based, then teams can identify athletes likely to succeed and nurture these individuals.

Personality

Our personality is who we are, rather than what we have become from interacting with our environment. Cattell's 16PF is an assessment of 16 personality factors that can measure an athlete's personality. They include: warmth, reasoning, emotional stability, dominance, liveliness and rule consciousness. This assessment can be used to produce a personality profile of an athlete or sportsperson. Another personality test used in sport is Eysenck's Personality Questionnaire (EPQ), which is a series of yes/no questions to identify aspects of personality such as extroversion and neuroticism.

Eysenck and Cattell both developed trait theories, where they tried to identify the characteristics which make up a person's personality. They believed it was inborn, whereas situational theories believe our personality is developed from our interaction with our environments. The social learning theory believes we learn our personality from significant others. Freud's psychodynamic theory identifies three different parts of our personality (id, ego and superego) and believes it is the interaction of these that develops our adult personality. Psychologists who adopt an Interactionist stance believe that both situational and trait theories explain our personality, each to a varying degree.

Kroll and Crenshaw (1970) used Cattell's 16PF to compare sportsmen and women from four sports and found that there were significant differences between the personalities of participants, although footballers and wrestlers didn't show a significant difference.

Aggression

Aggression can be defined as a deliberate act that causes harm to others. In sport there is often a debate between what is assertive and what is aggressive. **Freud's** theory of aggression identifies two unconscious conflicts – Eros (the life force) and Thanatos (the death wish) Thanatos causes us to be self-destructive but if Eros stops us from hurting ourselves then we will turn this destructive tendency towards others. We suppress this aggressiveness, but eventually it builds up and will need to be released. **Catharsis** is a way of releasing this pressure in safe environments, and Freud believed taking part or even watching sport can be cathartic and gently release the pressure of the built-up aggression.

However, some research suggests that participating in sport actually leads to an increase in levels of aggression. Berkowitz's **cue theory** (1969) is a social theory which assumes that our environment will provide triggers of aggressive behaviour. If we are highly aroused then we are more likely to be aggressive when there is a trigger present; in sport,

Checkpoint 1

What are the key theories of personality development?

The jargon

Extroversion. A personality with traits such as outgoing, assertive, and generally seeking out excitement.
Introversion. A personality with traits such as being reserved, less outgoing and less sociable.

Action point

Why do you think footballers and wrestlers didn't show significantly different personalty traits?

Checkpoint 2

What would Freud's theory suggest is the best type of sport to reduce aggression?

both participants and audience can be highly emotionally charged, so any trigger to aggression may lead to aggressive behaviour. Berkowitz's research showed that the effect might not be immediate but that a trigger later, such as a person's name, may cue a person's behaviour if it is linked with an aggressive situation.

To manage aggression in sport, the **social learning theory** suggests that introducing non-aggressive models will make children imitate their non-aggressive behaviour. This makes famous and influential sports people responsible for adopting non-aggressive behaviours when being watched by susceptible fans who might be tempted to copy.

Motivation

Motivation has various definitions within psychology, such as an internal state that triggers behaviour or a need that directs behaviour and in sport encourages participation.

McClelland-Atkinson (1953) investigated the **achievement motive** by carrying out a content analysis research using the TAT (Thematic Apperception Test). Subjects were shown standard pictures and asked to write their own stories based on four questions. They found that achievement-motivated people tended to avoid both low-risk situations because they are too easily resolved and high-risk situations because they think a positive outcome is due more to chance than their ability.

To investigate motivation specifically related to sports, Gill and Deeter's (1988) **Sports Orientation Questionnaire** was devised. The final version had 25 items which were rated on a 5-point scale from strongly agree to strongly disagree and it was tested on 237 undergraduates on sports and non-sports courses. They concluded that the SOQ was a reliable and valid measure of sports orientation. It showed that sportspeople were more competitive and that this varied depending on the sport.

Deci and Ryan (1985) formulated the **Cognitive Evaluation Theory** (CET) which looks at the effects of reward on intrinsic motivation. Intrinsic motivation is increased by competence and a sense of autonomy. Extrinsic rewards can reduce a person's intrinsic motivation, and negative aspects such as threats and deadlines, can also reduce intrinsic motivation.

Sportspeople often need to increase their motivation to chieve excellence and one of the theories for this is Ryan and Deci's (2000) **Self-Determination Theory**. There are three aspects to self motivation: competence, relatedness and autonomy.

The jargon

Participation. Taking part, in this case in a sporting activity.

The jargon

Excellence. The state of being superior to others. In this case performing a sporting activity as well as it can be performed, and better than others.

The jargon

Intrinsic motivation. Internal drives to behaviour.
Extrinsic motivation. Outside pressures, such as money for winning, gold medals or applause can motivate a sports person to perform well.

Action point

What intrinsic and extrinsic motivation might Olympic competitors have?

Exam practice   answers: page 171

(a) Describe theories of motivation in sport. (10 marks)
(b) Discuss the problems of researching motivation in sport. (15 marks)

Sport performance

Sportsmen and women have to perform feats of strength, endurance and co-ordination to enable them to succeed in their chosen activity. There are many factors which might influence the performance at any one time; arousal and anxiety are two which can have positive or negative effects on a participant.

Theories of arousal

Arousal can be considered as a **physiological**, possibly autonomic response but psychologists may also mean **cognitive** or **emotional** arousal. Yerkes-Dodson's (1908) **inverted U theory** shows the effect of arousal on performance. In the Dancing Mice study (1907), mice given electric shocks (arousal) took less time to learn a maze as the strength of the shocks increased. However, if the shock was too strong the learning decreased, so the resulting data graph would look like an inverted U.

Further research applied this to different skill levels and different sports. For example, a novice tennis player will reach the optimal point of arousal much sooner than an experienced player. The optimal point of arousal in golf is much lower than that for rugby as the skills are different. This means golfers need to learn how to keep their arousal under control, whereas rugby player must make sure they remain aroused throughout the match.

Lacey's (1967) research paper suggested **somatic response patterning**, in that for any situation there is a pattern of multiple physical responses. An understanding of this will increase our understanding of sporting performance. Oxendine's (1980) research suggests **emotional arousal** can be linked to motor performance. High arousal can increase performance, although levels of arousal may be too high, and the optimum arousal level may differ depending on the task. Even in the same situation the optimum level of arousal will vary from day to day with the same person.

Generally, the more complex the task the lower the arousal level for optimum performance, whereas for a simple task high levels of arousal are more likely to lead to better performance. With reference to sport, high arousal is necessary for sports involving strength, endurance and speed, but not for those involving co-ordination, speed and fine muscle movements.

Anxiety

If arousal levels become too high and are above the optimal point for performance, the levels of anxiety in the sportsperson increases. This in itself can increase the arousal further and so lead to a downward spiral of performance. Speilberger (1966) identified two types of anxiety – trait and state. **Trait anxiety** is where anxiety is an integral part of an individual's personality, whereas **state anxiety** is where a situation results in an anxiety response. There can be physical anxiety levels, which will be a biological reaction, and cognitive anxiety levels such as self-doubt.

Marten's **Sports Competition Anxiety Test (SCAT)** was planned to be objective, unambiguous, easily scored and with a reduced response bias. Fifteen items are rated and this has been tested for reliability and validity and found to be a good measure of anxiety.

There are some measures of anxiety which include more aspects and

The jargon

Somatic. Relating to the body (biological) rather than the mind (psychological).

Checkpoint 1

What are the different types of arousal?

still maintain reliability and validity. Marten's (1977) original **Competitive State Anxiety Inventory** (CSAI) is one of these used to measure state anxiety. Speilberger's **Trait Anxiety Inventory** (TAI) and his **State Anxiety Inventory** (SAI) test trait and state anxiety respectively. Using Martens et al's Competitive **State Anxiety Inventory-2** (CSAI-2, 1990), it was found that physical anxiety had an inverted-U shaped relationship with performance, self-confidence had a positive correlation with performance; and cognitive anxiety had a negative correlation with performance. Also, by giving the CSAI-2 to a selection of athletes 48 hours, 24 hours, two hours and five minutes before a critical event, they noted that cognitive anxiety stayed the same but that physical anxiety increased just before the sports event.

The inverted U model suggests a gradual tailing off of performance once the optimal point of arousal has been passed but Fazey and Hardy felt that in reality there is a 'catastrophe' effect where performance drops rapidly. The optimal performance can be regained at this point by the sportsperson tweaking the stress level back down to the optimal level. The cognitive aspect of arousal is what determines whether it is possible for the athlete to regain the optimal level of arousal.

Lynette Craft's study (2003) was a meta-analysis which looked at the effect of state anxiety on athletic performance. It was found that high self-confidence displayed the strongest and most consistent positive relationship with increased performance.

Improving sport performance

Boyd and Munro (2003) carried out research on 86 athletes from track and field and from climbing, using Hall's **Sport Imagery Questionnaire** (SIQ). This is a 30-item questionnaire which measures imagery use with a 7-point likert scale. It was adapted for climbers so that the specific events were related to climbing rather than competing. The results showed that athletes had a higher score for use of imagery than climbers, although there were differences in the types of imagery used by all athletes. The reason why imagery can have an effect on performance could be that imagined events cause the muscles to respond in the same ways as the actual physical act, so the acts are being practised. It may also be that a coding system used when imagining an act can help people develop mental skills such as concentration. Woods (2001) identifies four functions of imagery in sport. These are: mental practice, increasing self-confidence, controlling arousal and understanding and retaining information.

Vealey's (1986) research has always been grounded in sports psychology rather than in general psychological theories applied to sport. She identified **sports confidence**, which has a trait (an individual's personality) aspect, a state (individual's situation) aspect and a competitive orientation (individual's definition of success) aspect. They are combined in such a way that an athlete's self-confidence and competitiveness combine to produce a situation where they feel confident and their outcome will have an effect on their self-confidence next time.

Checkpoint 2

Describe the different ways anxiety can be measured in sports people.

Action point

Sketch the graphs to represent the relationships between physical anxiety and performance, self confidence and performance and cognitive anxiety and performance.

Link

Bandura's theory of self sufficiency is also found in health behaviours – see page 140.

Exam practice   answer: page 172

Describe and evaluate internal factors affecting sporting performance.

(25 marks)

Social psychology of sport

Sports often take place in a team setting, so psychologists are interested in the social interactions between team members, between sportspeople and their coaches, and between those participating in sport and the audience. Leadership is an often-discussed factor in sports teams, for example when deciding who will make the best captain.

Group cohesion

Tuckman's (1965) theory of small group formation identified five stages, commonly known as **Forming**, **Storming**, **Norming**, **Performing** and **Adjourning**. The sum performance of a team may not be the total of all the members put together. There can be a reduction in performance from **social loafers**. Latane's (1979) study showed this by setting up an experiment where participants had to clap and cheer and judge how noisy they had been. This was done alone, or in groups of two, four or six participants. The level of noise didn't increase in proportion to an increase of people, as each person produced less noise as the group got bigger. This showed the presence of social loafing in a group.

Checkpoint 1

What are the stages of group formation?

There are many aspects which can make for **group cohesion** (being bound together) or not. Carron looked at previous theories from social psychology and identified how rewards would influence the way the groups worked together and how much they stayed on task. From a sports perspective, Martens et al's (1972) **Sport Cohesiveness Questionnaire** is used to measure different aspects of cohesiveness, such as friendship, attraction, and a sense of belonging to the team. However, groups with high levels on these measures of cohesion do not necessarily perform the best and the best-performing teams do not necessarily have high levels of group cohesiveness.

Audience effects

Link

See Arousal and sports performance on page 162.

Audience effects are simply the effects on a person's performance due to other people being present, even if it is only one person. Whether that person is passive or active there is still some effect. Zajonc thought this was due to arousal by the presence of an audience even if there is no interaction with the performer.

Cottrell et al (1968) thought that Zajonc was wrong to assume a passive audience would have any effect. Their research compared the effect of a passive audience with that of an interactive audience. He found that a passive audience had little effect on the performance but an interacting audience made a significant difference to the performance.

Zajonc's (1967) own studies on cockroaches tried to investigate the effect on performance with and without an audience. By using a cockroach's natural tendency to run from light, he set up a cockroach run and a cockroach maze (where the escape from the light meant negotiating a maze). He then built a 'grandstand' which was a row of boxes each big enough to take one cockroach who had to face the runner. He timed the runners in the maze and the run, both with and without an audience.

He could also have cockroaches running alone or alongside another cockroach. Using the lone cockroach for a baseline time, he found the cockroaches in front of a grandstand ran quicker and those running alongside another cockroach were quickest in the run. However, in the 'maze' condition, the cockroach running against another was slower and the cockroach in front of the grandstand ran slowest.

Schwartz and Barsky's (1977) study into **home advantage** looked at 1880 major league baseball games in 1971 and found that home victories exceeded 50% of all games won. Looking at other sports, they found that home advantage has most effect in indoor settings such as basketball and ice hockey and had the most effect in indoor hockey. Playing at home seems to increase offensive rather than defensive play, and a hostile crowd has a negative effect rather than a supportive crowd having a positive effect. So it may be 'away disadvantage' rather than 'home advantage' – this could be linked to theories of arousal.

Theories of leadership

There are two types of leadership theories in social psychology – trait and type theories. Trait theories believe it is personality characteristics that make a great leader. An example is Stogdill's (1948) **Great Man theory**. He found several factors which might be thought to influence a group's choice of leader: age and physique (which had little effect), height and weight (which showed a weak link), and appearance, communication skills, intelligence and knowledge (which were positively linked with choice of leader).

Feilder's (1967) **contingency theory** was that, in addition to the traits, the choice of leader was dependent upon things such as how well they got on with the team members, and the type of task.

Chelladurai (1978) considered there are many dimensions to leadership and identified three factors:

→ whether the leader conformed to the team's view of what a leader should be
→ what type of behaviour the team expected a leader to show
→ what type of behaviour the leader actually showed.

In sport, the role of the leader is often that of being the coach, so the effectiveness of the leader is reflected in their **effectiveness as a coach**. Smith et al (1979) studied training for coaches and how this increased their effectiveness. They researched Little League Baseball coaches from Seattle, who were observed and assessed by self-report of team players and the coaches themselves. They found training increased the self-esteem of coaches, especially in those with low self-esteem at the beginning and that the percentage of games won was higher for the trained coaches. The trained coaches became more effective leaders and so their teams had more success.

Action point

Draw the four conditions of Zajonc's cockroach study.

Checkpoint 2

What effects does an audience have on sports performance?

The jargon

Contingency – depending upon factors and circumstances .

Check the net

Referee training for football association: www.footballreferee.org/better_refereeing.php

Grade booster

Apply the theories of leadership to the nature-nurture debate. Efectively using different issues to evaluate research will demonstrate the valuation skills needed for full marks.

Exam practice   answers: page 172

(a) Outline **one** theory of leadership that you have studied in sport psychology. (3 marks)
(b) Evaluate the theory of motivation you outlined in (a). (4 marks)

Exercise psychology

The impact of exercise and sport on the individual can be both physical and psychological. Positive benefits such as better mental health and mood states, and fewer diseases, are often used to promote exercise. However, negative consequences of exercise such as burnout, eating disorders and drug abuse, are of concern.

Exercise and health

Strenuous exercise could be one factor that might influence the incidence of breast **cancer**. Bernstein et al (1994) set out to investigate the potential relationship between different levels of exercise and the risk of breast cancer. He looked at newly-diagnosed breast cancer patients and a matched control group of 545 women without breast cancer. He used interviews to find out the average number of hours of physical exercise per week from their first period to within one year of diagnosis of breast cancer. The results found that one to three hours of exercise per week could reduce the risk of breast cancer in young women by around 30%. This figure rose to over 50% if the participant had regularly maintained four or more hours of physical activity.

Another effect can be with the infection **HIV – 1**. Lox, McAuley and Tucker (1995) used an experiment with 3 groups of HIV patients who were given a 12-week programme of aerobic exercise, weight training or flexibility. They found that participants in the aerobic and weightlifting conditions reported significantly higher levels of physical self-efficacy, positive mood and life satisfaction than the flexibility programme control group. Physical self-efficacy levels, positive mood and life satisfaction also increased for aerobic and weightlifting groups between pre- and post-programme measures.

Hausenblas and Carron (1999) carried out research to find out if athletes were more likely to have **eating disorders**. They thought this could be due to social pressures, pressure from coaching staff or excessive dieting and exercise needed for training. They also showed there might be personality traits in athletes that make them more vulnerable to eating disorders.

Exercise and mental health

Many theories have been created to explain why people who exercise feel better psychologically. One biological theory is the **endorphin hypothesis** (Steinberg and Sykes 1985). Beta-endorphin, produced naturally as a result of exercise to kill the pain of exercise, can have the same effect as opiates, and may result in an endorphin high. A negative side to this is when a person becomes addicted to this high in the same way as drug addicts do to opiates. Many studies have analysed blood and found that levels of beta-endorphins increase with exercise, and animal studies have found that mice can become swimming junkies, when they have regular exercise in the form of swimming. Other biological reactions such as increased temperature and the relaxation effect of hot showers afterwards can all have a positive effect on mood.

By exercising we can also be distracted from stressors and feel better, so it may not all be due to biological changes. Leith and Taylor (1990) wanted to study the effects of exercise on mental health and reviewed 81

The jargon

Matched control group. A group of participants who are similar in key characteristics to the experimental group but who don't experience the experimental condition.

Action point

What are the strengths and weaknesses of using self report methods to gather data?

The jargon

Meta-analysis. Research which looks at the results of several studies with the same research hypotheses.

The jargon

Opiates. Drugs, such as heroin, produced from opium, which have a sedating effect on users. They can be highly addictive.

research projects. 70% of studies reported significant improvements in mental health, which rose to 80% if partial improvement was considered.

Mood states might predict performance by sports people. Morgan and Johnson (1978) used the Minnesota Multiphasic Personality Inventory to test rowers before their training camp where they would be selected for the national team. The hypothesis was that rowers selected for the national team would have high scores in positive mood states such as vigour and extroversion, and low scores on negative mood states such as in anxiety, tension and depression. Using these predictions and the MMPI, the researcher could identify those who would and wouldn't make the team and they were correct 41 out of 57 times.

Issues in exercise and sport

The consequences of too many demands in sport may be **burnout and withdrawal**. Costill et al (1991) wanted to find it there was an optimal amount of training. By studying college swimmers who had either long or short training, they found that measurements of swimming power – heart-rate, blood samples and swimming technique – and success in competitions showed that shorter training sessions did not disadvantage the athlete in terms of performance improvement. Biological measures such as of cortisol showed there were fewer negative consequences (e.g. stress and fatigue) in the short training group and measures of mood states showed no differences between the two groups.

Another issue which has come to light in sports is that of body **image**. Hart, Leary and Rejeski (1989) developed The Social Physique Anxiety Scale (SPAS) which has 12 questions with a 5-point Likert-type rating scale. Fifty-six female undergraduates had their fitness evaluated and were then given the SPAS to see how stressed and uncomfortable they felt due to the fitness evaluation. Women in the high social physique anxiety (SPA) group scored significantly higher stress scores, felt less comfortable and recorded more negative thoughts about their body image than the low SPA group. However, women in the high SPA group did weigh more and had higher body fat percentages than the low SPA group.

Performance enhancing drugs may have a psychological as well as physiological effect. Maganaris, Collins and Sharp (2000) looked at how weightlifters would feel if they were told they had taken performance-enhancing drugs. They were given a drug which they thought was an oral anabolic steroid but which was in fact a saccharin placebo. Although the placebo would have had no effect on weightlifting performance, the participants showed significant improvements in all three lifts for both trials compared to the base-line recording at the starts of the study. For the participants who were told about the placebo after the first lift, they only showed improvement in weightlifting trails for the first lift. The perceived expectation of improved performance was therefore shown, although there was no reason for improvement. Several participants moved up to international competitions as a result of their improved performance.

Checkpoint 1

What beneficial effects might exercise have?

The jargon

Burnout. Physical or emotional exhaustion.

Action point

What are the advantages of objective data such as biological measurements?

The jargon

Saccharin. A calorie-free sweetener.

Checkpoint 2

What issues are related to exercise?

Exam practice   answers: page 172

(a) Describe **one** theory of exercise and mental health. (10 marks)

(b) Evaluate theories of exercise and mental health. (15 marks)

Answers
Health, clinical and sport psychology

Stress as a biological response, factors affecting stress

Checkpoints

1 Physiological symptoms include gastric ulcers. The body's stress response increases heart rate, pumping blood around the body faster and at higher pressure. This increased mechanical pressure may lead to damage and a shorter life. If the stress is prolonged, reabsorption of carbohydrates and fats into the bloodstream is compromised and these can fur up the cardiovascular system. Immuno-suppression caused by stress can make people vulnerable to illness.

2 Holmes and Rahe used the SRRI retrospectively and prospectively and found that the higher the score the more likely they were to be ill. Johansson et al 1978 found the 'finishers' in a sawmill had raised levels of stress hormones on work days, they had a higher incidence of stress-related health problems and there was a higher rate of absenteeism for this group than for a control group of cleaners in the sawmill. Friedman and Rosenman discovered that people with Type A personality were more likely to suffer from CHD. Geer and Meisel showed perceived control over something aversive reduces stress.

Exam practice

This question is asking you to do two things. The first is to describe research, which can be theories, studies or models. The research to include could be Johansson's research on sawmills, Holmes and Rahe's research on lifestyles, and Geer and Maisel's research on control. Three studies written in detail should gain high marks. Don't try and write about too many studies in less depth as your answer will appear superficial. The second thing you have to do is to evaluate research. This is not asking for your personal opinion but an informed argument based on evaluation issues such as ethnocentrism, reductionism and research methods.

Measuring and managing stress

Checkpoints

1 Physiological measures of stress include using a polygraph or GSR. Self-report methods can include questionnaires, interviews and diary-keeping. It is possible to combine methods of measuring stress, which should increase the validity of their measures.

2 To increase sources of social support, such as family, work, friends, support groups. These different types of social support were shown by Waxler Morrison to increase survival rates for women with breast cancer, and so we may assume reduce their stress levels.

Exam practice

This exam question is in two parts and should be divided into about 15 and 25 minutes respectively. This will include reading and planning time. In the first part the question asks for a description which means facts about the research.

Research might be theories, models of studies; in this case some description of the technique and why they are thought to measure stress would be appropriate, in addition to empirical evidence. When asked to evaluate the effectiveness of the techniques, the issues you could use include individual differences, validity (especially related to self-report), objectivity and samples they have been tested on. Make sure you use examples to illustrate each evaluation issue.

Healthy living

Checkpoints

1 Different methods of promoting healthy lifestyles include media campaigns such as Cowpe's research into chip-pan legislation, shown by Dannenberg's study into cycle helmet fear arousal, researched by Janis and Feshbeck's study on dental hygiene.

2 The health belief model might explain adherence and show how rational non-adherence is the logical decision that the cost of the side-effects of taking drugs may outweigh the benefits.

Exam practice

This essay is asking you to discuss factors. This means you have to describe and evaluate. The description is probably going to be worth about 10 marks and the evaluation worth about 15 marks. For the description you need to describe about three factors such as fear arousal, legislation, culture, planned actions, costs/benefits analysis, self-efficacy, and locus of control. Don't just describe theories, but make sure you answer the question about how the factors identified by the theories affect health behaviour. You can use empirical evidence to show the effect these have had. The evaluation might include: evaluation of the supporting research evidence (if it is only carried out on a small sample it may not be generalisable); individual differences (why some people might be less influenced than others by legislation); and the method used to gather the data may be flawed, which would question the factors' effect on behaviour. Give clear examples from the research and don't forget to compare and contrast.

Definitions of abnormality

Checkpoints

1 The four definitions are: deviation from statistical norms, where people fall outside of a normal point on the curve of normal distribution; deviation from social norms, which makes the abnormality culture-specific; failure to function adequately, where someone is unable to adapt to society; and deviation from ideal mental health. (Johoda's definition of ideal mental health is used to give a clear idea as to what individuals should be – if not, that is considered abnormal.)

2 Culture and gender bias, the validity and reliability of diagnoses shown by Rosehan's study, and the ethics of labelling someone could all affect the diagnosis of dysfunctional behaviour.

Exam practice

One of the four definitions from Seligman: statistical deviation, lack of ideal mental health, deviation from social norms or failure to function adequately. Give a brief example to illustrate your definition and show understanding. The evaluation is not going to be long, so two points should be the maximum. Points could include the anomalies such as many people having depression but that this is still labelled as abnormal. Individual differences might also impact on the definition.

Models of abnormality – assumptions

Checkpoint

The biological model of abnormality proposes that psychological disorders have underlying biological or biochemical causes. The behavioural model of abnormality makes two major assumptions: that all behaviour is the product of learning even if it is maladaptive and that what has been learned can be unlearned. Cognitive psychology suggests the information processing approach, which views the person as similar to a computer and abnormality as a malfunction in processing at one or more of the stages of input, storage, manipulation or output – the 'faulty cognitions' approach. The psychodynamic approach suggests psychic energy may be fixated at an early stage of development and unbalance the adult personality. Anxiety that threatens to go out of control could be traumatic.

Exam practice

This question appears to be complicated but – broken down – it asks you to evaluate the appropriateness of the biological explanation of dysfunctional behaviour. This could be done by showing the biological approach is appropriate by using empirical evidence to support it. However the evaluation of this research might reduce the strength of this approach. Another way of evaluating is to use psychological explanations which may have more to offer as an explanation, or the effectiveness of their treatments might show them to be more appropriate as explanations for dysfunctional behaviour. If you have time a good answer would use both ways of evaluating the biological approach.

Models of abnormality – treatments

Checkpoints

1 ECT may cause death in one in 200 patients over 60 or irreversible cerebral damage (Breggin 1979). Small et al (1986) found that ECT produces some short-term intellectual impairment but that this is not inevitable and rarely permanent.
2 Biological, or biomedical, treatments of mental disorder aim to reduce symptoms by addressing their underlying biological or biochemical cause. Behaviourists believe abnormal behaviour is open to the same laws of learning as normal behaviour and can be shaped and changed using the same principles. Restructuring thoughts which are illogical is the key component to cognitive therapy. In psychodynamic therapy the emphasis is on the unconscious and the therapist tries to bring into the consciousness the feelings of conflict the patient has.

Exam practice

This question is in two parts, making the skills required for each part very clear. A description of the biological treatment is straightforward – drugs, ECT and even surgery could be used – but make sure you only relate it to *one* disorder. Evaluation might include effectiveness shown by empirical research (although restriction of the sample may reduce the generalisability of the effectiveness); problems of reductionism; individual differences. Make sure you include examples (usually from part a) to illustrate the points you are making.

Psychotic disorders – schizophrenia

Checkpoint

Biological explanations support a genetic link and most schizophrenics show symptoms which suggest that they are suffering from brain damage. Cognitive psychology proposes that delusional thinking is a result of perceptual disorder. Family explanations of schizophrenia suggest that the family environment contains such confusing elements as a schizophrenogenic mother and double-bind communications. Behaviourism suggests that, since people with schizophrenia can learn less maladaptive behaviours, the maladaptive behaviours must have been learned in the first place.

Exam practice

You are asked in this question to describe and evaluate, and it is worth spending about equal time on these two skills. Describe one explanation. It must be biological, so chemical imbalance and brain structures are both equally valid. It is possible to get full marks for one, so if you know one in depth that is fine. If you are a bit vague on two then put both in, there is a depth/breadth trade off: more depth on one requires less depth (or none) on a second one. For evaluation the points could include: research evidence in support; evaluation of that research; reductionism in biological approach. The empirical research must be included in either or both of the description and evaluation.

Mood disorders – depression

Checkpoint

Psychological explanations: cognitive theories emphasise the role played by irrational thoughts and beliefs in influencing the emotional state of the individual. According to the learned helplessness view of depression, people become depressed when they perceive a loss of control and feel helpless about preventing future negative outcomes, and so may experience unipolar depression.

Exam Practice

The injunction 'Explain' is asking for more than a description of the therapy, it also requires some explanation of how it works. So not only do you need to include a description of a therapy such as Rational Emotive Therapy but also to show you understand what it is hoping to achieve, in terms of restructuring faulty cognitions. Make sure that you relate the treatment to depression. The second part is asking for an outline of biological therapies (did you spot the different approaches in the two parts of the question?) and this is much briefer than a description, it is more an overview. The evaluation might include: specific disorders they are more/less effective for; supporting empirical evidence and its limitations; approach bias; the evaluation of that approach.

Anxiety disorders – phobias

Checkpoints

1 An original bee sting will produce an unpleasant effect, so the bee is the unconditioned stimulus and the pain/fear is the unconditioned response. However the bee will produce the pain/fear on its own in future so it becomes the conditioned stimulus, because you have learned to fear the bee. It will bring about a learned response of fear, which is the conditioned response.

2 The presentation of dinner naturally makes us feel good, so the dinner is the unconditioned stimulus and feeling good is the unconditioned response. The rabbit is the object that is going to be learned to associate with the feeling good and so is the conditioned stimulus which is presented at the same time as the dinner. As we naturally feel good with the dinner, we learn to associate the feeling good with the rabbit so the rabbit can now produce a

learned response of feeling good. So no fear/feeling good when presented with the rabbit is a conditioned response.

Exam Practice

A question like this is asking for a detailed essay on one anxiety disorder. As research can refer to theories, models and empirical evidence, you could include theories which explain an anxiety disorder, theories which might explain treatment of the disorder, and empirical evidence which supports both. So you might look at the theory of classical conditioning (relating it to an anxiety disorder such as phobia) and some specific research showing how this has been illustrated, such as Little Albert. Then you could describe the treatments which arise out of classical conditioning, such as systematic desensitisation, and some evidence such as Little Peter, which shows the effectiveness of this treatment. Then all you have to do is evaluate the theories and the research, using your favourite issues such as reductionism, methodology, individual differences and so on.

Eating disorders

Checkpoint

The differences between the two disorders can be seen in the table in the text. They include the differences in body weight, attitude to hunger, how society views it, the effects on menstruation for women, and the role of family conflict. There are some gender and cultural differences as well.

Exam Practice

The first part of the question is only worth 5 marks and only asks for an outline, so a brief description of factors such as the role of the family and media is what is required. The majority of the marks are for evaluating explanations. Remember it is asking for psychological explanations, so social learning theory may be one that could be considered. Cognitive and psychodynamic approaches can also explain this disorder. The evaluation for 15 of the 20 marks can consider empirical evidence, the evaluation of such research, reductionism, determinism, individual differences, etc. Don't forget to give examples from your description to illustrate your evaluation points.

Autism

Checkpoints

1 Kanner (1956) identified five areas that define autism: lack of affective contact, obsession with keeping things the same, a fascination with particular objects, communication difficulties and often looking and behaving as if cognitive functions are normal. The triad of impairments which are prevalent in most children with autism are: deficits in social interaction, deficits in communication and a restricted repertoire of activities and interests. The DSM criteria for autism include: qualitative impairment in social interaction; qualitative impairments in communication; restricted repetitive and stereotyped patterns of behaviour, interests and activities; abnormal functioning in at least one of the following areas – social interaction and language as used in social communication or symbolic or imaginative play.

2 The Lovaas technique is based on the behaviourist approach, both operant and classical conditioning. It considers the role of rewards and punishment as necessary to teach people correct social behaviours.

Exam Practice

The theory of mind is considered a core deficit in children with autism, and this can be explained, along with a study which can show this. This could be the Sally Anne test used in Baron-Cohen's study, or the Smartie tube test. The evaluation may include the problems of linguistic understanding needed for these tests, bearing in mind the communication difficulties of children with autism. The ecological validity of the studies and individual differences may also be valid evaluation points for this answer.

Substance abuse

Checkpoints

1 Explanations for substance abuse include the behaviourist social learning theory and the biological genetic and mode of action explanations. Within individuals there might be peer pressure or role models, and attributions about the behaviour may differ. A cognitive approach could be the theory of reasoned action.

2 Advice to someone on giving up smoking might include: to resist peers, models and media through practice or to sit in a closed room and smoke a cigarette, taking one puff every 6 seconds, until the smoker cannot smoke any more.

Exam Practice

There is a clear indication of what is required: description, evaluation, at least one explanation, and specifically for substance abuse. Don't forget to refer to evidence. The breadth/depth trade off of one explanation in detail or more than one but done in less depth, is your choice. Your decision might be based on how much you have revised. But you can get full marks for detailed description of *one* explanation. The

social learning theory is a good one to use as it encompasses operant conditioning, classical conditioning and imitation, so there is scope to write a really detailed answer. You could equally well describe the biological explanation of genes, mode of action, etc. Evaluation might include problems of empirical evidence, reductionism and individual differences – and don't forget to refer to empirical evidence somewhere in the answer.

Sport and the individual

Checkpoints

1 The trait theories of personality development are Eysenck and Cattell, whereas the situational or state theories are the Social Learning Theory. Freud's psychodynamic theory of personality development is down to instinctive drives combined with interaction with the environment.

2 Fast, action-packed sports such as rugby and ice hockey might be good releasers of aggression (cathartic) and sports such as chess or darts might not release so much aggression. This would mean that football fans or players are less aggressive than chess fans or players.

Exam practice

This question is broken into two sections. Some exam boards may ask the same question but in one part with 25 marks. What you are being asked to do is describe theories of motivation in sport. It is important that you write a detailed description of at least two theories as the question asks for 'theories'. If you can add a third that would be better. You need to show you understand the theories by given appropriate examples from research in the sport setting or sports-specific examples. You will often be marked for quality of written communication so make sure you write in sentences and your answer is grammatically correct. For the evaluation section you are being asked to identify, explain and comment on the problems involved in trying to carry out research. This might be methodological problems, issues of validity and even the limitations of psychological research, for example in relation to individual differences. Use examples from section A to illustrate each point you make.

Examiner's secrets

Don't describe studies if the question asks for only evaluation. You will not get credit. The description should be in part A for OCR exams and the evaluation is asking you to make a value judgement on the theories. Use your issues, debates, strengths and weaknesses of approaches, etc., to judge the theory. When the questions have more than one part, the time you spend on each section will depend on the marks for that section. In this case the essay has a time limit of 45 minutes, so you would expect to spend just under 20 minutes on part a and just over 25 minutes on part b. Remember that this includes reading and planning time so you won't be writing for that long.

Sport performance

Checkpoints

1 Theories of arousal include physiological arousal, which is a result of adrenaline production, but also cognitive arousal, which is where thoughts are anxiety-provoking, and emotional arousal when feelings are making a person anxious.

2 Psychometric tests of measuring anxiety in sportspeople are: Competition Anxiety Test (SCAT), Martens original Competitive State Anxiety Inventory (CSAI), Speilberger's Trait Anxiety Inventory (TAI) and his State Anxiety Inventory (SAI) test trait and state anxiety respectively Martens et al's Competitive State Anxiety Inventory-2 (CSAI-2.)

Exam practice

This question is asking for a detailed essay on internal factors affecting sporting performance. You can refer to theories, models and empirical evidence, but you must relate them to internal factors such as anxiety, arousal and intrinsic motivation. The evaluation might be of the theories and the research, using issues such as reductionism, methodology, individual differences and so on.

Social psychology of sport

Checkpoints

1 Tuckman's theory of group formation has five stages:
   Forming – the coming together of a team
   Storming – identifying roles and actions which may cause conflict
   Norming – establishing the groups norms and values
   Performing – carrying out the task set
   Adjourning – the breaking up of the group.

2 The presence of an audience has most effect on the performance if it is an interactive audience rather than a passive one. It will increase arousal but this may tip over beyond the optimal point. An audience seems to have a positive effect on simple tasks and a negative effect on complex tasks (at least in cockroaches!). A hostile audience, e.g. at away matches, may reduce performance especially in inexperienced or less able teams.

Exam practice

One theory of leadership could be Feilder's contingency theory, or Stogdill's great man theory. As this is in the sports section, make sure you give examples from sports to illustrate your points. Evaluation might include points such as: difficult-to-measure leadership; the fact that supporting research might be only situation specific; it ignores individual differences; and why some seemingly non-great people will become leaders. There may be too many factors to really be able to identify what makes a leader. The social or biological aspect of the theory could also be used to evaluate it.

Exercise psychology

Checkpoints

1 Some of the benefits which could be attributed to exercise are the reduction of breast cancer in young women, higher levels of physical self-efficacy, and positive mood and life satisfaction as shown in HIV patients. Refer to the endorphin high although this might be linked to a negative effect of addition. High scores in positive mood states, such as vigour and extroversion in rowers, might also be the effect of the exercise. Of course it is difficult to see cause and effect in some of these; it is possible that extroverts might be more likely to become rowers.

2 This checkpoint could include factors from other areas, such as motivation arousal and anxiety, personality, etc but also included in this section is the idea of burnout and withdrawal, how body image is related negatively to sport, and the issue of performance-enhancing drugs.

Exam practice

The essay question is asking for one theory only, so it is not worth mentioning more than one in this section. A detailed description of a theory such as the endorphin hypothesis can be supplemented by a description of research such as the swimming mice. In the evaluation the question specifies theories, so more than one should be evaluated. This might be done effectively by comparing and contrasting two theories using evaluation issues such as supporting evidence, reductionism, application and their ability to account for individual differences.

Revision checklist
Health, clinical and sport psychology

By the end of this chapter you should be able to:

1	Describe and evaluate theories and causes of stress.	Confident	Not confident **Revise** pages 136–137
2	Describe and evaluate techniques of measuring and managing stress.	Confident	Not confident **Revise** pages 138–139
3	Describe models of health belief.	Confident	Not confident **Revise** page 140
4	Describe and evaluate methods of health promotion and education.	Confident	Not confident **Revise** pages 140–141
5	Describe and evaluate reasons for adherence, and techniques to measure and improve adherence.	Confident	Not confident **Revise** pages 140–141
6	Describe and evaluate definitions of abnormality and biases in diagnosis.	Confident	Not confident **Revise** pages 142–145
7	Describe and evaluate perspectives on dysfunctional behaviour.	Confident	Not confident **Revise** pages 146–147
8	Describe and evaluate characteristics, explanations and treatments of psychotic disorders, i.e. schizophrenia.	Confident	Not confident **Revise** pages 148–149
9	Describe and evaluate characteristics, explanations and treatments of mood disorders, i.e. bipolar/unipolar.	Confident	Not confident **Revise** pages 150–151
10	Describe and evaluate characteristics, explanations and treatments of anxiety disorders, i.e. phobias.	Confident	Not confident **Revise** pages 152–153
11	Describe and evaluate characteristics, explanations and treatments of eating disorders.	Confident	Not confident **Revise** pages 154–155
12	Describe and evaluate characteristics, explanations and treatments of autism.	Confident	Not confident **Revise** pages 156–157
13	Describe and evaluate characteristics, explanations and treatments of substance abuse.	Confident	Not confident **Revise** pages 158–159
14	Describe and evaluate psychological research into personality, aggression and motivation in sport.	Confident	Not confident **Revise** pages 160–161
15	Describe and evaluate psychological research into anxiety, arousal and improving performance in sport.	Confident	Not confident **Revise** pages 162–163
16	Describe and evaluate psychological research into group cohesion, leadership and audience effect in sport.	Confident	Not confident **Revise** pages 164–165
17	Describe and evaluate the link between health and exercise and psychological research into eating disorders and drug abuse in athletes.	Confident	Not confident **Revise** pages 166–167

Educational and forensic psychology

This chapter looks in depth at two of the applied options in psychology. There is a wealth of research, much of it recent, which investigates the human behaviour involved in crime and education, though the research may also come from other areas of psychology, such as social psychology, and be applied to the crime or educational setting.

Educational psychology looks at the learning experience for individuals, using perspectives from psychology, and more specifically investigates what goes on in a learning situation.

Forensic psychology uses psychological evidence to show why a person may become a criminal. It includes the process of making a case against a suspect, what happens in the courtroom, and the options for society after a person is found guilty.

Exam themes

- Teaching and learning
- Social world of learning
- Student participation
- Causes of crime
- Profiling criminals
- Witnesses
- The courtroom
- Sentencing and treatments

Topic checklist

	Edexcel		AQA/A		AQA/B		OCR		WJEC	
	AS	A2	AS	A2	AS	A2	AS	A2	AS	A2
Teaching and learning			○					●		●
Social world of learning								●		●
Student participation								●		●
Enabling learning								●		
Causes of crime						●		●		●
Making a case						●		●		●
Reaching a verdict								●		●
Sentencing and treatments						●		●		●

Teaching and learning

Different psychological approaches have different explanations for human behaviour, and learning is one behaviour which can be explained using many approaches. This section focuses on the psychological explanations for learning, taking psychological theories and applying them to the educational setting. Individual differences in learning can also influence educational practice.

Stage theories of knowledge acquisition

Piaget's (1937) theory was a **constructivist** theory, as children construct knowledge by changing their existing schema to make sense of new experiences. He organised knowledge acquisition into four distinct stages: the Sensorimotor stage, the Pre-operational stage, the Concrete Operational Stage and the Formal Operational Stage. Bruner (1966) proposed three stages, and children's intellectual development is dependent on moving through these stages, called representations. They are: the Enactive stage, the Iconic stage and the Symbolic stage.

Social construction theories

Vygotsky (1962) suggested that a child's interaction with its surroundings is based on language which helps them make sense of their experiences. They can construct an understanding of the world and this is called social construction. He identified the Zone of Proximal Development, which is the difference between what a child could achieve alone compared to when given help. A teacher has to decide what each child's ZPD is, i.e. what they need help with, provide that support until the child has mastered that skill or concept and then provide help with the next ZPD.

Models of stimulus and response

Some behaviourists believed behaviour was learned by **association**, and Watson showed this in his case study of 'Little Albert'. Skinner's (1920) theory of operant conditioning said that, if the consequence of a behaviour was positive, that behaviour would be repeated but if it was unpleasant, the behaviour would be reduced. In schools this might be used in directed learning which is **reinforced** when a child shows correct understanding. This could take the form of gold stars or smiley faces which the child has learned to associate with being praised by the teacher.

Variations on learning strategies

Curry's (1983) model explained how the learner engages in learning activities. Each of us has a different strategy but our strategy has layers, like an onion. The model has three main layers:

→ Outer: how an individual would like to engage with the learning.
→ Middle: how individuals prefer to think about the learning task.
→ Inner: how individuals **assimilate and adapt** information.

Rezler and Rezmovic's (1981) Learning Preference Inventory (LPI) was linked to learners' **preference** for three things: tasks which are either abstract or concrete concepts; people working alone or in groups; and work which is teacher or student directed

The concept of **Visual, Auditory and Kinaesthetic** learning (VAK) (Rose, 1985) assumes each of us has a learning style that shows a preference towards one particular sense. Teachers often assess this in students and give a variety of learning activities to meet the three styles. Riding and Raynor (1998) thought that many of the existing learning styles had a little evidence to support them but that some **cognitive processes** did seem to be different but stable in individuals.

There are two dimensions of cognitive style, both of which are on a continuum – ways of organising information and ways of representing information – giving four possible combinations. Grasha (1996) identified the following five **teaching styles** as key aspects of a teacher in a classroom: expert, formal authority, personal model, facilitator and delegator. Teachers may use more than one of these at any one time. Over-reliance on one may not provide appropriate teaching styles for all learners. Ausubel (1977) placed the responsibility on teachers to use advance organisers to help learners make links between previous learning and the present learning situation.

Checkpoint 2

What different styles of teaching and learning are there?

Discovery and co-operative learning

Bruner (1966) argued that learning is not just about understanding facts and rules but also developing learning and problem-solving skills. He recognised the importance of thinking like an expert, so that learners discover ideas for themselves instead of just being told. This allows learners to explore materials or concepts at their own pace, with the materials provided being carefully selected by teachers to allow the **discovery learning** to take place.

Co-operative learning builds on Vygotsky's theory that we learn more effectively as a result of interacting and talking with others. This has led schools to encourage students to work in groups and to share tasks. It also develops social skills and can improve a child's self-esteem.

The jargon

Concept. An abstract idea or principle.

Multiple intelligences

Gardner's (1993) theory of **multiple intelligences** suggests that there are many types of intelligence and that we are all highly intelligent in some areas and lower in others. The seven core intelligences are: linguistic, logical-mathematical, spatial, musical, bodily-kinaesthetic, interpersonal and intrapersonal.

Action point

Try to plan how you would develop a child's understanding of conservation of volume using both discovery and co-operative learning.

Exam practice   answer: page 192

Critically consider individual differences in learning style. (25 marks)

Social world of learning

The interactions between students and their peers or between learners and teachers can have a great effect on the personal development of an individual. This will inevitably have an effect on a student's learning. Teachers are trained in how to communicate effectively with learners and how their communication and expectations will influence their students.

Developmental stages

Freud's (1898) theory of development is based on a series of **psycho-sexual stages** which might motivate learning. Erikson (1963) used Freud's ideas to develop his own theory of personality development, which did not focus on sexuality. He agreed with Freud that development took place in stages and that the negotiation of each stage had an influence on the development of personality. **Erikson** argued that there are eight stages throughout a person's life, all of which involve learning from experience and can have either a positive or a negative outcome. The stages of children in education are 1 Mistrust v. Trust, 2 Autonomy v. Shame, 3 Initiative v. Guilt, 4 Industry v. Inferiority, 5 Identity v. Role confusion.

Humanistic approach applied to learning

Rogers' (1961) central idea was that people need the **approval** of others and to be accepted by them. We are motivated to seek this from others and so will be motivated to learn to gain the regard of teachers. If children do not understand their task in class, their feeling of approval will be lacking and they may become needy and demand the teacher's attention. They have to learn that, in order to get the approval, they have to wait and take their turn.

The ideal self is what all of us aspire to be; as a learner this might be to get an A grade in a psychology exam. If the actual self is not near the ideal self (an E grade in the mock, for example) this could lead to low self-esteem. Teachers need to increase a student's self-esteem by giving positive regard and showing them how to become their ideal self.

Moral development, rules and empathy

Learners have to make decisions which are based on their understanding of right and wrong. Kohlberg (1958) tested boys' moral development and found three main levels: pre-conventional moral reasoning, conventional moral reasoning and post-conventional moral reasoning.

Kohlberg's ideas are used by teachers to help understand the learner's view of right and wrong which might influence their behaviour. For example, Kohlberg's stages show that teenagers will not just accept rules and will feel the need to question authority. Gilligan (1982) suggested that, as Kohlberg only used Western males in his study, it provided a biased view of moral decision-making.

Empathy is an important part of high **emotional intelligence** and is also linked to interpersonal intelligence, which is one of Gardner's (1993) multiple intelligences. The ability to be empathic would enable learners to understand how others were feeling and so would make for a more pleasant educational setting.

Action point

Make a timeline of a person's life and put in the all the stages you know, which are linked to chronological age. These might include cognitive theories as well as psychodynamic theories.

Action point

Make a diagram of Maslow's hierarchy of needs and apply each one to how a teacher might fulfil that need.

The jargon

Ideal self. What a person would see as the ultimate goal in terms of behaviour. **Actual self**. A person's perception of what they are actually capable of. This may be similar or dissimilar to the ideal self. If it is not accurate this could be due to other people's criticisms.

Link

Kohlberg's ideas are also seen as important in understanding criminal behaviour – see page 184.

The jargon

Empathy. The ability to understand how other people are feeling.

Link

See Gardner's multiple intelligences on page 177.

Friendship and bullying

A large support **network** of friends can provide cognitive and social scaffolding – Hartup (1996). Friends help in acquiring knowledge and can support someone worried about their learning. Demetrio et al (2000) found that teachers know friends are very important especially at stressful times like the transfer from primary to secondary school. Programmes have been developed to help reduce **bullying**, and strategies suggested include: raising awareness of bullying, incorporating bullying issues into learning programmes and promoting individual intervention with the bullies and victims. Smith and Shu (2000) found that if students tell someone about being bullied it is very effective at reducing bullying. Other useful strategies include peer support programmes and personal and social education programmes.

Student–teacher communications

The Flanders Interactional Analysis technique (Flanders 1970) is used to study the **communication** that happens in a learning environment. Flanders' ten categories cover all the types of communication that take place during the teaching and learning process. When teachers talk they: accept feelings, praise or encourage, accept or use ideas of pupils, question, lecture, give directions or criticise. When pupils interact they: talk as a response, initiate talk, remain silent/confused.

Observers can make a judgment on what type of communication is taking place every three seconds and it is possible to understand communications between teachers and pupils to help teachers develop their practice.

Teachers' expectations

Rosenthal and Jacobsen (1968) showed that, if primary school teachers are given information suggesting some of the children they teach will do better than others, then they will do better. The '**self-fulfilling prophecy**' occurs and the children do better than was expected. Rubie-Davies et al (2006) researched teachers' expectations for Maori children in New Zealand. Their expectations of the Maori students' reading ability were lower than for other ethnic groups. By the end of the year these students hade made the least progress in reading, despite being the same at the beginning of the year.

Types of questions used with primary and secondary pupils

Galton's study (2002) aimed to find out what had caused a negative attitude towards science at Key Stages 2 and 3. Observations of science teaching in Year 6 (KS2) and Year 7 (KS3) and records of classroom **interactions** including categories such as questioning, type of teaching activity and statements by teachers were used. They found that teachers gave more feedback to Year 6 and there was little cognitive demand and a decrease in enjoyment by students in Year 7, so secondary school students need to be encouraged to think independently.

Exam practice   answers: pages 192

(a) Describe a theory of moral development. (10 marks)

(b) Discuss the usefulness of research into moral development for teachers.

(15 marks)

Student participation

Students need to engage with their teachers in order to enhance their learning experiences. Finding ways to encourage students to participate in their education and adopt appropriate educational behaviours is important to ensure each individual fulfils his or her potential.

Motivation

Psychodynamic theories such as Freud's theory assume unconscious processes cause all of our behaviour. For example, we may be motivated by unconscious defence mechanisms which protect us. A child feeling inadequate may displace his or her feelings of inadequacy onto others and this could lead him or her to become a bully.

One of the most well-known **Humanistic** theories of motivation is Maslow's (1954) theory. We are driven by a hierarchy of needs, from basic physiological needs which, once met, lead on to the next level of safety needs, then esteem needs, and cognitive needs which drive us to learn. This theory of motivation assumes we are all striving to reach our potential or 'self actualisation'. This is important for teachers, who must ensure that they are meeting each of the needs of their learners. Breakfast clubs in schools can meet physiological, safety and esteem needs, before the teachers even become involved.

Cognitive psychologists such as Weiner believe that people use logical cognitive thoughts to determine a course of action (Weiner, 2000). This means that behaviour will depend on how an individual feels about behaviour, and what the person logically believes causes the behaviour. If a pupil does badly in a test they might decide this is due to their own lack of intelligence, and if they think they are incapable of doing well then they might not try, as it will just lead to failure. So they are motivated not to learn. If a student believes it is because the question was hard, they will be more motivated to learn for the next test.

Play

Guided play in early years education has long been seen as an effective way for children to learn. This means that children choose the activities but that adults play with the child and develop their learning in this way. Research such as that of Schweihart (2000), comparing guided **free play** with directed play where the child couldn't choose what they did, found that guided play led to children doing better in education.

Ability grouping

It is believed by some educators that ability grouping is the best way to ensure students are able to fulfil their potential. Able students can be stretched and less able learners can be supported. The DfES Research Report 796 (2006) looked at 24 schools and found that only the high ability groups gained, but rarely was there any difference. In fact sometimes ability grouping had a detrimental effect on students' learning.

Checkpoint 1

What are the key assumptions of the cognitive approach and the psychodynamic and humanistic perspectives about human behaviour?

Grade booster

Compare these three theories (Freud, Maslow and Weiner) using the evaluation issues from your specification. This will help with the analytical skills needed for a high grade evaluation answer.

Action point

What do you think are the strengths and weaknesses of ability grouping? Try and link them to psychological concepts such as labelling and self-fulfilling prophecy.

Link

Look at key social studies on pages 51 and 52.

Social roles and academic success

Learners have a difficult time working out what their role in a classroom is. Is it to be chatty or quiet, to ask questions or not to ask questions, to carry out tasks which they don't comprehend? There can be confusion if the expected behaviour changes from one learning situation to another. Social psychology explores the human tendency to obey and conform.

Riley (1995) found that children who adapted to the expected behaviours in school did better than those who didn't. It might be linked to better pre-school experiences such as pre-reading activities, and also the self-fulfilling prophecy that children who conform are expected by teachers to do well. There is a problem if students conform to the **social norms** of a group whose behaviour is not to learn. **Mentoring** can be helpful in this situation to enable the learner to conform to expectations of learning. Widmer and Weiss (2000) found that older siblings could encourage younger brothers or sisters to adopt positive behaviours towards schooling.

Action point

Make a note of the different roles there are in your school or college. Which ones are you involved in? Do you act differently in each role?

Learned helplessness

Seligman (1975) carried out research on dogs and found that they learned they were helpless in certain situations. In education this means that if a child fails at something several times they will learn they cannot do it and give up.

Hiroto and Seligman (1975) studied undergraduates and found that, although the participants never actually failed in a task to stop a noise; they were told they had and this '**failure**' led them to be unable to complete another simple anagram task.

Link

See page 151 where learned helplessness is included as an explanation for depression.

Self-esteem

A person's view of their own worth, or **self-esteem**, is important in influencing a student's learning. The self-esteem of students can be affected by the quality of the feedback from teachers, and teachers have to be seen to care about their students (this could link to Maslow's hierarchy of needs). So teachers don't have to concentrate on self-esteem but do have to show students what they can do well, and feed back on this. This increase in self-esteem can, like learned helplessness, be transferred to other areas of education.

Dweck links motivation with a learner's perception of whether they can do something. By increasing self-esteem learners may not be significantly more motivated but, by changing a learner's perception of their own ability by attributional training, their engagement with education will be improved.

Checkpoint 2

How could a teacher increase a student's self esteem?

Exam practice   answers: page 193

(a) Describe research into **one** method for improving a student's participation in learning. (10 marks)

(b) Evaluate methods of improving student participation. (15 marks)

Enabling learning

Individual differences mean that we all have individual needs that need to be met to enable us to learn effectively. These needs may be as a result of a specific learning difficulty such as dyslexia or due to culture or gender effects. Psychologists can research the factors which might hinder learning and provide strategies which can improve the learning not only of the individual but of all learners.

Individual support

Lewis and Norwich reviewed the **teaching strategies** used for pupils with additional needs, such as moderate, severe, profound and multiple learning difficulties and their overall conclusion suggests that successful teaching strategies are the same for all learners, whether they have additional needs or not. What this suggests is that good teaching strategies are helpful to all learners and not just those with additional needs.

They suggest that teaching strategies need to differ along a continuum and that certain areas require highlighting in order to meet the individual needs of those who have learning difficulties. Among their proposals are:

→ Provide more opportunities to use knowledge in more than one context.
→ Use more examples to learn concepts.
→ Provide more time to solve problems.
→ Ensure students have successfully mastered one stage before moving to the next.
→ Encourage students to think about their own learning strategies.
→ Have regular focused assessment.

The Rose report (2006) recommended that all schools adopt the '**synthetic phonics**' system to teach reading, although Wyse and Styles (2007) reviewed 30 years of research and found little evidence that this method was beneficial. The 'Reading Recovery' programme by Clay (1985) suggested one-to-one tutoring, for 30 minutes a day for 20 weeks would help remedial readers.

Ability grouping

The **Gifted and Talented** programme, introduced in 2002 provides for exceptional students in the UK. However it is difficult to identify what the special talents are that these students have, and it may differ from student to student, with some having talents in art, music, etc. and others having high IQs. The DfES (2002) produces specific criteria but such a label could lead to the self-fulfilling prophecy.

Ethnic minorities

Evidence may point to differences in the educational achievement of various ethnic groups. The DfES (2006) found that certain groups, such as Gypsy, Pakistani and Black students, tend to be reflected disproportionally in lower achievers. Consistently high achievers tended to include Indian, Chinese, Asian and White pupils. One key feature which might influence

---

The jargon

Strategies. Plans and methods used.

Check the net

Government site on using phonics to teach reading: http://www.standards.dfes.gov.uk/phonics/

Link

See more about ability grouping on page 180.

Checkpoint 1

What is the self-fulfilling prophecy?

---

attainment is ability in English. Strand and Demie (2005) found a strong link between **fluency** of English and Key Stage 2 test scores. Educational achievement may therefore not be linked to ethnic groups as such but more likely to the group's general ability in English language.

There is value in providing positive **role models** and teachers can fulfil that role, but positive role models can also be found where other students from ethnic minorities, such as African Caribbean students, are given positions of responsibility (school prefects, for example). The importance of positive role models within the family also shows how important other people are to learners' education. It is not just what happens in the classroom. The Aiming High project (2006) encourages schools to develop approaches such as taking students on trips; if the school is committed to a positive approach, the students and their parents became more positive themselves.

Gender differences

A report by the DfES (2007) found many differences in educational performance between the two genders. For example, pre-school girls have better communication, social and cognitive skills than boys, and at Key Stage 3 girls do better at English and Maths, though the differences for Science are very small. At A Level girls do better than boys in most subjects but again the gap is very small. Psychometric tests such as IQ or cognitive ability tests show very little difference in intelligence between the genders, so there should be no difference in the overall academic achievement of males and females. Strand et al (2006) suggest that there is another variable that affects educational achievement. The **brain structures** of males and females are very similar but there are some differences which might relate to educational performance. Men have larger brains, for example, but there seems to be no direct link to higher IQ.

What might make a difference is that females have a larger corpus callosum than males, and so can make better connections between the two hemispheres. This could help with processing language and increasing empathy. Females tend to favour **language-based** tasks, which are what our education system uses most of the time, so this disadvantages males who prefer structured, logical tasks. Younger and Warrington (2005) investigated methods of raising the achievement of boys in education. By carrying out an in-depth case study on 16 schools, they found that strategies that raise boys' achievement are also likely to raise girls' achievement. These strategies include teachers being creative, using ICT, and support from mentors for pupils.

There are some social reasons why boys don't achieve as well as girls. This may be due to boys joining groups with social norms of disrupting lessons, and disengaging from creative arts projects. There is little, if any, evidence that single sex schools raise the achievement of boys.

The jargon

Role model. Someone who is seen as an example of acceptable behaviour and who is therefore copied by others.

Grade booster

Review the strengths and weaknesses of the research methods used in this section. This will ensure your evaluation is wide ranging, which is necessary for top marks.

The jargon

Corpus callosum. This is the fibres which join the two hemispheres of the brain and so allow them to communicate. See the Sperry Key study on page 50.

Checkpoint 2

Make a note of the differences in educational performance found between different cultures and between male and female learners. Can you explain these differences?

Exam practice   answers: page 193

(a) Describe research into improving the educational performance of a minority group. (10 marks)

(b) Discuss how the problems of invidual differences might affect a student's ability to improve their educational performance. (15 marks)

Causes of crime

The jargon

Stereotyping. This is generalising about a person or group of people based on a standard image or idea. It can be based on our own experiences, on the media or on incidents which have been reported to us by friends and family

The jargon

Anti-social behaviour. A behaviour that can be verbal or physical and which harms others either people, animals, or property, but which may not break a specific law.

Checkpoint 1

Which side of the nature-nurture debate will social explanations adopt?

Link

See Criminal thinking patterns and moral development on pages 100–101.

Forensic psychologists try to find out what causes a person to adopt a criminal lifestyle. Is it something a person is born with or is it a factor in a person's environment that makes them more likely to become criminal? This has ramifications for the prevention of crime, and is linked to the nature-nurture debate.

Social explanations

David Farrington's (1994) study into **disrupted families** used a prospective study and followed boys from East London until the age of 48. They were then interviewed and criminal records were checked. His results found many factors linked with criminal behaviour. One of these is that 'chronic offenders' tend to have one or more of the following: parents with criminal convictions, a delinquent sibling, a young mother, a large and disrupted family, low popularity.

Other features of upbringing, such as **poverty**, have also been found to be linked to criminal behaviour. The Peterborough Youth Study (2006) by Per-Olof H. Wikström studied 2000 Year 10 (14- to 15-year-old) pupils. The research found that some youths who offend frequently have common risk factors, such as weak family and school bonds, poor parental monitoring and truancy, weak morality (anti-social values and low levels of shame) and poor self-control.

However, Sutherland (2000) believed that criminals also **learn from others**. This would mean that criminal behaviour is not inherited or a result of any other biological condition. His research showed nine principles of learning, such as criminal behaviour being learned through interaction with others, in groups, in much the same way as non-criminal behaviour. It only becomes criminal when society's laws are broken.

The **social learning theory** suggests that behaviours are learned through observation and imitation. Ray Surratt's research (1992) shows the media as only one factor in the generation of youth violence. Whether or not a particular media depiction will cause a particular viewer to act more aggressively depends on the interaction between each individual viewer, the content of the portrayal, and the setting in which exposure to the media occurs. So there may be some people who are influenced by the media, but by itself the media is not likely to promote criminal behaviour.

Gudjonsson and Bownes (2002) used a Blame Attribution Inventory (GBAI) to measure offenders' attribution of blame. They found that, with regard to external attribution, i.e. blaming something or someone other than themselves, the highest scores are found for violent offenders and the lowest for sex offenders. When compared with English prisoners, violent Irish prisoners showed higher external attribution scores.

Biological explanations of crime

Raine's (1997) research used PET scans of murderers' brains to investigate the link between **brain dysfunction** and criminality. It has been found that there are differences between the rate of glucose metabolism in murderers' and in non-murderers' brains. In his longitudinal studies other factors such as birth complications and increased body size have also been linked with aggressive behaviour, which may be related to criminal activities.

The role of inheritance in the **genetic transmission** of criminal behaviour has been studied by Brunner (1993). With his colleagues he studied males from one family who all showed violent behaviours such as impulsive aggression, arson and attempted rape. By analysing urine samples they found a deficit of the enzyme MAOA which is caused by a mutation of the X gene. This deficit leads to less than normal serotonin metabolism, and such a deficit is linked to aggression. This might explain a biological predisposition, but cannot rule out environmental factors being at least, if not more, important.

The difference in **gender** behaviours is clearly seen in criminal behaviour. Statistics generally show males are more likely to be involved in violent criminal behaviour. The evolutionary explanation that males might indulge in more risky behaviour is shown by Daly and Wilson (2001). By researching communities in Chicago they found that males had a lower than average life expectancy and this was linked to a higher murder rate. It may be that if young men expect to live for a shorter time they are more likely to take risks for short-term rewards. The communities are also less likely to be wealthy and so neither parents nor children are willing to consider their future (which is likely to be relatively short-lived) when engaging in violent criminal behaviour.

Atavism is the reappearance of genes which were thought to have died out, so the person appears to be an evolutionary 'throwback'. Lombroso (cited in Gibson, 2002) thought that people with atavism showed earlier evolutionary characteristics, such as protruding jaw, drooping eyes, large ears, flat nose, and long arms. He thought this type of person was biologically inferior and would act in a more animal-like way, not showing a conscience, and would therefore be more likely to become criminals.

The innate features of an individual's **personality** are thought to influence all behaviours, and have been linked to criminal behaviour. Eysenck identified three aspects of personality, one of which was extroversion/introversion. Extroverts have a biologically low level of arousal and so need stimulation to increase their arousal. He and colleagues devised the 'General Arousal Theory of Criminality' (1985), which stated that extroverts who are by nature impulsive and sensation-seeking will participate in high-risk activities such as crime.

Measuring crime

Crime can be measured in a variety of ways. Analysing statistics (of arrests, convictions or reported crime) is one way. Surveys are another and The British Crime Survey (2000) selected 16,000 households and asked one person from each household to provide details of any crimes in which they had been the victim. It was thought this might show an increase in the number of crimes, as many are unreported. The BCS found four and a half times more crime in this survey than had been reported to police.

Link

See the Locus of Control on page 140 as another example of attributing blame to others.

Action point

Compare and contrast one cognitive and one social explanation for crime.

Grade booster

Make a list of the strengths and weaknesses of the biological approach and apply each one to the explanations of crime. This will help to strengthen your evaluation and give clear analysis, which is needed for top marks.

Checkpoint 2

What aspects of biology are thought to contribute to criminal behaviour?

Action point

Make a list of the reasons why people might report different crime rates in the BCS than to the police. How can researchers overcome these problems?

Exam practice   answers: page 194

(a) Identify **two** methods which have been used to measure crime and give **one** limitation of each method. (4 marks)

(b) Briefly discuss **one** limitation of biological explanations of crime. (4 marks)

Making a case

Once a person has been arrested for a crime, the police have to gather evidence in order for the suspect to be charged and ultimately appear in court to be tried for the alleged crimes. There are many factors which police need to be aware of in order not to bias witness evidence, whilst at the same time gathering detailed and accurate information.

Witness recognition

When using photo-fit or, more commonly, **e-fit** techniques, witnesses are encouraged to construct a facial likeness of suspects. Sinha (2006) identified eight points which are useful when using e-fits. These include the ability to recognise poor (CCTV) images and the fact that some facial features such as eyebrows and hairline are most important.

Frowd et al (2007) carried out experimental research to see which **features** are needed for accurate facial recognition and used three sets of photographs of celebrities: one 'complete' set, a set containing the internal features (the eyes, eyebrows, nose and mouth) and another set containing the external features (the head shape, hair and ears). Whole faces and those with just external features were identified similarly at approximately 35% correct. The photos of just internal features were only 19.5% correct.

Cutler and Penrod's (1995) research into **identity parades** found that suspects are more accurately identified if the participants see a sequential line-up, where the faces are seen one at a time and the witness says yes or no, than a traditional line-up where all individuals are seen at the same time. Further accuracy could be obtained by hearing the voices of the people in the line-up, showing three-quarter poses and seeing the individuals walk in and out of the observation room.

The emotional context of the crime has been found to influence a witness's recall of the event. **Weapon focus** was studied by Loftus et al (1987) when they showed slides of a cash till in a restaurant and in one condition 'person B' has a cheque and in the other 'person B' has a gun. When shown photos of the suspects afterwards, of the participants in the cheque condition 38.9% chose the correct 'person B', whilst only 11.1% chose the correct person in the gun condition.

Interviewing

Mann et al (2004) researched police officers' **ability to detect lies** in suspects. In a field experiment in Kent, police officers were able to judge lies and truths in videos of real-life interviews, often using story cues (or discrepancies in their evidence) rather than body language. The process of **interrogating suspects** is shown in The Reid 'Nine Steps' of Interrogation by Inbau (1986), which gives guidelines on how police should interrogate. Step 1 is direct confrontation – telling the suspect that they are thought to have committed the offence and then ignoring any protestation of guilt or reasons why they couldn't have done it, then moving on to offering alternative actions (both of which assume guilt), to offering sympathy and understanding but in the end getting the suspect to sign a confession (Step 9).

The jargon

CCTV. Closed Circuit Television.

Watch out!

Make sure you don't confuse weapon focus with false memories, or with leading questions in other eye witness testimony research.

One problem with interviewing is that a person may give a **false confession** to committing a crime. Gudjonsson (1990) studied one case where, after 14 hours of continuous interviewing, a seemingly normal 17-year-old was pressured into confessing to two murders, which it was later found out he did not commit.

The **cognitive interview** (CI) is an interview governed by a set format which aims to reinstate the context of the original event and to search through memory by using a variety of retrieval methods. The guidelines are to set the interview in a similar environment to the original event by reinstating in the witness's mind the external emotional and cognitive features that were experienced at the time. The interview must generate focused concentration and encourage the witness to retrieve information as many times as possible. If the witness cannot remember they are asked to think of the event from a different angle. Fisher's (1989) research tested CI and found trained detectives using the CI gained between 47% and 63% more information without a loss of accuracy.

Profiling

Offender profiling means analysing a crime scene and the way the crime was carried out to ascertain likely aspects of the criminal's personality and characteristics such as occupation. This enables police to build up a description of the offender. **Top-down profiling** takes the 'fingerprint' of the scene, whether it is organised or disorganised and, using this information, identifies an organised or disorganised criminal. An organised offender is likely to live a routine life, but (often after a critical event) will carefully plan and execute a crime. This criminal is often highly intelligent, has a high level of social skills and is likely to be employed.

The disorganised criminal will be more likely to leave blood, fingerprints and the murder weapon at the scene, and be less intelligent and less socially skilled. A mixed offender cannot be put into either of these two categories, and it might be that something unexpected happens in an organised crime which can then cause the person to panic and become disorganised. David Canter (1993) used a content analysis of 100 cases to find out if the features of each type of criminal were consistently and distinctively different. He concluded that all crimes have an organised element to them and that a more effective way is to look at the individual personality differences between offenders. His cognitive social approach or **bottom-up** approach found that there are certain personality characteristics linked with certain offence behaviours and that an analysis of a computer database of cases can find such correlations.

John Duffy admitted committing 25 sexual offences between 1975 and 1986 which included 22 attacks on 23 women. Before Duffy's confession David Canter had worked on the case. From his analysis Canter drew up a profile of the suspect, including areas of residence, age, occupation and relationship status, all of which accurately matched Duffy.

Link

See Cognition and the law on page 100.

Checkpoint 1

Think of examples of internal emotional and cognitive features of an event.

Grade booster

Compare the top-down and bottom-up approaches to profiling. What are the strengths and weaknesses of each? You will need to be able to do a comprehensive analysis to gain high marks.

Checkpoint 2

What are the features of top-down and bottom-up profiling?

Exam practice   answers: page 194

(a) Describe research into witness interviewing. (10 marks)
(b) Evaluate the methods used by psychologists for researching witness interviews. (15 marks)

Reaching a verdict

In court, both the prosecution and defence counsel have to try to persuade the jury that their version of events is the truth. It is unlikely they can both be true and juries are influenced by many factors in terms of evidence presented and the person giving the evidence. The decision-making process also has many stages and influences.

Eye witness testimony

Loftus (1974) has carried out much research into the problems of eye witness testimony; she showed that it can be easily manipulated by leading questions. However, **Yuille and Cutshall** (1989) carried out research on witnesses to a fatal shooting and found that, even in interviews with leading questions, witnesses' recall was quite accurate, being rarely misled by the questions.

Cohen (1966) showed how **face recognition** should not be considered in isolation because it is influenced both by the event itself and by people's schema, social norms and values and therefore stereotyped images. Cohen suggested that people find it easier to identify people from their own race than people from a different race.

Much research highlights the **unreliability of eye witness testimony** but Cutler et al (1989) found that, even if this was pointed out to the jury, they were still likely to be confident in the witness's testimony. In a laboratory experiment, undergraduates viewed the video-taped trial of a robbery in groups of two to eight. They then completed a questionnaire on how confident they were in their verdict. Under the good conditions for the witness the jurors had more confidence in the accuracy of the identification. This effect was stronger if they had heard the expert witness and if the witness was 100% confident rather than 80% confident.

Presentation of evidence

Evidence ruled **inadmissible** by the judge should be ignored by the jury but research has shown that a judge's ruling of evidence being admissible or inadmissible has very little effect on the verdict of jurors. If the judge is direct and tells them they have no choice but to disregard the evidence, they in fact still use it. Pickel (1993) tested the effect of the judge's instructions on the ability of the jury to disregard that witness's testimony. He found that participants who were told the critical evidence was inadmissible but didn't have any explanation were able to ignore the evidence. Those who heard the evidence ruled inadmissible and who were given an explanation were not able to disregard it and were less likely to find the defendant guilty.

Something as simple as the **order of evidence** can have an effect on a jury's judgment of a case. Pennington Hastie (1988) investigated whether story order affects confidence in verdicts. In the story order condition, evidence was arranged in its natural order. In the witness order condition, evidence items were arranged in the order closest to the presentation at the original trial. He found that, if the defence presented its evidence in witness order, then even more jurors would find a guilty verdict; if the positions were reversed and the defence had the benefit of the story order,

Link

Read more about the study by Loftus and Palmer on page 45.

Action point

Make a note of Loftus and Palmer's research on eye witness testimony and leading questions.

the guilty rate dropped to 31%. Participants had most confidence in their verdict if they heard the defence or prosecution in story order.

The physical **attractiveness** of a victim or defendant can also influence the jury. Castellow (1990) found students in introductory psychology classes at East Carolina University gave guilty verdicts 56% of the time when the defendant was attractive against 76% for an unattractive defendant. When the victim was attractive, the guilty verdict followed 77% of the time with 55% for the unattractive victim.

One of the most convincing features of a witness is their **confidence** when giving testimony. Penrod, et al (1995) showed a video-taped trial of a robbery in which eye witness identification played a key role. The witness said she was either 80% or 100% confident that she had identified the robber. Participants were asked to decide whether the robber was guilty or not guilty after watching the film. The confidence of the witnesses significantly influenced the verdict.

Some witnesses, for whatever reason, don't want to give evidence in open court where the defendant may be in the same room as them. It was considered that this might affect the juries' perception of the witnesses. Ross et al (1994) carried out an experiment to see if this was the case and if a barrier would either inflate credibility or deflate creditably of a **child witness**. The judge read a warning before either a screen or a video monitor was used, clearly directing the jury not to infer guilt by their use. The guilty verdicts showed no significant differences between conditions and with no difference across the three conditions of the credibility of the witness.

Checkpoint

Identify some of the features of the presentation of evidence which could influence a jury's verdict.

Decision making

Jury's have to discuss the evidence they have heard when **making a decision** and Hastie et al (1983) identified three stages in this discussion. In the orientation period jurors have relaxed and open discussion, they will set the agenda, explore facts and voice opinions which might be different. The second stage of open confrontation will include fierce debate with concentration on details. Here, there might be pressure on the minority to conform to the majority opinion. Finally, the reconciliation stage attempts to resolve any conflicts or tensions, often using humour.

Asch's (1955) study on **majority influence** on conformity shows how people can be convinced by others to agree with something they don't actually believe. Moscovici's (1985) research, however, shows that the **minority view** can prevail and he believes that the consistency of the minority is most likely to achieve this. Nemeth et al (1974) studied this in relation to trials and found that the person in the mock trial and juror discussion who was a confederate was more influential if he was consistent and when he was thought by the other jurors as having chosen his seat, whereas when he was seated by the experimenter he had little influence.

Link

Read more about the core study by Asch on page 51.

Action point

Look at all the factors which can influence a jury. What research evidence is there for each of these?

Exam practice   answers: page 194

(a) Describe relevant research which informs us about how a jury reaches its verdict. (10 marks)

(b) Discuss the problems of conducting research into courtroom behaviour. (15 marks)

Sentencing and treatments

Once a guilty verdict has been recorded, there are many options for the magistrate or judge to apply to the criminal. The idea of punishment versus treatment or rehabilitation is one to be considered. The recidivism rates need to be considered to ensure the safety of society balanced with the need to ensure criminal behaviour has negative consequences in order to reduce crime rates.

Prison

The effects of prison were studied by Zimbardo (1974), who set up an experiment using students. The 'prisoners' became withdrawn and submissive and the 'guards' more authoritarian.

Cullen and Seddon (1981) studied a **token economy** used with young male offenders aged 16 to 21 in a UK Young Offenders Institution. They found that a points incentive scheme was used as this was seen as the most tangible widespread reward for good behaviour. Six behaviour contracts were designed so that offenders could deal with specific behaviour problems and trainees were awarded a star for successful completion of each contract. The results showed improvements in terms of not offending and the acquisition of new skills.

There are many factors which might affect **recidivism** and Gillis and Nafekh (2005) investigated one of these, namely a community-based employment scheme. Content analysis of data from Canada looked at offenders who took part in an employment programme prior to finishing their sentence, compared with a matched group of offenders who had not. They found that offenders on employment programmes were more likely to remain on conditional release and less likely to return to custody with a new offence.

Suicide is relatively common amongst prisoners, as is self-harming, and a study by Dooley (1990) attempted to investigate this by looking at all unnatural deaths in prison between 1972 and 1987. Using a content analysis of Prison Department papers, he found 442 unnatural deaths were recorded in prisons in England and Wales during this period. Of these, 300 were suicide and 52 were from consciously self-inflicted injury. This is obviously a problem and the present level of suicide in British jails is much higher than in previous years. This could be due to overcrowding causing more stress on the prisoners. Also, many prisoners do have mental health problems, including addiction, when they are admitted, which might make them more susceptible to suicide.

Alternatives to prison

Being on **probation** means that an offender is released into the care of the Probation Service who monitor their behaviour whilst they are rehabilitated into society. Mair and May (1997) interviewed offenders on probation, and found that 88% of the sample felt probation was extremely or very useful. Over 60% of the offenders had felt they could talk to their probation officer who would help sort out their problems. However, only 37% felt it would stop them re-offending. It would appear that providing someone independent to talk to is the most useful aspect of the probation officer.

The jargon

Token economy. A method of encouraging desirable behaviour, for example in a prison, by offering rewards that can be exchanged for privileges such as special food, access to television or sport facilities.

The jargon

Recidivism. The tendency to relapse or return to previous criminal behaviour.

Checkpoint 1

Why might prisoners be more likely to die by suicide?

Restorative justice (RJ) works on the principle that the victim of a crime has some input into the justice system. An impartial facilitator will work with the offender to encourage them to accept responsibility. Sherman and Strang (2007) reviewed the content of research where a sample of offenders on a RJ program was compared with a similar sample who did not experience RJ. They found that there were reductions in re-offending for some crimes such as property crimes but not for all. It was more effective if there was a personal victim and if violence had been involved. The victims reported better mental health and fewer symptoms of Post Traumatic Stress Disorder.

Capital punishment or execution is still used in many states in the USA. However, there appears to be a bias towards the execution of black offenders. Research by Jennifer Eberhardt et al (2006) found that murderers of white victims are more likely to get the death sentence than murderers of black victims. Analysis also showed that the most stereotypically black defendants were 57.5% more likely to receive the death sentence than less stereotypically black defendants at 24.4%. Other researchers have found that criminality is associated with the black facial stereotype and that these criminals get eight months' longer sentences on average.

The **anger management** programme used by the Prison Service has six modules which look at:

➜ motivating prisoners
➜ identifying physiological responses to anger
➜ understanding how their behaviour affects others
➜ learning skills to help with communication
➜ practising those skills
➜ identifying future situations when they might need those skills.

Ireland's (2000) research assessed whether anger management programmes work, with a group of young male offenders. His sample of 50 prisoners who had completed an anger management course was compared with a matched group who did not attend the course and he found a significant reduction in prison wing-based aggression in the experimental group but not in the control group.

Cognitive psychology would say that crime is caused by faulty thinking and that **cognitive skills training** is one way to stop criminal re-offending, by stopping these faulty thinking patterns. Early research in the USA found that reconviction rates of people on the programmes went down 10%, while research in the UK by Caroline Friendship (2003) found that offenders having CBT showed a reconviction rate two years after leaving prison that was 14% lower than in the control group. However, more recent research has failed to replicate these findings and the reasons for the success and subsequent failure of these programmes is still being investigated.

An alternative treatment used in prisons is ear **acupuncture**. Wheatly (2007) found that prisoners who received acupuncture reported better sleep, were more relaxed and staff could tell which prisoners had had acupuncture as the wing was calmer. There were also improvements to their physical health.

Action point

What might be the problems of a victim meeting the criminal responsible for the crime against them?

The jargon

Post Traumatic Stress Disorder. Feeling grief stricken, depressed, anxious, guilty and angry after a traumatic experience. There are three main types of symptom: flashbacks and nightmares, avoidance and numbing and being 'on guard'.

Grade booster

Identify which approach each treatment is based on. This will help as you can use analysis of the approach bias to show excellent evaluation skills.

Checkpoint 2

What alternatives to prison are there that have been shown to reduce re-offending?

Exam practice   answer: page 194

John is a prisoner serving an eight year sentence for violent behaviour. Describe and evaluate **two** psychological treatments which might be used with violent offenders. Refer to evidence in your answer. (12 marks)

191

Answers
Educational and forensic psychology

Teaching and learning

Checkpoints

1 Cognitive theories include Piaget's theory and Bruner's representations. Vygotsky's theory of social constructionism and SPD are also cognitive theories, as are co-operative and discovery learning. Behaviourist theories of learning are based on the concept of conditioning, both operant and classical.

2 Individual differences will include how individuals prefer to assimilate and adapt information, for example either abstract or concrete concepts; people working alone or in groups; and work which is teacher or student directed. Visual, auditory and kinaesthetic learning styles place the emphasis on which sense learners use when learning. Dimensions of cognitive style include ways of organising information and ways of representing information. Grasha identified five – Teaching Expert, Formal Authority, Personal Model, Facilitator, Delegator.

Exam practice

This essay will give credit for describing and evaluating individual differences in learning style. The description could include: research by Curry on learning styles; Grasha and teaching styles and the effect on individual differences of learning; the visual, auditory and kinaesthetic learning styles of Rose and the Learning Preference Inventory (LPI) of Rezler and Rezmovic, which was linked to learners' preference for abstract or concrete concepts; working alone or in groups; and teacher or student directed learning. You could also gain credit by including Riding and Raynor's identification of two dimensions of cognitive style, ways of organising information and ways of representing information; the evaluation points can be anything from the inability to define and measure learning styles, the usefulness of learning styles, empirical research which supports these ideas, and the evaluation of that research. Comparisons and contrasts between the different methods of categorising learning styles are valid evaluations.

Social world of learning

Checkpoints

1 Gardner's multiple intelligences are:

Linguistic	Using words, reading, writing and has a high verbal memory.
Logical-Mathematical	Numbers, abstract thought, computers.
Spatial	Good hand to eye co-ordination, clear visual memory of places.
Musical	Identify notes, pitch, rhythm.
Bodily-kinaesthetic	Dexterous, good at movement and balance.
Interpersonal	Often extroverts and can empathise with others.
Intrapersonal	Ability to be introspective, very self aware of own emotions and goals.

2 Direct influences on a student's learning can be due to the teacher's expectations; if they are low the student's performance is likely to be low. This can be linked to the self-fulfilling prophecy. Also, the communications between teachers and learners can be analysed to see whether students might feel too frightened to answer a question, or not understand what the teacher is saying, both of which are detrimental to the learner. Finally, the type of questions asked by the teachers has been shown to influence performance and attitude to a subject.

Exam practice

(a) This exam question asks for a theory of moral development, so the key point is to describe just one theory such as Kohlberg's. You are asked to describe and not evaluate, so make sure it is very detailed, with stages clearly identified, the characteristics of each stage detailed, and with examples from educational settings. Write in prose and don't bullet point your answer as you will gain credit for quality of written communication.

(b) The evaluation part is specifying how you should evaluate research into moral development. You must make sure that you only concentrate on the usefulness of these theories, so must think about issues which might affect that. For example, a theory that is reductionist is less useful, if it doesn't account for individual differences. It might also be less useful if it doesn't have empirical research or has flawed empirical research to support. Four points would be a good number to aim for.

Student participation

Checkpoints

1 The cognitive approach is concerned with the logical processing of information in order to structure a schema of the world. The thought processes are what direct our behaviour. The psychodynamic approach believes that unconscious drives motivate us to resolve conflicts and protect ourselves from emotional harm.

The humanistic perspective looks at individuals and their drive to self-actualisation, which is founded on a hierarchy of needs and positive self-regard.

2 A teacher might use extrinsic rewards to show that they value a student's work. Lots of praise and accepting what the student says will also bolster the student's self-esteem. Setting tasks that the student can achieve and supporting them in their learning as they need it will also mean that the student will feel able to achieve and so will value themselves. If a student's ideal self is too far removed from their actual self, teachers can either help the student to a more realistic ideal self, or show that they are capable of achieving their ideal self.

Exam practice

(a) This question gives you a range of methods to choose from. It might be improving motivation, extrinsic rewards, boosting self-esteem or using one of the strategies which have been shown to improve performance in genders. It is important that you refer to educational practices in your answer. The question only asks for one method, so don't be tempted to write about more than one.

(b) You need to evaluate methods, so now you can introduce other methods, but don't describe them in detail. The evaluation points might include empirical evidence (or the lack of it) to support them, individual differences, reductionism. Aim for four points, with examples.

Enabling learning

Checkpoints

1 The labelling of a person as either gifted, intelligent or conversely less able, will ultimately lead to that person acting as the label would indicate. Research has shown that this is often as a result of how people who know about the label behave towards the person. For example, a teacher may think a child is highly intelligent and so spend more time with that pupil, or extend their learning through questions.

2 Ethnic differences – Gypsy, Pakistani and Black students tended to be reflected disproportionally in lower achievers. Consistently high achievers tended to include Indian, Chinese, Asian and White pupils. Gender differences show that pre-school girls have better communication, social and cognitive skills, whilst at Key Stage 3 girls do better in English and Maths, with Science showing little difference. At A Level girls do better than boys in most subjects but the gap is very small. The reasons why this might be are: women have larger a corpus callosum than males; females tend to favour language-based tasks, which are what our education system uses most of the time; strategies that raise boys' achievement are also likely to raise girls' achievement; and boys become members of groups with social norms of disrupting lessons. Ethnic minority differences tend to be caused by less ability in English.

Exam practice

(a) This is a very specific question on ethnic minorities, so make sure that the strategy you describe is appropriate. It could be inter-group tasks, role models or positive support. The question doesn't limit you to one method, so a broader approach to this would be perfectly acceptable, writing about two methods in less detail. Don't be tempted to write for more than the time allocation of about 12 minutes.

(b) The problem of individual differences is one for all areas of psychological research. The problems include individual needs and skills, different backgrounds and the emphasis they place on education. Any education system that looks to change performance is going to be reductionist to some extent, and can't take into account other factors. Individual teaching and learning styles could also be a problem. Aim for four problems and give examples from education practice or research to illustrate them.

Causes of crime

Checkpoints

1 The social explanations show the influence people in our society can have on us and so will be firmly on the nurture side of this debate. However, the role of biology cannot be ignored and may identify those people genetically predisposed to criminal behaviour who would be more likely to become criminals when exposed to social stimuli associated with criminality.

2 The evidence described considers brain structures, body size, genes, innate personality traits, and behaviours which have evolved over time. Other factors could include the role of hormones.

Examiner's secrets

Check your specification to see if there are studies or theories that MUST be learned. Make detailed notes on these; the more you know about these studies the better marks you will get for description.

Examiner's secrets

Being able to compare and contrast theories, research or explanations is a valuable skill in essay writing. A Venn diagram showing two sides of one issue can be a useful visual way of comparing (the similarities which appear in the overlap) and contrasting (the differences applying to only one explanation). For example, put biological, cognitive and social explanations into the Venn diagram below.

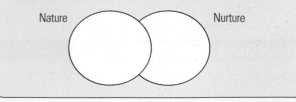

Exam practice

(a) The first part of this question is clearly asking for a short answer as it is using the injunction 'Identify', so naming and very briefly explaining this would be sufficient. Try to give a different limitation for each method.

(b) The second part of the question is not asking for description but for limitations of the biological explanation. You will need to refer to examples from your knowledge of biological theories of crime, such as personality, but the marks will be awarded for your knowledge of the limitations not your knowledge of the theory.

Making a case

Checkpoints

1 The features of an event which will help a witness recall details of that event are external (such as weather), emotional (how the person felt, afraid or angry) and cognitive (the thoughts the person had, such as 'How can I get out safely? What is the criminal likely to do?'

2 The top-down approach looks at the evidence in light of previous crimes, psychological theories of criminals and theories that have identified a link between evidence and an offender's personality. The bottom-up theory profiles a criminal in the opposite way. It takes the evidence and data and builds up a piece by piece picture of the offender until a clear profile of the suspect is reached.

Exam practice

(a) This question is asking you to describe research. Remember that this can refer to theories, models and research. For this answer you might consider weapon focus, leading questions and the cognitive interview. Don't be tempted to write about interviewing suspects (Inbau) as this will not gain credit. You could outline the cognitive interview, and also refer to research which shows its effectiveness. There is no limit to the number of pieces of research you can refer to but be aware of the time constraints on this section.

(b) For the evaluation, this is a simple use of your knowledge of research methods but it must be applied to research on interviewing witnesses to gain full marks. You could consider ecological validity of methods, validity of methods, and issues such as demand characteristics and social desirability bias, in addition to the evaluation of methods such as experiments and observations. Try to make four detailed points with examples.

Reaching a verdict

Checkpoint

These factors that have been shown to influence juries include order of evidence, witness confidence and expertise of witness. However, a barrier such as a video or screen does not inflate credibility or deflate credibility of a child.

Exam practice

This question has two parts, firstly a description of research and secondly an evaluation of the problems of carrying out research. For section (a) you should describe at least two pieces of research – there is a depth/breadth trade off so more research in less detail is acceptable but don't write too superficial an answer. Two pieces of research in detail would be a good approach. You will only have about 15 minutes writing time, so there is a limit to what you can put in. Don't put any evaluation is this section, not even a throw-away line like 'but it did not take part in a real-life setting so lacks ecological validity'. This is evaluation and should be kept for part (b). You can describe any research which might be specifically carried out in a courtroom setting, such as Hastie, or general decision-making research, such as Asch, but make sure you relate it to the courtroom, at least in the conclusions.

In part (b) the problems of conducting research are many, and general points such as reliability, ethics, validity and sampling can all be used but must be related to the courtroom setting for full marks. There are also specific problems with courtrooms as it is illegal to carry out research in a real court, so any research is going to suffer from lack of ecological validity and possibly demand characteristics.

Sentencing and treatments

Checkpoints

1 Criminals are more likely to suffer from mental health problems and addiction. This would make them vulnerable and susceptible to suicidal tendencies.

2 Evidence has shown that the following alternatives to prison are effective: being on probation, restorative justice, anger management programmes, cognitive skills and acupuncture.

Exam practice

Longer essay-style questions are going to require structure and good quality of written communication. The main part of this answer is going to be the description and evaluation of treatment programmes. These could include rehabilitation and cognitive restructuring. To gain full marks you will need to refer each one to how it would relate to the stimulus material about John.

Examiner's secrets

If an exam question asks for a specific number of pieces of research, e.g. two treatment programmes, then you must write about two, although they may not be equally detailed. If you only write about one you will be limiting the number of marks you can gain, and if you write about more then you will not gain any more credit, but may have written a superficial answer and so done less well on the two that are credited.

Revision checklist
Educational and forensic psychology

By the end of this chapter you should be able to:

1	Describe and evaluate psychological research into perspectives on learning, multiple intelligences and learning strategies.	Confident	Not confident **Revise** pages 176–177
2	Describe and evaluate psychological research into personal development, teacher expectations, bullying and student–teacher interactions.	Confident	Not confident **Revise** pages 178–179
3	Describe and evaluate psychological research into ability grouping, self esteem, play, social roles and motivation.	Confident	Not confident **Revise** pages 180–181
4	Describe and evaluate psychological research into individual support, gender differences in educational performance and ethnic minorities.	Confident	Not confident **Revise** pages 182–183
5	Describe and evaluate psychological research into biological, social and cognitive explanations of criminal behaviour and measuring crime.	Confident	Not confident **Revise** pages 184–185
6	Describe and evaluate psychological research into witness identification of suspects, profiling and police interviews.	Confident	Not confident **Revise** pages 186–187
7	Describe and evaluate psychological research into eye witness testimony, evidence presentation and decision making.	Confident	Not confident **Revise** pages 188–189
8	Describe and evaluate psychological research into prison and alternatives to prison.	Confident	Not confident **Revise** pages 190–191

Resources

It is important to know what can appear on your exam paper and what the questions will look like. This can help you revise appropriate material and practise answering possible exam questions. The specification of your exam board will contain all the topics you can be asked about. Specimen assessment material is also often available and is useful for seeing how the question paper will be constructed and what techniques and content are needed in your answers. The exam technique is almost as important as your knowledge of psychology.

Exam board specifications

It is useful to have a copy of your exam specification. You can obtain one from the board's publication department or by downloading the specification from the board's website. The boards will also supply copies of past papers.

Edexcel
One90 High Holborn, London WC1V 7BH – www.edexcel.org.uk

AQA (Assessment and Qualifications Alliance)
Publications Department, Stag Hill House, Guildford,
Surrey GU2 5XJ – www.aqa.org.uk

OCR (Oxford, Cambridge and Royal Society of Arts)
1 Hills Road, Cambridge CB1 2EU – www.ocr.org.uk

WJEC (Welsh Joint Education Committee)
245 Western Avenue, Cardiff CF5 2YX – www.wjec.co.uk

Synoptic assessment

The jargon

Synoptic is demonstrating a comprehensive mental view of something.

Watch out!

Synoptic assessment is not necessarily part of every section. Most examination boards restrict this requirement to a 'perspectives' section.

Action point

On a piece of paper, make a note of the different ways that you might explain issues connected with each of these behaviours.

Take note

When revising for those areas of your specification that assess your synoptic understanding, try to develop a spread of explanations and issues.

Synoptic assessment is taken to mean your understanding and critical appreciation of the breadth of theoretical and methodological approaches in psychology.

The nature of synoptic assessment

Most examination boards have decided to place the major part of their synoptic assessment in a 'perspectives' section of the exam. The term 'perspective' is used here to refer to the various theoretical approaches in psychology. These may be major orientations such as the *psychodynamic* perspective or *behaviourism*, or they can refer to a particular field of psychology, such as *social psychology* or *abnormal psychology*. There are also a number of important 'issues' and 'debates' (*nature versus nurture*, *ethical issues*, *cultural bias* etc.), and these permeate the perspectives and methods used in psychological inquiry. The idea of synoptic assessment is that it tests your knowledge of psychology as a whole, and your ability to make links between the different things you have learned.

What counts as synoptic assessment?

Synopticity can be demonstrated in many ways, including the following:

→ demonstrating different explanations or perspectives relating to a topic area (e.g. different explanations of schizophrenia, drawn from biology, social learning etc.)
→ demonstrating different methods used to study a topic area (e.g. experiments, clinical studies, epidemiological studies etc.)
→ overarching issues relating to a topic area (e.g. ethical issues, issues relating to free will and determinism, reductionism etc.)
→ links with other areas of the specification (e.g. with evolutionary explanations in comparative psychology, or methods of studying the brain in physiological psychology).

Explaining psychological phenomena from multiple perspectives

To fully appreciate the synoptic nature of psychology, it is necessary to explore the breadth of explanations for different areas of behaviour. The exam will usually require you to use your knowledge of different 'approaches' in psychology to explain novel areas of behaviour. The main approaches to psychology include:

→ biological
→ evolutionary
→ psychodynamic
→ behavioural
→ cognitive
→ humanistic
→ social.

Index